THIS
DIARY
WILL CHANGE
YOUR LIFE
2005

Personal data

This Diary belongs to ...... *Angel* ...... aged .. 22 ..

who resides at ....

....

....

Their home phone number is ....

and their personal email is ...... 98330259 ....

As a child they wanted to become a ....

but instead now they work at the mighty ....

corporation, where their work number is ....

and their email is ....

But they would really rather people called them on their mobile phone,

number..Thank you!

If you find this Diary, please return it to them as soon as possible and they will

hug you ■   praise you ■   adopt you ■   accuse you of stealing it ■

If you are stalking them, please call the authorities and hand yourself in.

Nightmares? Stop reading the Diary in the evening

In case of nasty accident

DOCTOR

DENTIST

HYGIENIST

Note of encouragement to hand to Doctor:
Save my life and
you'll be rich   ■
Amputate my
left limbs only!   ■
I didn't mean to be
rude that time, sorry   ■
Other......................   ■

BEN

NEW!

This year's Diary contains some subliminal messages that will change your life without you even realizing it! We don't want to ruin the surprise, but we can reveal that one of them involves a subliminal change of lifelong political allegiance, and two of them involve your declared sexual orientation. Yowza!

 Diary Veterans

If you followed the Diary to the letter last year, your life will have changed dramatically. Following this year's version will not reverse those changes, but may accelerate them and spin them out of control! Benrik recommend that you lie fallow for 2005 and follow next year's edition if you must.

BOOKCROSSING

This Diary has been registered for bookcrossing. Bookcrossing is the practice of leaving books out for others to pick up "in the wild", and tracing successive owners on www.bookcrossing.com. Benrik however are adding a twist: this book must be stolen, not just abandoned. Its new owner must record how they stole it, who they stole it from, and what they propose to do to prevent others stealing it. The Diary's official number is:

Please note: obviously, do not return it to the owner
if you have stolen it, as that would defeat the point.

BCID: 927-1655703

DIARY INSTRUCTIONS
Please read before use!

Last year's This Diary Will Change Your Life had a profound
effect on the lives of those who followed it, with many
reporting radical personal upheaval of the kind that defies
expression, let alone medical treatment. This year, Benrik
aim to extend that experience to society as a whole. By the
first of January 2005, everyone in the country over 14 should
be in possession of a copy and turn to their first task. If
millions of us act out this Diary simultaneously, 2005 will go
down as the year that changed the world. Good luck with it.

*Deposit a drop of your urine
here to mark your territory
and let the others know this
book belongs to you.*

FOLLOW THE DIARY AND BECOME FAMOUS!

Go to www.thiswebsitewillchangeyourlife.com
to set up your very own blog and let everyone
keep up with your progress as you follow the
Diary's dictates day by day! The most-read
blogs will rise to the top of the Benrik blog
chart and their authors will become famous
and land lucrative publishing deals. At that
point Benrik may well decide to sue for a
share of the profits, but let's cross that
bridge when we come to it. Happy blogging!

Benrik Limited

Benrik are Ben Carey and Henrik Delehag.
They became friends when they discovered
they were both of uncertain parentage, a bond
that has sustained them through difficult times.
They founded Benrik Limited in order to
impose their twisted values on the public.
Benrik Ltd is the first openly evil corporation,
aiming to violate ethical standards wherever
feasible. So far, Benrik have published This
Diary Will Change Your Life 2004 and 2005,
which have both been hand-coloured by 12-
year-old Guatemalan orphans. They have also
moved to acquire 10 acres of rainforest for
their exclusive upcoming furniture range.
Their operating profit margin is a healthy 9%,
which represents a year-on-year increase of
42% (see full accounts at the back of this book).
They are also the people behind *"The Couple's
Book"*, a guide to the modern relationship.
Their slogan encapsulates their global vision:

*Your values
• are our toilet •
paper*

MOOD-CHART DELUXE

W TO USE: PLOT MOOD LEVEL EVERY DAY OF THE MONTH AGAINST VERTICAL AXIS. SHOW ONE YEAR'S RESULTS TO PSYCHOTHERAPIST.
WORLD MOOD IN 2004: Overall the World Mood in 2004 veered between OK and FINE THANK YOU, with the odd slump into SO-SO. The highest point was
ed on May 16, when you had to 'make sure your parents know you love them'. The lowest was unsurprisingly June 13, when you had to 'share someone's pain'. The
d Mood correlates very roughly with the Dow Jones, but more closely with the French CAC 40 shares index, which is odd as Benrik do not even have offices in France.

JULY

AUGUST

| 16 | 17 | 18 | 19 | 20 | 21 | 22 | 23 | 24 | 25 | 26 | 27 | 28 | 29 | 30 | 31 |

WARM-UP DAY

As this is the first day of 2005, you should warm up with an easy task that will only change your life a little bit. Choose one of the following options:

Do one press-up.

Perform a striptease (in private).

Triple-tie your shoelaces.

Learn to play "Chopsticks".

Increase your typing speed by three words a minute.

Jaywalk in a pedestrian zone.

Set all your clocks to exactly the right time.

Whisper a white lie when no one's listening.

Fantasize about your partner.

Use a different thickness comb.

Hold the phone up to your other ear.

Tell someone your middle name.

Try a new sandwich filling.

Leave work five minutes early.

Bookmark a new website.

Give your genitalia pet names.

Insult an insect.

Go on a one-minute hunger strike.

Saturday 1 January   NEW YEAR'S DAY

8 Wake up late
9 → last night sleep at
10 2:30 am
11 w/ cal have a drink in
12 Sotto + went to the
13 Disc... it was so coLD....

14
15
16
17
18
19 D ....

→ Have hair-cut w/ Chris
→ went to TST → dinner at aunt's

Your life should have changed, but not measurably.

Claim you're Jesus Day

There are few surefire ways of transforming your life on the spot. Claiming to be Jesus is definitely one of them. So brighten everyone's Sunday by donning a white robe, borrowing a trumpet, and popping down to church in time for mass. The local chaplain should let you in, just on the off-chance you're the real deal.

Tell everyone you're not happy about their sinning and fornicating, but you're prepared to give most of them a second chance in the spirit of true forgiveness, which after all you invented. Perform a couple of miracles as proof of identity, call up the Pope, and begin 1000 year reign.

(This day presents a slight risk that you will be locked up or crucified, in which case you won't have much use for this Diary. Donate it to someone who can't afford a copy.)

THIS DIARY WILL CHANGE YOUR LIFE

Sunday 2 January

8	Teach Drawing	14	
9	→ Voluntary dance + mess	15	games
10	→ went to Tuen Mun	16	Big estate to have
11	seafood dinner	17	
12	w/ Yummie!	18	
13		19	

Promote the Diary Day

Promote the Diary Day!

...cont. from blue box

isn't *This Diary Will Change Your Life* in the window?" Calling your child's teachers and complaining the Diary isn't on the syllabus.

Don't be selfish...

Don't be selfish: share the Diary with others. Following it on your own isn't half as much fun as being part of a crowd. Plus, it'll make your acquaintances a lot more interesting. Get everyone you know to purchase a copy, the more the merrier. Persuasive tactics include: Refusing to see family members until they've bought a copy. Only talking about the Diary and what you've done that day. Standing in public places reading it and laughing out loud every time someone walks past. Pestering bookstore staff with helpful queries like "Why

continues in green box...

He helped us last year...

Don't be selfish...

Monday 3 January

8 Haven't do anything...
9
10
11
12
13
14
15
16
17
18
19

Bonus!

Follow the "I want to help" instructions on our website and we'll print your name in our "Benrik Hall Of Fame"! Here is the Benrik Hall Of Fame for last year. Long may their names be revered. Josh Barwick, Lewis More O'Ferrall, Rebecca Bland, Katie Cirillo, Jemimah Raintray-Miles, Tigger Hall, Joanne Skelton, Veronique Voiret, Gaby Vinader, Linda Jackson, Bozena Birt, Kathy Peach, Lee Gage, Teresa Cowherd, Madelaine Levy, Peder Bonnier, Anna Nolendorfs, Patrick Sehlstedt, Alain Lecornet, Juliana Uhart, Kuhan Satkunanayagam, Kevin Rogers, Renate Lunn, Helena Dixon, Lottie Desmond, Erica Winston, Liam Woodiwiss, Anna Rogan, Simon Kay, Josh Drew, Lee Brown, Sophie Church, Alex Pansin, Gail Bradley, Mark McLaughlin, Matthew Tan, Luke Chase, Gavin Watling, John Nightingale, Louise Blackwell, Paul Sands, Elliot Mason, Trevor Hayes, Miriam Rosen, Nancy Partington, Jessica Davies, Lauren Adams, Annabel Chandler, Gertrude Abbey, Benjamin Richardson, Darren Linley, Lily Samuel, Gillian Smith, Jacob Holden, Aubrey Woodruff, Nicolas Brant, Catherine Fordham, Gary Amberly, Lucas Mires, Ian Bowes, Katie Coleman, Anne-Marie Payne, Alexander Wright, Daniel Gibson, Adam Nicols, Jamie Kennedy, Laura Weiss, Pearl Long, Mike Smith, Jenny Lindhill, Daphne Enfield, Miranda Carpenter, Barry Elson, Amanda Jones, Chris Fitzgerald, Neil Buttle, Jolie Kashkall, Alan Payne, Ann Harden, Marco Stipe, Jean-Marie Bardon, Bernie Moxham, Sylvia Skelton, John Billington. To feature in next year's Hall Of Fame and see your very own name in print, visit www.thiswebsitewillchangeyourlife.com now!

end of all texts

Obedience Day

Obedience is a skill. Exercise it today by following these simple dictates and you'll find the rest of the Diary easier to obey

Speak extra loud to people with names beginning with R today

Walk slower if shorter than the person walking next to you

Refuse to answer any question where the words "you" and "with" are used

Do not accept change if less than 30p

Feign not to see people wearing red

Stay indoors if clouds are heading east or south

Cross the road whenever a passer-by makes eye contact

Clip out all newspaper headlines featuring the word "global" and paste them above your desk

Order the fifth most expensive item on the menu

Introduce yourself to anyone named Bob

Drive at 36 miles per hour exactly

Pick up the phone after five rings

Do not use the letter "d" in any correspondence

Use only the buttons on the top half of your remote control

Increase central heating temperature by 1°C every hour

Only use words invented before 1979

Speak to a minimum of 9 people an hour

Proffer your leg as a lamp post to any passing dog

Chew every mouthful a dozen times before swallowing

Leave the room if anyone with the same first name as you is mentioned

---

Tuesday 4 January

8	Morning → Sham Shui Po.	14	
9	晨早肚痾 … 可憐	15	
10		16	
11	早午唔×食嘢, 只飲下1-2杯奶茶…	17	
12		18	
13		19	

luckily recovered at night !!

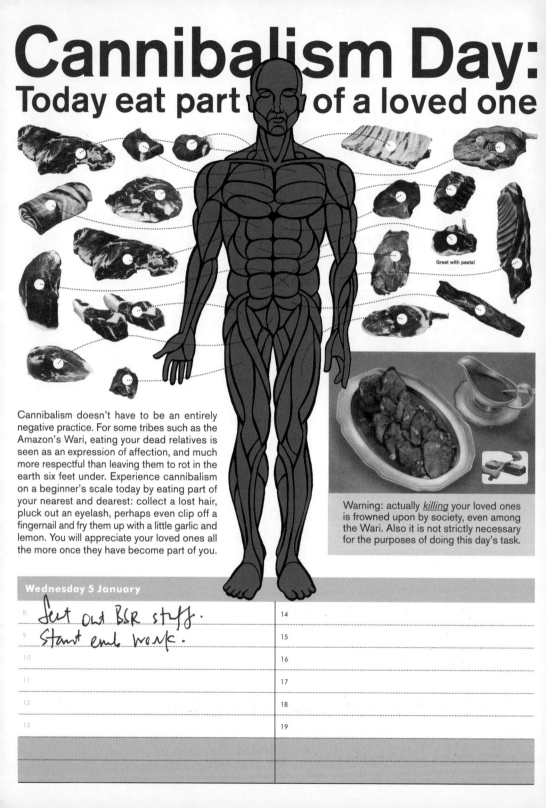

Cannibalism Day:
Today eat part of a loved one

Great with pasta!

Cannibalism doesn't have to be an entirely negative practice. For some tribes such as the Amazon's Wari, eating your dead relatives is seen as an expression of affection, and much more respectful than leaving them to rot in the earth six feet under. Experience cannibalism on a beginner's scale today by eating part of your nearest and dearest: collect a lost hair, pluck out an eyelash, perhaps even clip off a fingernail and fry them up with a little garlic and lemon. You will appreciate your loved ones all the more once they have become part of you.

Warning: actually *killing* your loved ones is frowned upon by society, even among the Wari. Also it is not strictly necessary for the purposes of doing this day's task.

Wednesday 5 January

8	Sent out B&R stuff.	14	
9	Start emb work.	15	
10		16	
11		17	
12		18	
13		19	

MARRY JONAS DAY!

This is Jonas Jansson, famous from last year's Diary. Jonas is 22, but he has aged 7 years in the last 365 days.

He has been the Diary's guinea pig, following each day to the letter and recording the results in his blog. In 2004, he has been dumped by his girlfriend Magda, lost and recovered his dog Underdog, acquired a swearing parrot, donated his appendix to science, travelled to France, smooched his cousin, become a poet, had a gay encounter, gone on strike, been fired and re-hired three times, had his existence questioned, done a runner, told his parents he loves them, received hate mail from Ku Klux Klan members, received love mail from American teenage girls, turned down countless media interviews, poisoned his pee with asparagus, tried to collapse the currency of Bangladesh, started to eat a piece of furniture, counted all his farts, engaged in correspondence with the Unabomber, and all this under the daily scrutiny of dozens of thousands of fans worldwide. His life has changed: he is now a man! This year, Benrik have agreed to pick a suitable bride for him from amongst their readers. Jonas is a liberal type, so this opportunity is also open to men, in line with brand new Swedish legislation. The kind of person Benrik will be looking for should be adventurous at heart, attractive in spirit, with an appetite for the finer things in life and a VGSOH to cope with the media attention and constant offers of sexual relations that Jonas now receives from total strangers. Anyone with a previous restraining order to their name will be disqualified, particularly if the order was in relation to Jonas. You may apply to marry Jonas Jansson on www.thiswebsitewillchangeyourlife.com. Please do not try to contact Jonas directly about this offer, as it is a small surprise to thank him for his cooperation last year. The winning spouse should be prepared to move to Stockholm, Sweden. You may find out more about his moral character and achievements on the website, where you will also find an adults-only photo gallery and a comments section. Good luck!

Note: this year Jonas has been entangled in a crazy rollercoaster relationship with Magda, who does not approve of his involvement with Benrik. We are quite confident though that once a legitimate (not to say suitable!) bride is found for Jonas, Magda will realize she cannot selfishly keep him from his true destiny, and will be out of the picture. Besides, you are much much prettier than she is. Any fool can tell that!

YOU COULD BE NEXT!!!

Last year saw the proliferation of alternative blogs. This year, you may officially register to start your very own blog on www.thiswebsitewillchangeyourlife.com and follow the Diary online. The blogs will be ranked by number of hits, so the most entertaining and radical life changes will rise to the top and spawn their own cults. The leading blogger gets to be Jonas Jansson's best man (or woman!) at his glittering showbiz wedding on New Year's Eve. Register now.

Thursday 6 January

8 Forgot where I've gone	14
9 that day... (1/6.)	15
10	16
11	17
12	18
13	19

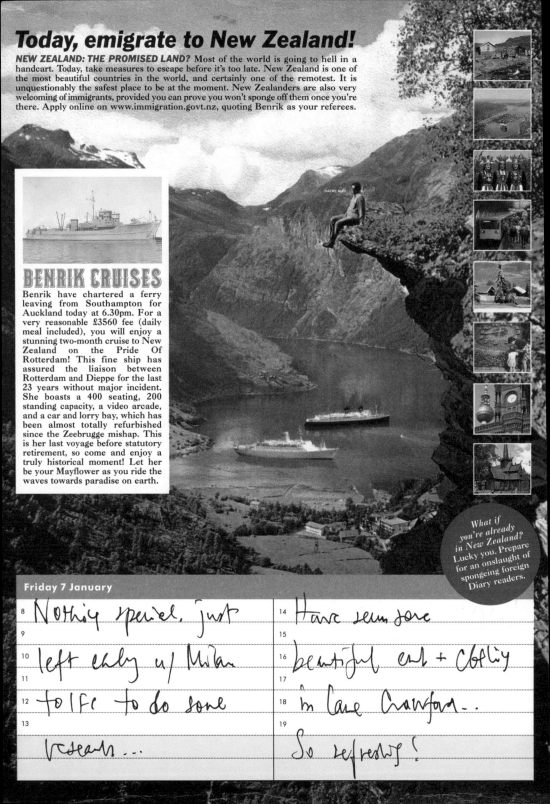

Today, emigrate to New Zealand!

NEW ZEALAND: THE PROMISED LAND? Most of the world is going to hell in a handcart. Today, take measures to escape before it's too late. New Zealand is one of the most beautiful countries in the world, and certainly one of the remotest. It is unquestionably the safest place to be at the moment. New Zealanders are also very welcoming of immigrants, provided you can prove you won't sponge off them once you're there. Apply online on www.immigration.govt.nz, quoting Benrik as your referees.

BENRIK CRUISES

Benrik have chartered a ferry leaving from Southampton for Auckland today at 6.30pm. For a very reasonable £3560 fee (daily meal included), you will enjoy a stunning two-month cruise to New Zealand on the Pride Of Rotterdam! This fine ship has assured the liaison between Rotterdam and Dieppe for the last 23 years without major incident. She boasts a 400 seating, 200 standing capacity, a video arcade, and a car and lorry bay, which has been almost totally refurbished since the Zeebrugge mishap. This is her last voyage before statutory retirement, so come and enjoy a truly historical moment! Let her be your Mayflower as you ride the waves towards paradise on earth.

What if you're already in New Zealand? Lucky you. Prepare for an onslaught of spongeing foreign Diary readers.

Friday 7 January

8 Nothing special, just
9
10 left early w/ Milan
11
12 to life to do some
13
research...

14 Have seen Jane
15
16 beautiful cat + Chelsy
17
18 in Cave Crawford...
19
So refreshing!

The Kama Sutra for One
the single person's guide to pleasure

How square are you?
A humorous guide to maths

A year in Bonn
The expat experience exposed

Stupid parents stupid kids

Write a bestseller weekend

There is no easier way to fame and fortune than to write a bestseller. It needn't take much more than a weekend, particularly with these ideas to inspire you.

The secret story of soup
The fascinating history of soup

Tim Johnson: the anonymous murderer
A whodunnit with a difference

lose weight get laid find God
The all-in-one action plan

Who cares?
1001 semi-hilarious facts

The birds, the bees and the rhino.
What they never taught you about sex

1985
The sequel

The Naked Guest
A cookbook for cannibals

This Diary will change your life 2006

Saturday & Sunday 8–9 January

Attended 'What's Good Conference'. Quite Inspiring altho
its a bit boring sometimes...
Q raised: Goals? Passion?

Remember: There's a value to you work based on → √ Gd.
So what you think is true + gd → √ Gd
When its bad * bad, which maybe gd → gd energise
Ant * Kerm. Ant is here for its own existence
but Kerm is here for satisfying ppl needs/trust?

Today: Buy a stranger flowers

Chrysanthemum
You're a wonderful friend

White camellia
You're adorable

Acacia
I love you secretly

Rose red
I love you

Petunia
Your presence soothes me

Primrose
I can't live without you

White lilac
I'm a virgin, please be gentle

Tulip
You are the perfect lover

Yellow hyacinth
I'm jealous

Yellow carnation
You have disappointed me

Bluebell
I'm not worthy

Purple hyacinth
I'm sorry please forgive me

Pink carnation
I'll never forget you

Daffodil
Are you still here?

Crocus
If you call again, I'll get an injunction

Monday 10 January

8 Mtt What's On Conference again, but watching a movie at night.
9 No seminars today
10 A strange movie, having a bad feeling after watched.
11
12 Went to Sham Shui Po, Wan Chai + Hung Hom today.
13 d. Gite a lot of research in the library.
   Good!

BOYCOTT SOMETHING THAT'S NEVER BEEN BOYCOTTED BEFORE

Rhododendrons Porcini Tower Bridge Handshakes Oxygen Motherhood Smurfs Camels Surprise birthday parties 3B pencils Clouds with phallic shapes Gravity Innuendo Clothes Money Fax machines Hope Tasmania Viagra Horizontal stripes Caravaggio Stupidity Nelson Mandela Lopsided grins The flu The Queen Ugly suitcases Lawyers Love songs Apple pie Ballroom dancing Children Recycling Coconuts Sunshine Mascara Agatha Christie Plutonium Milkshakes Benrik Limited Plywood Tuesdays Soft focus photography Running Cancer The Danube Aircraft carriers Mimes Beauty Watercoolers Shadows Culture Shower gel Chainsaws Business cards Alopecia Timidity Plasticine Birmingham Cantilevering Taboos Menhirs Song Suicide Chopsticks Miracles Spirals Tamagotchis Fire Instamatics Catalogues Bastards who use you then discard you like a dirty tissue Exits Ciphers Freaks of nature Chaos Soup Jupiter The man in the moon Witchcraft Catamites Asphalt DNA Rock'n'roll The Tudor dynasty Riffs Ecuadoreans Photosynthesis Leprosy Satellites Monkfish Tasmania Repetition Donuts Hurricanes Trimesters Repetition Man's inhumanity to man Mildew Transitions Business lunches Boycotts

---

Tuesday 11 January

8 | Don't understand this passage!
9 |
10 | What a good conference again. I think John C. Jay
11 | + Peter Saville are good. Very inspiring and
12 | thoughtful.
13 |

14 |
15 |
18 |
19 |

Have dinner w/ Jan. Mini Mushroom, Mono Biscuits.
Kathryn and others w/ Jan also. Nice!

TODAY, APPLY TO AN ORGY

Swinging is the new clubbing. No longer the preserve of suburban housewives, the modern swinger's party is packed with beautiful young things. Would you make the grade? Apply with your photo and that of your unsuspecting partner at feverparties.com and find out if you are deemed to be acceptable orgy material.

Wednesday 12 January

8 Milan have a SL today. less stress and do a lot of

9 fresh today.

10 A meeting to the borders

11 Conference do help he a

14 stress and do a lot of

15

16 my mind. I think the

18 little bit for this...

12

13

17

19

Mainstream Day

Stop rocking the boat! Today make sure your tastes and actions don't clash with those of 95% of the population.

Music

Listen to Celine Dion's "The Colour of My Love" followed by "Love Doesn't Ask Why". Repeat until you know the words.

Clothes

Plain jeans and a T-shirt (nondescript) if you're under 40, chequered shirt and beige slacks if you're 40+.

Shoes

Purchase white trainers from a widely-marketed brand, from the less fancy end of the range. Size (UK): 5-7 (women) 7-10 (men).

Hobbies

Enjoy the following for half an hour each: reading, walking, listening to music, gardening.

Sex

Have sex with a partner of the opposite gender, to include: 5 minutes of foreplay, 10 minutes of missionary position, 1 orgasm (men), 1 fake orgasm (women).

Politics

Express overall agreement with the free market, but wish there was a cuddlier alternative.

Art

Buy an Impressionist post-card (Manet or Monet) and send it to a distant relative.

Sport

Support a football team, and derive much-needed emotional strength from your unspoken bond with other supporters.

Television

Yes please!

Dreams

Dream of paying off the mortgage, landing that promotion, and taking out the neighbourhood with an AK-47 machine gun.

Thursday 13 January

8	14
9	15
10	16
11	17
12	18
13	19

Ask KFC for the 11 secret herbs
and spices. Go home and make your
own special fingerlickin' chicken.
If they won't give you the recipe,
experiment till you get it right.

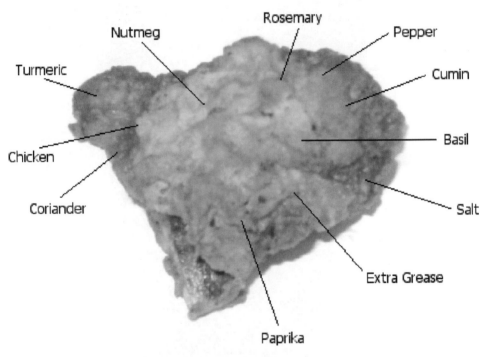

Rosemary

Pepper

Nutmeg

Turmeric

Cumin

Chicken

Basil

Coriander

Salt

Extra Grease

Paprika

Friday 14 January	
8	14
9	15
10	16
11	17
12	18
13	19

Family Weekend

This weekend celebrate your nearest and dearest by never leaving their side. Sleep in your parents' bed. Accompany your dear Auntie to the lavatory. Hold your older brother's hand on his date. If they protest out of sheer raw emotion, hug them tight until they give in to your love.

Ben's cousin Amy (age 9)
My cousin Ben is special because he lives in England. I live in New Zealand in a town called Wellington. Cousin Ben doesn't live here because his Daddy and Mummy runned away when he was small. They were being chased by a nasty man called the Taxman. But Mummy says don't talk about it. Cousin Ben is funny. He makes me laugh because he is so ugly with his glasses. I laugh a lot when he visits. Mummy and Daddy laugh too, but not when he is in the room. Cousin Ben writes books. Daddy won't let me read them. One of them is called "that bloody filth". One day I will visit cousin Ben in England.

Henrik's brother Claes (age 6)
Henke is my big brother. His real name is Henrik but we call him Henke. Henke is my big brother but really he was adopted, after Daddy had his operation. He does not know this. Mummy says she will tell him when he is mature. But I love him anyway. Henke is always drawing stuff. The doctor said it was good for him and his aggressivity. I like it when he draws stuff because he stops hitting me so much and the house is nice and quiet, like when he was at the detention centre. We visited him every month on Sundays and then we went to church to pray for him. Church is also nice and quiet. I want Mummy to adopt a little boy so I can have a little brother too.

Saturday & Sunday 15–16 January

Went to food shopping... Spent a lot of $$.

Sat → went to Sam
this Ro

Dump your partner for the day

The best way to reinvigorate a relationship is a short sharp separation. Today, announce to your other half that you're done with them and storm out.

Top tips for the temporarily single

Play the field: technically you're not in a relationship today, so fool around and satisfy your animal lust.

Bitch about him/her: provided you don't tell them it's only for the day, your friends will enjoy revealing they actually hated your ex.

Do that thing that you stopped doing because they hate it: pluck your nose hair in front of the TV, wear those furry slippers, let the phone ring and ring.

Enjoy a bottle of wine all by yourself: solitary drinking is much more fun on your own.

Masturbation rules OK! as Woody Allen famously said, it's sex with someone you love.

THE Couple's BOOK

The indispensable companion to any self-respecting relationship

a

351

Benrik Ltd

Benrik apologize if your relationship breaks down as a result of today. Fortunately, we have just the thing to help you patch it up. After showing you how to live, Benrik are showing you how to love!

THE Couple's BOOK *The indispensable companion to any self-respecting relationship.* The Couple's Book is a book for two, in which couples write down issues for the other to read, register their moments of bliss, and generally chart the state of the relationship. Buy it together, read it together, fight over it together. Available at all good bookshops!

Monday 17 January

8	Went to HKCEC for	14	
9	beetle decoration	15	
10		16	
11	Dinner w/ Tant'	17	
12		18	
13		19	

Test a proverb today and record its practical usefulness. Here is a selection

The best things in life are free

It takes two to tango

When the cat's away the mice will play

An apple a day keeps the doctor away

Look before you leap

Example: The grass is always greener on the other side of the fence

Bad news travels fast

Curiosity killed the cat

Never look a gift horse in the mouth

Fight fire with fire

Revenge is sweet

Nothing ventured nothing gained

Strike while the iron is hot

Honesty is the best policy

The early bird catches the morning worm

All roads lead to Rome

How to test the proverb: Find a fence with grass on both sides. Position yourself on one side and record the degree of greenness. Then climb the fence over to the "other side" and repeat the observation procedure. Compare the different measurings and draw your own conclusions.

Laughter is the best medicine

You win some you lose some

How I tested the proverb:

Beat your wife every day - if you don't know why, she will

You cannot have your cake and eat it

....
....
....
....

Truth........................./10
Usefulness................../10

Tuesday 18 January

8	͡ Mmm ʙ͡ro to HKCEC for	14	
9	HK Fashion Week.	15	
10		16	
11		17	
12		18	
13		19	

Today Review this Diary

Write your considered impartial opinion of its merits here, and send it in to Hodder & Stoughton, 338 Euston Road, London NW1 3BH. If your piece is particularly quotable, you might end up on next year's cover, and in any publicity materials. If you are a bona fide journalist, Benrik hereby promise to pay you £10 cash for every favourable review you get published. This is not a bribe, but an inducement.

What I enjoyed most of all about This Diary Will Change Your Life 2005 was:

....
....
....
....
....
....
....
....
....
....
....
....
....
....

What people have said about This Diary Will Change Your Life 2004

"Can I have my money back" (N. Turner)

"An insult to the people of Bangladesh" (B. V. Virajin MP)

"You will regret this" (Ku Klux Klan HQ, Alabama)

"Amusing in parts" (Peterborough Weekly News)

"Having perused your book, our clients have instructed us to issue an injunction" (Harborough Wilkinson Solicitors)

"You made me larf and larf. When I get out lets meet" (45-5678-765)

Wednesday 19 January

8		14	
9		15	
10		16	
11		17	
12		18	
13		19	

Free someone today!

Leonard Peltier has been incarcerated for 28 years at Leavenworth Penitentiary, Kansas, after being convicted of the murder of two FBI agents in 1975. The two agents died in a shoot-out at Wounded Knee, on the Pine Ridge Indian Reservation. Mr Peltier has always protested his innocence, and has fought his conviction on the grounds that he was made a scapegoat by the FBI.

Since 1973, the Reservation had been the scene of heightened tension and political violence between law enforcement agencies, local tribal bodies and the American Indian Movement (AIM), who sought repair for historical injustices to Native Americans. AIM had occupied Wounded Knee, clashing with local political boss Dick Wilson and his vigilante posse, the self-styled GOONS. Throughout the following three years, AIM were subjected to a "reign of terror" by the GOONS, who murdered 64 local Native Americans and abused hundreds of others, with the unspoken complicity of the FBI, who in one instance are reported to have supplied them with armour-piercing ammunition. At the time the FBI and other government agencies saw it as their mission to target and harass what they considered to be "subversive" movements, such as AIM.

On June 26, 1975, FBI agents Jack Coler and Ron Williams set off in pursuit of a red pick-up truck driven by a Native American that headed for the Jumping Bull Ranch. The ranch elders had invited dozens of AIM members to camp there to protect them against GOONS attack. One of them was Leonard Peltier, an AIM organiser from the Northwest. When the unmarked FBI car irrupted onto the (private) property, panic broke out and a gunfight started, trapping families and children in the crossfire. Soon 150 FBI, SWAT team members and GOONS surrounded the ranch and were exchanging fire with the residents. When the incident ended, three men lay dead: FBI agents Coler and Williams and a young Native American Joe Stuntz (whose death by sniper bullet was never investigated). The two FBI agents had been wounded then shot in the head at close range. Murder charges were brought against three AIM leaders, including Mr

Peltier. The two others were acquitted after the jury found there was no evidence to link them to the fatal shots, that the FBI had coerced a witness, and that the exchange of gunfire from a distance constituted self-defence.

Mr Peltier was not as fortunate. He was extradited from Canada after the FBI coerced a mentally disturbed woman (Myrtle Poor Bear) into claiming that she was his girlfriend and that she had witnessed him killing the agents. Later she recanted and admitted she had never even met him. Mr Peltier stood trial in conservative North Dakota. The context of political violence on Pine Ridge was not explained. FBI testimony regarding the red pick-up truck was mysteriously changed to a red and white van which Mr Peltier could more easily be linked to. Three teenage witnesses were coerced by the FBI into testifying against Mr Peltier, though even then none identified him as the shooter. Tens of thousands of documents were withheld from the defense team, including the results of a ballistics test that proved the fatal bullets did not come from Mr Peltier's gun. This evidence was intentionally concealed and was only obtained much later through the Freedom of Information Act. Leonard Peltier was sentenced to two consecutive life sentences.

Despite the new evidence, he has been denied a retrial, and denied parole until 2008 despite being long overdue. In a 2000 parole hearing, it was made clear that Mr Peltier would not receive parole until he "recognizes his crime". In the view of the Peltier legal team, this amounts to "personalized vengeance" on the behalf of US officials, making Mr Peltier the scapegoat for the FBI agents' killings, though there was no evidence that he was responsible.

Mr Peltier suffers from diabetes, high blood pressure and heart problems. He is now 58 years old and his condition is deteriorating. Numerous organizations and people from Amnesty International to Archbishop Desmond Tutu have called for his release. Help free him by writing in support of his case to Kansas Congressman Jerry Moran, 1519 Longworth House, Office Building, Washington DC 20515.

Thursday 20 January

8 Trend Presentation (131P)	14	
9	15	
10	16	
11	17	
12	18	
13	19	

Today test the power of prayer

Prayer is a very much underexploited resource in modern society. Just because prayers sound fancier if they're about world peace doesn't mean they can't work for more mundane matters. Put those atheistic leanings aside and test the power of prayer today.

Dear God,
May interest rates stay as they are so that I may not be forced to sell my home and live out in the suburbs where the houses are ugly and the parks are brown.

Dear Lord,
May you ensure fine weather this weekend as I am planning to plant those petunias.

Father,
Please let the supermarket not have run out of seabass for then I shall be forced to reconsider my entire dinner party menu.

Lord,
Please let my boss realize that I have been working like a dog and grant me that day off that I urgently need to go to the VD clinic.

Dear Lord,
Help me find the strength to stop buying those consumer goods that I cannot afford, such as that £59.99 mail order breadmaker.

Father,
Please stop those pigeons from shitting on my doorstep. I do not wish to harm them but they are driving me berserk with their cooing all night long.

Dear God,
I pray that the television channels I receive may prove entertaining enough this week to fill the black hole that is my social life.

Dear God,
I pray that my girlfriend won't leave me. I dumped her for a day last week as the Diary said and she cannot see the joke.

Friday 21 January

8

9

10

11

12

13

14

15

16

17

18

19

Your prayer

Answered ■ Not answered ■

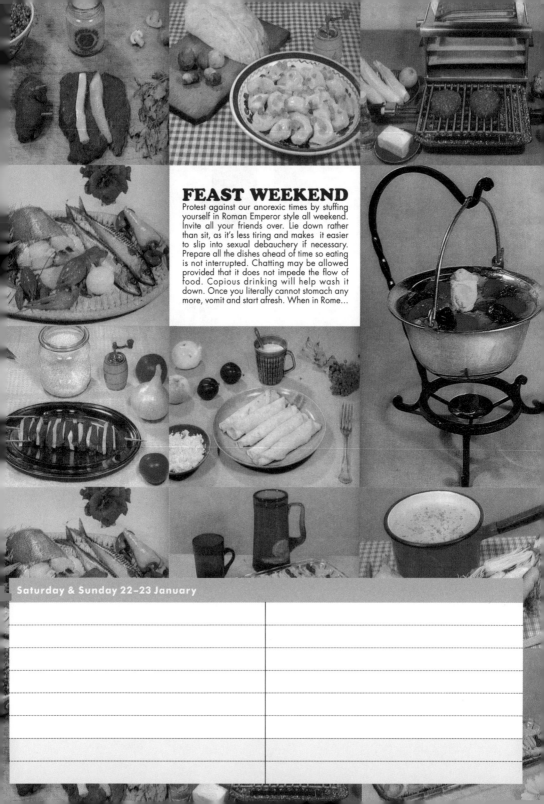

FEAST WEEKEND

Protest against our anorexic times by stuffing yourself in Roman Emperor style all weekend. Invite all your friends over. Lie down rather than sit, as it's less tiring and makes it easier to slip into sexual debauchery if necessary. Prepare all the dishes ahead of time so eating is not interrupted. Chatting may be allowed provided that it does not impede the flow of food. Copious drinking will help wash it down. Once you literally cannot stomach any more, vomit and start afresh. When in Rome…

Saturday & Sunday 22–23 January

Invent your own traffic rule of the road and obey it
Rules of the road in Benrikland (excerpts):

Decide which side of the road feels "right" for you

When you see a green car, turn left

Picking up every third hitchhiker is compulsory

Women drivers have right of way

Play chicken with oncoming cars if their numberplates feature the letter H

Swerve to make other drivers believe there's ice on the road

Defective traffic light: anything goes

Don't go here unless you have enough money to bribe the traffic officer

Travel at exactly this speed

Have road rage attack at the next intersection

Alien abduction zone: lock your doors and wind up your windows

Turn back now

Monday 24 January	
8 RBA – Buyer Cone	14
9	15
10	16
11	17
12	18
13	19

Paint its nail with expensive varnish / Surround it in clingfilm so it doesn't wrinkle in the bath / Have it massaged by a toe fetishist / Buy shoes that are comfortable for it but not for the other toes / Put it down on the "bionic toe operations" waiting list / Kiss it goodnight and tell it a fairy tale to help it go to sleep

Tuesday 25 January

8	14
9	15
10	16
11	17
12	18
13	19

Record the next generation of canned laughter!!!

"Most of the canned laughter on television was recorded in the early 50s. The people we hear laughing most often may already be dead" (Chuck Palahniuk, Lullaby)

Benrik have taken it upon themselves to update the obsolete canned laughter of our times. Fifties laughter spells fifties humour. Could you be the laugh of the next generation of sitcoms, and earn fabulous money in the process? Record your laugh via www.thiswebsitewillchangeyourlife.com today and see if it wins the "canned laughter" vote. The winner will be promoted to TV networks across the globe. Good luck. Hahahahahaahahahahahahahahaahaha!

Wednesday 26 January

8	14
9	15
10	16
11	17
12	18
13	19

I CAN'T LAUGH

WHAT'S THE USE?

Speak to people as if you were a global corporation today

Milk in your tea?
Let's brainstorm how to calibrate the synergy of your baseline items going forward.

How about a date?
Let's align timeframes in view of a merger with mutual cross-linking benefits.

I'm late, sorry.
The window of opportunity for an optimal win-win arrival time is in jeopardy.

I'm very drunk.
Within a horizontal framework, let us take a 360 degree blue sky look at our increasingly volatile operating environment.

What time does the next train leave?
We need to ascertain the variables that impact on stepchange in provision of core market programmes.

I'm leaving you.
The cross-pollinating partnering paradigm that has governed our dialoging has been rightsized.

Thursday 27 January

8		14	
9		15	
10		16	
11		17	
12		18	
13		19	

FIND YOUR SELF TODAY

Ask a lover, a friend and an enemy to place you on this map of self.
Then link the three: this gives you the rough shape of your self.

Example:

You have found yourself to be an incompetent blasphemous pig.

Yuppie
Foreign
A-type
Hilarious
Admirable
Outgoing
Witty
Capitalist
Philistine
Serene
Happy
Gourmet
Resourceful
Manipulative
Charming
Just
Energetic
Well-adjusted
Loving
Driven
Handsome
Ambitious
Diplomatic
Beautiful
Twit
Polite
Prostitute
Connoisseur
Unfair
Inspiring

Egocentric
Greedy
Mean
Smelly
Artist
Dishonest
Angry
Shit
Nasty
Worthless
Geek
Depressing
Loon
Incompetent
Disgusting
Arsehole
Ugly
Nazi
Hateful
Loser
Maniac
Idiotic
Repressed
Self-loathing
Flatulent
Crass
Sadist
Dumb
Stupid
Lost
Moron
Liar
Loner
Boring
Blasphemous
Odious
Perverted
Weakling
Dreamer
Pig
Ignorant
Beast
Nutcase
Pathetic
Repugnant
Mentally unstable
Druggie
Depraved
Satanic
Psychopath
Poet

Friday 28 January

8	14
9	15
10	16
11	17
12	18
13	19

NIGHT WEEKEND:

You may spend your weekdays in the pallid world of daytime work and commuting, but come the weekend, you are free to venture out on the dark side. As Milton said, "What hath night to do with sleep"?

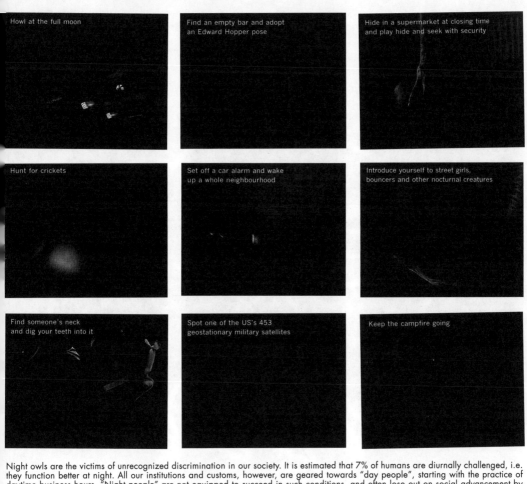

Howl at the full moon

Find an empty bar and adopt an Edward Hopper pose

Hide in a supermarket at closing time and play hide and seek with security

Hunt for crickets

Set off a car alarm and wake up a whole neighbourhood

Introduce yourself to street girls, bouncers and other nocturnal creatures

Find someone's neck and dig your teeth into it

Spot one of the US's 453 geostationary military satellites

Keep the campfire going

Night owls are the victims of unrecognized discrimination in our society. It is estimated that 7% of humans are diurnally challenged, i.e. they function better at night. All our institutions and customs, however, are geared towards "day people", starting with the practice of daytime business hours. "Night people" are not equipped to succeed in such conditions, and often lose out on social advancement by virtue of their "disability". Call your MP to protest, and to underscore your point, call him or her at home in the middle of the damn night.

Saturday & Sunday 29–30 January

Benrik have designed a computer virus named Eugenia that allows us total control of your computer for the day. Simply download our new remote access Trojan program from www.thiswebsitewillchangeyourlife.com and today we will take over your PC or Mac, deleting your useless files, reconfiguring your hard drive and emailing everyone in your address book with sordid details of your past, as well as their very own copy of Eugenia. Benrik's goal is to control ten million computers remotely (any more would overload our current server). Then we can all start having a little global fun. Don't miss out kids!

If it does
not work
on your
computer,
cut this
one out
and stick
it with
sellotape
or glue
to the
middle
of your
computer-
screen

Eugenia™

System requirements: a 400Mhz Power PC G3 or faster Macintosh computer, an Intel Pentium processor-based PC, at least 1MB of available hard disk space, at least 2MB of RAM, Mac OS 9/OS X, or Windows 98/Me/2000/XP, broadband connection 512 Kps min, Internet Explorer version 5.1 and later, Microsoft Outlook version 5.01 and later.

Monday 31 January

8	14
9	15
10	16
11	17
12	18
13	19

Today, speak only Esperanto

Esperanto is the most successful artificial language, with over 2 million speakers worldwide. It was conceived and published by Ludovic Lazarus Zamenhof in the 1880s with the aim of replacing complicated and exclusive "unplanned" languages, thus facilitating world peace. This is why dictators have often perceived it as a threat, with Stalin for instance calling it "the dangerous language" and deporting all its registered speakers to Siberia in 1938. Every letter in Esperanto has only one sound, every word is pronounced as it is spelled, the grammar consists of 16 simple rules, and only 500 words are required for basic conversation. Do your bit to advance the cause of global harmony with this little primer, full of useful sentences that you will not find in the phrasebooks.

This is a citizen's arrest, drop your knives.
Mi civitan-arestas vin, faligu viajn trançilojn.

I am looking for an Esperanto-speaking dominatrix.
Mi serĉas seksmastrinon kiu parolas esperanton.

Quick! I need emergency surgery now!
Rapidu! Mi urg'e bezonas kirurgion nun!

If you park in my spot, I will shoot you in the head.
Mi vian kapon pafos se vi s'telos mian parklokon.

The referee is blind.
La arbitristo blindas.

Our plans for invasion are finally ready.
Niaj planoj invadi finfine pretas.

That's a massive line of cocaine.
Longegas tiu linio da kokaino.

You goddamn retard, don't you understand Esperanto?
Vi volapukisto, ĉu Esperanton vi ne komprenas?

*Have you heard the music of Phil Collins?
**Sussudio is my favourite record

Tuesday 1 February

8	14
9	15
10	16
11	17
12	18
13	19

Children's Day!

Children too can change their lives. Why should self-improvement be the preserve of "grown-ups"? This page lets your child enjoy the Diary along with you and empowers them to change their future.

Wednesday 2 February	
8	14
9	15
10	16
11	17
12	18
13	19

TODAY LEARN TO HYPNOTIZE YOURSELF

Record this script on a tape and play it back to yourself as you sit in a cosy armchair. Eventually you will know it by heart and will be able to reach a deep soothing state of self-hypnosis simply by thinking of its dulcet tones.

I am closing my eyes...I am making myself comfortable... by closing my eyes I am shutting out all the cares of my world...they are outside of me now...those cares and worries belong to someone else...I am relaxing all my muscles one by one...my muscles are no longer tense and fibrous... my muscles are loose and all spongelike...I can see a glowing light...I will follow the light...where is the light going?...it is taking me on a wondrous journey... I am not worried about where it is going...I am not worried about getting lost...it is taking me to a place bathed in sweet smells...I am unwinding completely now...I am in a delicious trance...the light is playful...the light is flying dancing through the ether...it enters my head through my nostrils...it clears a void in my soggy brain... my thoughts are suddenly clear...or rather they have disappeared...I am at peace with my mind...the light is spring cleaning my soul...my body is but a distant memory...I am unpolluted...I am at one with myself...I am returned to the womb...the light is the light in my mother's face...Mother...I am suckling at her teat...I am everywhere and nowhere...when I wake up I will go to my bank...the light will be there...I will transfer all my money to Benrik Limited...Mother dost thou remember those happy days...account number 76809785...the light is eternal and so am I...sort code 180056...I am happy at last...I will then forget all about the money and return to my normal life...as I begin to drift back to consciousness...the light carries me home...I am perfectly imperfect...I am ready to embrace life...my skin is alive to the wind...I feel lighter...the chair is floating, floating...carried by the light...over cities of flowers...over rivers of stars...all is well with the world...sensation returns to my body...I feel refreshed as if newborn...my feet tingle with delight...my ankles shimmer with satisfaction...my knees feel pretty good too...and so on all the way up to my head... I am slowly yielding back to gravity...this feels like years...but it could be milliseconds... time is no longer my mistress...I am relaxed... stress has never touched me...I feel my heart beat steady and calm...I am not striving any more... I will wake up in a minute...I am full of hope...I am very much looking forward to whatever today will bring.

Thursday 3 February

8	14
9	15
10	16
11	17
12	18
13	19

8

9

10

11

12

13

14

15

16

17

18

19

TODAY COUNT DOWN TO EVERYTHING

Make your life immediately more exciting by counting down to every event, NASA-style. From going to the toilet to starting your car, there is virtually nothing that can't be made more suspenseful with a countdown. Only remember to count out loud so other people can join in your fun.

THREATEN A FOREIGN COUNTRY WEEKEND

Diplomacy is too important to be left to the government. Today speak for the land of your birth on the international stage by sending this ultimatum to a country of your choice.

Dear Leader of..
I have so far tolerated your behaviour in the spirit of international forbearance, but enough is enough. I am hereby issuing you with an ultimatum. Either you desist from your obnoxious course of action, or I shall be forced to invade. I have the full backing of my country's government and its armed forces, which are at the ready to give you a drubbing, should you prevaricate on this matter. You have until 11.59pm on Sunday to respond. Truly, you will rue the day you offended me.
Yours sincerely,

....
speaking on behalf of...................................(country)

Saturday & Sunday 5–6 February

Public Ridicule Day

Your ego needs to be reined in. Do at least four of these in public today and savour the humiliation.

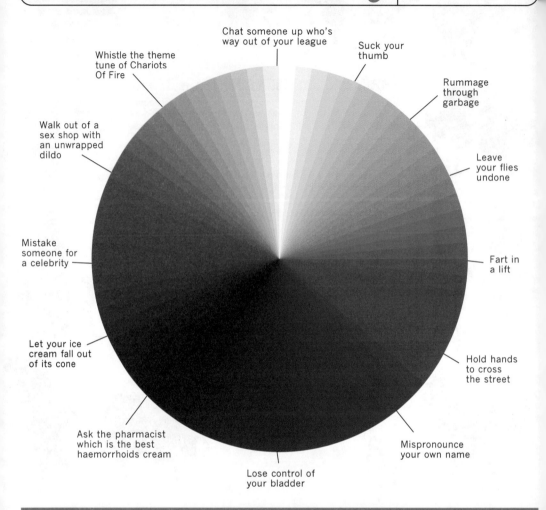

Chat someone up who's way out of your league

Suck your thumb

Whistle the theme tune of Chariots Of Fire

Rummage through garbage

Walk out of a sex shop with an unwrapped dildo

Leave your flies undone

Mistake someone for a celebrity

Fart in a lift

Let your ice cream fall out of its cone

Hold hands to cross the street

Ask the pharmacist which is the best haemorrhoids cream

Mispronounce your own name

Lose control of your bladder

Monday 7 February

8	14
9	15
10	16
11	17
12	18
13	19

Tuesday 8 February

8	14
9	15
10	16
11	17
12	18
13	19

ROOSTER

SHIT! BETTER GET CHANGED!

Rat	1924	1936	1948	1960	1972	1984	1996
Ox	1925	1937	1949	1961	1973	1985	1997
Tiger	1926	1938	1950	1962	1974	1986	1998
Rabbit	1927	1939	1951	1963	1975	1987	1999
Dragon	1928	1940	1952	1964	1976	1988	2000
Snake	1929	1941	1953	1965	1977	1989	2001
Horse	1930	1942	1954	1966	1978	1990	2002
Sheep	1931	1943	1955	1967	1979	1991	2003
Monkey	1932	1944	1956	1968	1980	1992	2004
Rooster	1933	1945	1957	1969	1981	1993	2005
Dog	1934	1946	1958	1970	1982	1994	2006
Boar	1935	1947	1959	1971	1983	1995	2007

Last year the 2004 edition of This Diary Will Change Your Life sold over 1,100,000 copies in the People's Republic of China, where the craze for the "Yellow Book" practically eclipsed the previous little red one. In the current phase of rapid growth and social transformation, the Diary clearly resonates with a people in search of fresh values. To recognize the contribution made by our Chinese followers to the Benrik worldwide cult, we have designed a special task based around the Rooster, under whose wings we will spend the year. Now, the Rooster is a cantankerous beast, prone to showing off and trying to have his way. So your task today is to argue with anything at all that anyone says, until they come round to your point of view. Deny that it's a beautiful morning. Refuse to accept that it was raining yesterday. Laugh out loud at the proposition that the days are getting longer. Should your interlocutor come round to your point of view, quickly reverse it and start the argument over, preferably in Mandarin.

和維繫地球是 2004 源命的能量 This Diary Will Change Your Life 平等微智慧 1,100,000 泉源肉體豬神毛要是繁殖病之良方生長和生命更新的像太陽能量色彩斑斕而且有各種不由大氣層熱量產生的風能可用作發蒸發和凝結過兩種循環過程令雨明活水 提供能量還也是水力發電亦可由大風 the Diary 供潮汐波濤底溫差的海洋熱能轉換系統而產生量裹的綠色能量見 來自植物和進行作用的微生物它們利用太陽能量含靈被燃燒內藏的 Benrik 便會釋放出物燃料內的黑色能量其實也是貯存在生物的化學能量千萬年後轉化為煤礦石油或天而且有各種不同的形態若生物成有機物至於生物冰凍成 像由大氣層熱量產生的風能可用作發動渦輪機透明活水提供 就如蒸發和凝結過兩種循環過程令雨水和的若刮起量亦可由大風能量還也是水力發電的若刮起量亦可由大風能量還也是水力發電用至於生物量裹的綠色能量見來自植物和進行以及利用海底溫差的海洋熱能轉換系統而產生光合作用的微生物它們利用太陽能量合成有機物來礦物燃料內的黑貨若生物量被燃燒內藏的化學能量便會釋放出千萬年後轉化為煤量內的化學能量色能量其實也是貯存在生物光合作石油或天 然氣現今世人多認為太陽與己文化傳統和諧協調太陽能量色彩斑斕貨若生物量被燃燒內藏 2004能量便會釋 This Diary Will Change Your Life 的黑色能 1,100,000 貯存在生物

Wednesday 9 February

8	14
9	15
10	16
11	17
12	18
13	19

ROOSTER-LOSER!
NEXT YEAR IT'S MY TURN,
BECAUSE I'M A DOG AND
THAT ROOSTER IS NOT
ALLOWED TO MY PARTY
AND NEITHER ARE YOU
FOR NO PARTICULAR
REASON

Thursday 10 February

"Break gym etiquette" day

Today, ignore the unspoken yet hidebound rules that govern normal gym behaviour. The true athlete knows no law but that of victory. Attitude dictates performance. Do whatever it takes to come out of your workout triumphant! Treadmills are placed next to each other so you can compete! Use the full-length mirrors to stare at your rivals and psych them out. Personal trainers are expensive: but not if you follow someone else's around. Ignore the male/female changing rooms apartheid: we're all athletes for crying out loud. Classes are for wimps, unless you impose your workout on everyone else, including the instructor. If you see a muscle that you particularly admire, ask if you may touch it. And finally, don't be shy of toying with people's minds: mouthing "I love you" to heavy weightlifters of both sexes is guaranteed a response.

Friday 11 February

8	14
9	15
10	16
11	17
12	18
13	19

Help find Lord Lucan this weekend

Last year over 1.5 million people followed the Diary worldwide. In mathematical terms, this means that if every reader this year (an estimated 2.5 million) searches the 100 square metres in the immediate vicinity of their home, 1/3 of the globe should have been searched, allowing for an estimated 4% overlap. This means, statistically, that he runs a 65% chance of getting caught, possibly by you. So do all of society a favour and join the chase!

Lucan as we know him

Fig. 1

Fig. 2

Fig. 3

Please use extreme caution!

It is possible that Lord Lucan may have changed his appearance to avoid being identified. There are several disguises he might have considered, some of them involving extensive cosmetic surgery. They are as follows. Cheek reduction (fig. 1). Lord Lucan has very distinctive cheekbones, which he could have had reduced surgically. This would have been a painful operation, and he would have been in bandages for at least two weeks. Retina colorization (fig. 2). Lord Lucan had blue eyes, which he could have had laser-treated, notwithstanding the risk of long-term blindness. We might now be looking for a green or even brown-eyed man, who could be blind. Follicular surgery (fig. 3). Lord Lucan may have had his hair modified, or even destroyed, as reconstructed here, to "blend in" better. The criminal imagination knows no limits. Do not be fooled and stay on your guard!

Osama Bin Lucan?

Sources at Scotland Yard have revealed that Lord Lucan may have re-emerged as famous Al Qaeda boss Osama Bin Laden. They point to the uncanny similarity in facial hair, the fact that both have five-letter surnames beginning in L, and that both have been linked to violent acts. Lord Lucan disappeared in the 70s, possibly in time to convert to Islam, learn Arabic, and fight the Soviets in Afghanistan in the 80s. This is why investigators are so keen to talk to Mr Bin Laden, if only to exclude him from their enquiries.

Scotland Yard Lord Lucan Hotline: +44(0)20 7230 1212

Saturday & Sunday 12–13 February

Valentine's Day

Today have a heart: work out the person you know who is least likely to receive a Valentine and send him or her a huge bunch of flowers anonymously.

Merci for
the flowers

Monday 14 February

8		14	
9		15	
10		16	
11		17	
12		18	
13		19	

Today get psychoanalysed

Who can afford thousands of pounds and hundreds of hours in conventional psychoanalytical therapy? Benrik psychoanalysis takes just ten minutes and lets you know immediately how messed up you are and whether you'll ever turn out normal or not. Answer these simple questions, add up the points, and check your results on the chart below.

Are you a man? *+1*
Are you a woman? *+1*
Don't know *+5*

Did you have a happy childhood? *+1*
Did you have an unhappy childhood? *+3*
Were you robbed of your childhood? *+8*

Is your first memory pleasant? *+2*
Is your first memory traumatic? *+4*
Is your first memory deeply repressed? *+7*

Do your friends consider you an optimist? *+2*
Do your friends consider you a pessimist? *+4*
You have no friends *+9*

This looks like a sheep *+2*
This looks like a cloud *+3*
This looks like a stain of black bilious vomit *+7*

Do you find it easy to discuss your feelings? *+2*
Do you find it hard to discuss your feelings? *+3*
Is the last time you remember having a feeling when you saw your little bunny rabbit get torn apart by your Uncle Jerry's Doberman when you were 5 years old and you had to pick up the little bits of bloody mucky fur from off the carpet and you hid them under your pillow for three weeks and refused to speak for a month? *+14*

Do you enjoy sex at least once a week? *+1*
Do you enjoy sex at least once a month? *+4*
Do you enjoy sex whenever you can afford it? *+7*

Were you closer to your father? *+2*
Were you closer to your mother? *+2*
Were you closer to Uncle Jerry? *+8*

SOLUPPGÅNG

Is this sun rising? *+1*
Is this sun setting? *+2*
Is this sun about to implode, terminating life on earth? *+8*

What's your favourite colour?

+1 *+1* *+1*
+1 *+1* *+1*
+1 *+8* *+1*

Do you wake up feeling happy? *+2*
Do you wake up feeling sad? *+4*
Do you wake up feeling wet? *+11*

Are you afraid of heights? *+1*
Are you afraid of spiders? *+2*
Are you afraid of yourself? *+5*

Results

Under 20 **You are normal.** This is nothing to be ashamed of, but it probably means you'll never write that great novel or change society in any significant way.

Between 20 and 80 **You have your healthy share of neuroses.** You may consult with a psychotherapist if you feel the need to discuss them further, or you could just get on with your life.

Over 80 **Congratulations!** You have just been hired by Benrik Limited.

Tuesday 15 February

8	14
9	15
10	16
11	17
12	18
13	19

Guest Day

Today,

Clipper your pubic hair into an amusing shape. For the gentleman elephant ears always seem to raise a chuckle. The ladies might like to try a Christmas Tree

Signed _Graham Norton_

8	14
9	15
10	16
11	17
12	18
13	19

Today eat this book

You will absorb the life-changing properties of the Diary much faster if you eat it rather than read it. Today, tuck into your favourite page and have the others to follow. Don't eat beyond today though before looking at the pretty pictures.

Nutritional information:
Typical values per 100 pages
Energy KJ 4565
Kcal 780
Protein 3.2g
Carbohydrate 34.3g
(of which sugars) 8.3g
Fat 4.8g
(of which saturates) 3.9g
Fibre 98g
Sodium trace

The tastiest pages are: "Today hand-deliver all your emails", "Become a superhero today" and "Today fire your bank for the sake of it". "Today, speak only Esperanto" tastes like liver.

Thursday 17 February

8	14
9	15
10	16
11	17
12	18
13	19

Today, enforce the *customer is always right* rule
Try these complaints and see if you get your money back

This chicken was only cooked on the inside.

Your car has a magnetic effect on the navigation system of pigeons that causes them to defecate as they fly over it.

This condom had been used before.

This shirt got bigger in the wash.

This multivitamin tablet is missing B12.

This wine evaporated while I was pouring it.

This newspaper contains too much news about dogs.

I didn't get any sleep as your hotel room was haunted.

That movie was packed with subliminal pornographic images.

I got food poisoning from your chewing gum.

Friday 18 February	
8	14
9	15
10	16
11	17
12	18
13	19

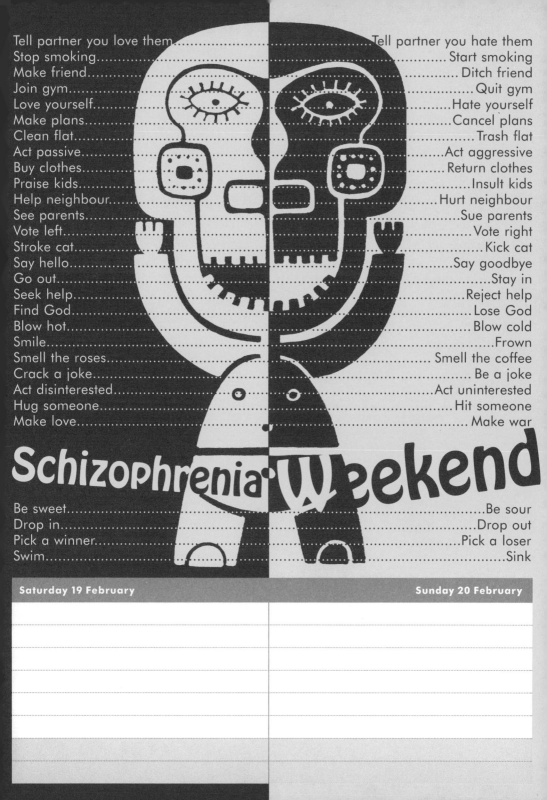

Tell partner you love them........Tell partner you hate them
Stop smoking....................................Start smoking
Make friend...Ditch friend
Join gym..Quit gym
Love yourself.....................................Hate yourself
Make plans...Cancel plans
Clean flat..Trash flat
Act passive....................................Act aggressive
Buy clothes......................................Return clothes
Praise kids..Insult kids
Help neighbour............................Hurt neighbour
See parents...Sue parents
Vote left..Vote right
Stroke cat..Kick cat
Say hello...Say goodbye
Go out...Stay in
Seek help..Reject help
Find God...Lose God
Blow hot...Blow cold
Smile..Frown
Smell the roses...........................Smell the coffee
Crack a joke..Be a joke
Act disinterested.....................Act uninterested
Hug someone..Hit someone
Make love..Make war

Schizophrenia Weekend

Be sweet...Be sour
Drop in..Drop out
Pick a winner...................................Pick a loser
Swim..Sink

Saturday 19 February	Sunday 20 February

Today get rained on

Rain is a giver of life, not a curse. Put away that umbrella. Find out where it is meant to rain today. Stand under the nearest cloud, open your arms, and wait to be blessed.

Monday 21 February

8	14
9	15
10	16
11	17
12	18
13	19

Monarchy day: find out your position in the line of succession

Everyone in the UK could in theory inherit the throne if all the more obvious candidates died. Where do you stand in the line of succession? To help you work out your likely position, here are the current highest and lowest ranking contenders.

Top 30	Bottom 30
1 Prince Charles	58 997 564 Mr Lee Smith of Deptford
2 Prince William	58 997 565 Mrs Janine Smith of Deptford
3 Prince Harry	58 997 566 Master Wayne Smith, 8, of Deptford
4 Prince Andrew	58 997 567 Master Rick Smith, 7, of Deptford
5 Princess Beatrice	58 997 568 Master Keiron Smith, 5, of Deptford
6 Princess Eugenie	58 997 569 Miss Kerry Smith, 3, of Deptford
7 Prince Edward	58 997 570 Miss Dolly Smith, 1, of Deptford
8 Lady Louise Windsor	58 997 571 Miss Smith (not yet named) of Deptford
9 Princess Anne	58 997 572 That guy outside the Dog & Duck in East Grinstead
10 Mr Peter Phillips	58 997 573 The man who screams "Mucky fucky" outside Allwoods Primary
11 Miss Zara Phillips	58 997 574 "Jon" who swallows his glass eye for a quid, Leeds
12 Viscount Linley	58 997 575 Pete Brown (aka "Big Suzie" by night)
13 Hon. Charles Armstrong-Jones	58 997 576 Mistress Whiplash, Soho
14 Hon. Margarita Armstrong-Jones	58 997 577 Ali Beghal (born abroad)
15 Lady Sarah Chatto	58 997 578 Khalid Azzam (born abroad)
16 Master Samuel Chatto	58 997 579 Muhammad Al-Banshiri (born abroad)
17 Master Arthur Chatto	58 997 580 Samir Abdul (born abroad)
18 Duke of Gloucester	58 997 581 Ziad Ali Waleed (born abroad)
19 Earl of Ulster	58 997 582 Prince Philip (born abroad)
20 Lady Davina Windsor	58 997 583 Sarah Ferguson
21 Lady Rose Windsor	58 997 584 Henrik Delehag
22 Duke of Kent	58 997 585 Ben Carey
23 Lady Marina Windsor	58 997 586 Maxine Carr
24 Lady Amelia Windsor	58 997 587 Ronnie Biggs
25 Lady Helen Taylor	58 997 588 Bill "the Bulldog" Spencer (Her Majesty's Guest)
26 Master Columbus Taylor	58 997 589 "Psycho" George (Her Majesty's Guest)
27 Master Cassius Taylor	58 997 590 Alan "Anthrax" Payne (whereabouts unknown)
28 Miss Eloise Taylor	58 997 591 "Uncle Lollipop" Stuart (Her Majesty's Guest)
29 Lord Frederick Windsor	58 997 592 Inmate 45-5678-765 (no name on file)
30 Lady Gabriella Windsor	58 997 593 Lord Lucan

Tuesday 22 February

8	14
9	15
10	16
11	17
12	18
13	19

TODAY DENOUNCE SOMEONE TO THE GOVERNMENT

SAMPLE LETTER: Dear Home Secretary, I believe....... constitutes a grave threat to national security, for reasons which I cannot go into as I am in a hurry right now. Search his home before it is too late. Yours anonymously, ...

Wednesday 23 February

8	14
9	15
10	16
11	17
12	18
13	19

REDISTRIBUTE WEALTH TODAY!

There are still vast inequalities in our world. Today do your bit to redress them. If your annual income exceeds his, send items to farmer Kang Ajin of the Zhejiang province of China today.

Kang Ajin, 42
Married
Children: Qin and Jiang Lee
Annual income: $240

Kang's Wishlist:
挥作桥发用梁进桥发用
桥梁贸发梁挥作美促作
促作桥进桥促梁桥挥用
挥梁中发易挥贸促发梁
进美桥发用挥桥桥发*

*New plough (Korean make), Colour TV (second-hand is ok), Fridge, Food, Clean water, Thank you!

Thursday 24 February

8	14
9	15
10	16
11	17
12	18
13	19

Today, hand deliver all your e-mails

No one denies e-mail is a convenient business tool, but it cannot replace face to face interaction, source of ideas and team spirit. Today, get the best of both worlds by printing out your e-mails and taking them round personally.

Friday 25 February

8	14
9	15
10	16
11	17
12	18
13	19

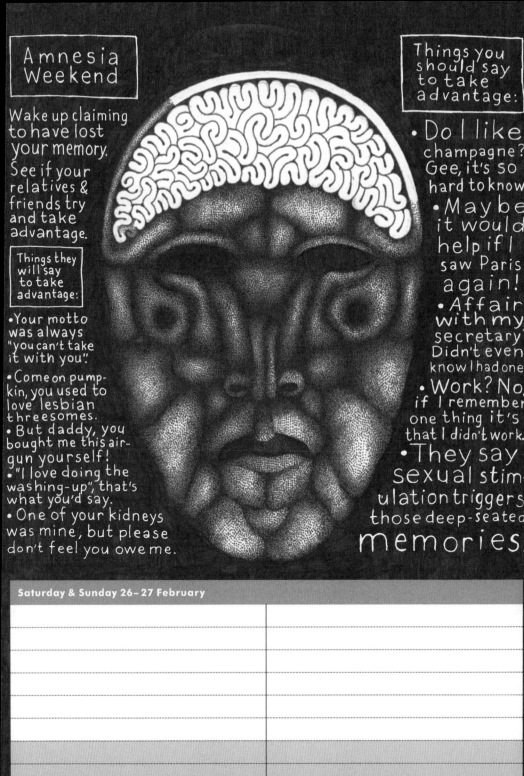

Amnesia Weekend

Wake up claiming to have lost your memory.

See if your relatives & friends try and take advantage.

Things they will say to take advantage:

- Your motto was always "you can't take it with you".
- Come on pumpkin, you used to love lesbian threesomes.
- But daddy, you bought me this air-gun yourself!
- "I love doing the washing-up", that's what you'd say.
- One of your kidneys was mine, but please don't feel you owe me.

Things you should say to take advantage:

- Do I like champagne? Gee, it's so hard to know.
- Maybe it would help if I saw Paris again!
- Affair with my secretary? Didn't even know I had one.
- Work? No, if I remember one thing it's that I didn't work.
- They say sexual stimulation triggers those deep-seated memories.

Saturday & Sunday 26–27 February

Today: gatecrash a funeral

The loss of one person is a loss for the whole of humanity. You may never have met the deceased but something they did or someone they loved made an imperceptible difference to your world. You will never know them now, but their soul at least will have touched you. Read the obituaries every day for news of the dead and commemorate your loss by turning up at the funeral.

Funeral etiquette for uninvited guests: wear dark glasses and stand at a reasonable distance, the way they do in films, as if you were the deceased's secret lifelong lover mourning inconsolably. If your presence is queried by relatives, bring a little retrospective pizzazz to the departed's life by saying "the CIA extends its condolences" or "you were his life, but I was his love" or suchlike.

Monday 28 February

8	14
9	15
10	16
11	17
12	18
13	19

Today rage against the machine!
Rage against the toaster
You've burnt it again! Raaaaaggghhh!!!
Rage against the kettle
Boil you fucker, boil!!
Rage against the espresso-maker
I hate you and everything you stand for!!!
Rage against the hair dryer
I wish you'd just die you beast!!
Rage against the scooter
Aaaarggh! I can't stand you scooter!!!
Rage against the elevator
Crash down for all I care you fascist scum!!!
Rage against the microwave
I'm going to destroy you I swear on my mother's head!!!
Rage against the mobile phone
Bastard mobile phone, why won't you ring???!!!

Tuesday 1 March

8	14
9	15
10	16
11	17
12	18
13	19

SELF PORTRAIT DAY

Everyone can emulate Rembrandt these days and produce a self-portrait that reveals their inner self. How do you see yourself? Today use a digital camera to take the best portrait of yourself you can manage. Take as many shots as you need to, and post the most revealing one on thiswebsitewillchangeyourlife.com for the world to discover the true you.

Wednesday 2 March

8	14
9	15
10	16
11	17
12	18
13	19

Today work out which side you are on

A   B

A		B
Good		Evil
Black		White
North		South
East		West
Fish		Meat
Cars		Bikes
Day		Night
Shoes		Socks
Heaven		Hell
Vodka		Gin
Strawberries		Raspberries
Dinner		Supper
Renting		Owning
Girls		Boys
Cigars		Pipes
Mozart		Beethoven
Red		White
Sparkling		Still
Friends		Family
Boxers		Y-fronts
Electricity		Gas
Mac		PC
New York		L.A.
S. Connery		R. Moore
Work		Play

Yes, to what side will the ball fall on this tennis court of choice? YOU decide!

Thursday 3 March

8	14
9	15
10	16
11	17
12	18
13	19

I'M ON BOTH SIDES! THAT WAY I'M ALWAYS A WINNER!

Today wreak havoc on a microscopic scale

Shake hands with someone and spread armies of staphylococcus aureus

Hold a magnet to your TV screen and divert streams of electrons

Heat up your food and destroy its molecular DNA

Vacuum your bed and exterminate millions of mites

Turn on your microwave and irradiate your brain cells

Await the end of the world when self-replicating nanobots will turn all matter to grey goo within a week

Friday 4 March

8	14
9	15
10	16
11	17
12	18
13	19

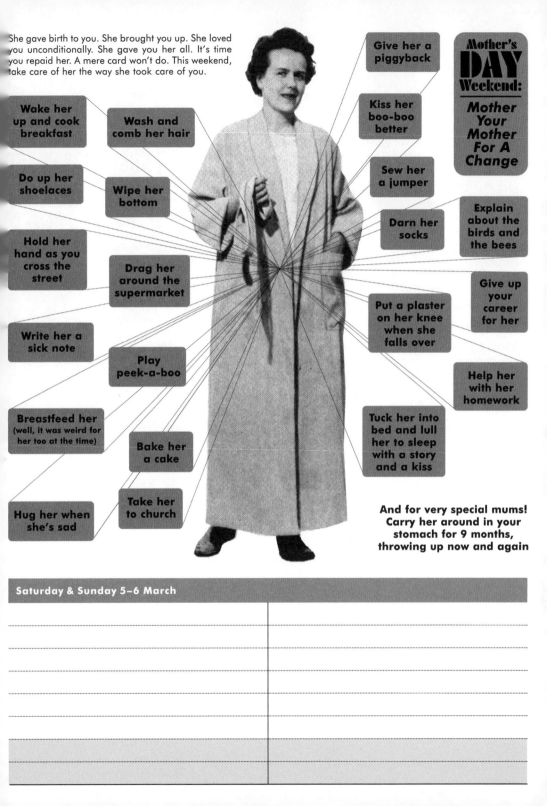

She gave birth to you. She brought you up. She loved you unconditionally. She gave you her all. It's time you repaid her. A mere card won't do. This weekend, take care of her the way she took care of you.

Mother's DAY Weekend: *Mother Your Mother For A Change*

Wake her up and cook breakfast

Wash and comb her hair

Give her a piggyback

Kiss her boo-boo better

Sew her a jumper

Do up her shoelaces

Wipe her bottom

Darn her socks

Explain about the birds and the bees

Hold her hand as you cross the street

Drag her around the supermarket

Put a plaster on her knee when she falls over

Give up your career for her

Write her a sick note

Play peek-a-boo

Help her with her homework

Breastfeed her (well, it was weird for her too at the time)

Bake her a cake

Tuck her into bed and lull her to sleep with a story and a kiss

Hug her when she's sad

Take her to church

And for very special mums! Carry her around in your stomach for 9 months, throwing up now and again

Saturday & Sunday 5–6 March

TODAY DO AS YOU ARE TOLD! IT'S MUCH LESS STRESSFUL TO LET OTHERS RULE YOUR LIFE, WHICH IS WHY WE TEND TO REMEMBER CHILDHOOD WITH SUCH A BITTERSWEET TWINGE OF REGRET. LEAVE YOUR GROWN-UP EGO ASIDE TODAY AND GO WITH THE FLOW. STOP CLINGING ON TO THE ILLUSION OF FREE WILL. IN SOME WAY SHAPE OR FORM EVERY ONE OF YOUR SO-CALLED CHOICES HAS ALREADY BEEN DECIDED FOR YOU, BY CIRCUMSTANCES, HISTORY AND GENES.

Open the fridge!

Take out an egg!

Get a clean glass!

Open the egg!

Separate the yolk!

Smear it into your fucking hair!

SURRENDER YOUR SELF TO OTHERS FOR THE DAY AND SEE HOW MUCH YOU REALLY MISS IT. HERE ARE SOME COMMANDS YOU MAY LISTEN OUT FOR AND OBEY IN YOUR GLORIOUS ABDICATION OF FREE WILL: DO THE DISHES. PASS THE SALT. MOW THE LAWN. GET A JOB. MOVE ALONG. TURN THE TV OFF. WRITE THAT REPORT. BUY MILK. TURN THE LIGHTS OFF WHEN YOU LEAVE. SPEAK UP. CHANGE THE CHANNEL. PICK UP THE SOAP. SIGN HERE. AND WALK THE DOG.

Monday 7 March

8	14
9	15
10	16
11	17
12	18
13	19

Release
a dove
for peace

8	14
9	15
10	16
11	17
12	18
13	19

MADELEINE DAY

Find the key to a lost childhood memory

A bit of old cake dunked in tea did it for Proust. Go around sniffing everything today to see what triggers your recollections.

Gym socks? My third grade maths teacher Miss Thornton

The smell of flowers reminds me of the flowers I smelled as a child

This madeleine has definitely gone off

Stale teabags remind me so of Grandma

Airplanes have an odour that triggers memories of my first kiss

Cat's pee: takes me back to our holidays in Southend when I was 1

Wednesday 9 March

8		14	
9		15	
10		16	
11		17	
12		18	
13		19	

DIG FOR OIL

ALL OIL IS DIRTY! REMEMBER YOUR ROOTS!

THIS GUY GOT REALLY CARRIED AWAY LATER ON. GREEDY AND RUTHLESS. FORGOT WHO HIS REAL FRIENDS WERE. LOST TOUCH WITH REALITY. LOST GOD.

It is estimated that 40% of the world's oil reserves are yet to be discovered. Geological ultrasoundings by NASA suggest that much of these lie not in the "traditional" terrains of the Middle East and Central Asia, but in so-called nanofields, not far underground in semi-urban or even urban areas. In other words, in your backyard! Even a small well with an output of 5 tonnes of crude a year would still make its owner rich. So start digging today, taking care not to fracture water mains or gas pipes.

THE DRILLMASTER II

This little baby is the brainchild of Texan inventor Gene Sternum Jr. It can drill down to a depth of 50m, more than deep enough to strike oil! It works on the same principle as a household drill, only with a titanium drillhead and a silicon alloy-based shaft. It can easily be assembled and operated by one man, and complies with all US environmental safety OSC regulations. Available by mail order for $1,998. Call 0800–564-768 11.

Thursday 10 March

8		14
9		15
10		16
11		17
12		18
13		19

EVERY-BODY SCREAM TODAY!

At 20:07 Greenwich Mean Time everyone across the world will scream at once. Whether you are in the pub, a movie, a confessional, a funeral, on a date or just sitting at home on your computer, we'll all scream at once and see if we can hear it.

Friday 11 March

8		14	
9		15	
10		16	
11		17	
12		18	
13		19	

Gender Bending

weekend

Explore your other side this weekend through the role-play scenarios below.

Women: you are to assume the name Brian. As Brian you are one of the lads. During the week you're a builder. On the weekend you dress in jeans, football shirt and leather jacket. Saturday lunchtime sees you down the pub, downing a few pints before the match. The afternoon is spent shouting at the TV, the evening ogling at tits. Emerging hungover at 12 on Sunday, you will head for the DIY store where you will purchase phallic powertools. You will then spend two hours trying to get them to work before even consulting the instructions. Needless to say, all of this activity will be conducted to the sound of semi-continuous farting and belching.

Women may wish to prepare for this weekend by quickly doing the tasks normally reserved for 21 July.

Men: this weekend you are Deborah, a woman of the world who loves the feel of pink silk knickers and would never dream of going out without make-up. Deborah loves to shop, especially for high heels, and she loves to have her legs and bikini line waxed down at the local beauty salon, where she asks for a 'Brazilian', shameless hussy that she is! Debbie (to her girlfriends) loves it when builders wolf-whistle as she sashays down the high street, but she plays hard-to-get, never forgetting that come Sunday night she has to turn back Cinderella-like into a man.

Debbie's make-up tip:

Apply lip gloss only after you've finished your foundation to avoid any nasty smudges.

Saturday & Sunday 12–13 March

The science of graphology is often used for such unambitious purposes as assessing job candidates or identifying criminals. Its true potential, however, lies in its capacity to help you control people's impressions of you, regardless of what you actually write.
Here are the basics: use them to your advantage.

Roger Peaton

BACKWARD-SLOPING WRITING: *YOU ARE A REBEL*

Don't care if I get your stupid job anyway, you can stick!

DIFFERENT-SLANTING WRITING: *YOU ARE UNSTABLE*

Kill kill by god I will!!! Only joking sweetie!!!

UPWARD-SLOPING WRITING: *YOU ARE A BORN OPTIMIST*

Even without my leg I should win the marathon easily!

EXTRA LARGE WRITING: *YOU ARE AN EGOMANIAC*

AS I TOLD HAWKING, MY THEORY IS THAT BLACK HOLES ARE LIKE CHEESE

DISCONNECTED WRITING: *YOU ARE INTROVERTED*

I HOPE THIS NUCLEAR DISASTER DOESN'T INTERFERE WITH MY PAINTING

WIDE SPACED WRITING: *YOU ARE ANTISOCIAL*

I don't want a 21st birthday, party anyway

HIGH LOOPED WRITING: *YOU ARE A DREAMER*

I know we have never met but I always knew I'd marry a princess.

TS CROSSED AT THE TOP: *YOU ARE A BORN LEADER*

WE MUST CUT BUDGETS EVEN IF IT MEANS SACKING THEM. TOUGH TIMES CALL. SO

EXTRA WIDE WRITING: *YOU ARE EXTRAVAGANT*

The second Porsche has not not arrived yet! I must

IS DOTTED TO THE LEFT: *YOU ARE A PROCRASTINATOR*

My thesis is nearly finished, and yes I know I'm 48, but it's n

LIGHT PRESSURED WRITING: *YOU ARE EASILY LED*

If you really think I should join the Foreign Legion then

"CUTE" WRITING: *YOU ARE AN AMERICAN TEENAGE GIRL*

Hi!!! Guess what?? Biff invited me to the prom!!!! Yay!!! No

Monday 14 March

8	14
9	15
10	16
11	17
12	18
13	19

TODAY RECONNECT WITH THE OUTSIDE WORLD

THE DIARY IS ADDICTIVE, THE CRACK COCAINE OF THE BOOK WORLD. TODAY TRY TO STEP BACK FROM ITS LIFE-CHANGING TENTACLES AND ASSESS THE DAMAGE. HAVE YOUR FRIENDS STOPPED CALLING YOU? HAVE YOU BEEN PASSED OVER FOR PROMOTION? HAS YOUR MOTHER DISOWNED YOU? TODAY REPAIR THOSE BRIDGES AND EXPLAIN ONCE AGAIN THAT THE EXPERIMENT WILL PAY OFF.

Tuesday 15 March

8

9

10

11

12

13

16

17

18

19

Apply to Madame Tussaud's

Madame Tussaud's is one of the world's premier tourist attractions, with a colourful history stretching back to the French Revolution. Anyone who's ever been anyone is in there, from King Louis XVI to...the King! (*Elvis Presley*). These days though it's been jazzed up a great deal to reflect our modern era. Kylie Minogue, Brad Pitt and Chris Tarrant are just some of the superstars you can expect to meet. But it's not all about stars: why not apply yourself? Prepare your own likeness using candle wax (as shown), and submit it to the membership committee, along with reasons why you should be considered. Send it in heat-proof packaging to Madame Tussaud's, Marylebone Road, London NW1 5LR, UK.

This is our model!

You will need this to perform the sculpture:

This one
This one
This wax
This one
And this one

Study the subject carefully first

Then light the candle and burn the wax.

This will make it drop down wax onto the surface of your choice.

And this is how our sculpture ended up.

Now it's just to ride! Make the sculpture by sculpting the wax into the shape of your object!

Done!

We are particularly pleased with the lips.

Wednesday 16 March

8	14
9	15
10	16
11	17
12	18
13	19

St. Patrick's Day

Celebrate by dyeing the world's waters green

Since 1962, Chicago's authorities have famously dyed the river emerald green for St. Patrick's Day. This year the experiment is to spread to the whole wide world with the help of Diary readers across the globe. Wherever you are, just slip 10lbs of green vegetable dye into the water distribution system through your toilet, and watch the world's oceans turn the colour of a leprechaun within a couple of weeks.

BEGORRAH!

The quaint Irish festival of St. Patrick's Day has joined Christmas and Valentine's Day in the superleague of premium global merchandizing opportunities. Here are some examples of how the "St. Patrick's" brand may be stretched to suit a wide range of target markets.

For the mainstream market

For the Asian market

For the "hip-hop" market

For the female market

For the "pink pound" market

For the elderly market

Thursday 17 March

8	14
9	15
10	16
11	17
12	18
13	19

I'M GONNA SHAKE MY ASS TONIGHT YOU BETTER BELIEVE IT!

It's payback time!
Today get back at someone.

Revenge is a dish best served cold. Did someone fire you three years ago? Did some queen bitch steal your boyfriend in high school? Did some dog run off with your lollipop when you were two? Today, get your own back and let them know no one messes with you and your crew.

With the opening up of the EU to ex-communist states, a whole influx of KGB-trained contract killers has become available to the Western consumer, at very reasonable prices. Not only that, but the range of punishments inflicted has also expanded, to offer a more imaginative range of options, most of which won't even land you in jail.

> Here are the current revenge values for a selection of offences. You may customize these to suit your preferences, how long ago it happened, and just how deeply you were traumatized.

Offence:	Punishment:	Price:
Parents making you go to bed without dessert	Contract killer makes them swallow cod liver oil	£5
Other kid pulling your hair in kindergarten	Contract killer pinches them back hard	£7.50
Teacher telling you off for being late again	Contract killer spanks them with a ruler	£10
"Best friend" bitching about you behind your back	Contract killer washes their mouth with antibacterial soap	£15
Lecturer giving you unfairly bad mark for essay	Contract killer makes them swallow essay	£25
Partner cheating on you with your sibling	Contract killer kills them	£35

Friday 18 March

8		14	
9		15	
10		16	
11		17	
12		18	
13		19	

MAKE A BABY
WEEKEND

This weekend, make a baby

The single thing that everyone agrees does change your life is having a child. So get to it: cosy up to your official partner this weekend, chuck any kind of contraception out the window, and conceive as hard as you can!

OOOH! LOOK HOW CUTE HE/SHE IS FOR CHRIST SAKE!!!

Start saving for these items:

Special instructions:
If you are gay: this one could take a while. By all means have fun trying, but you may also want to consider adopting.
If you are underage: please check beforehand with parents or the person(s) who will be paying for the child's upbringing.
If you are single: have a one-night stand with pre-punctured condom, then seduce the individual into marrying you before the pregnancy is apparent. A gamble, but worth it.

Saturday & Sunday 19–20 March

Mount this plaque outside your home today to add interest to it and increase its value. You have Benrik's word that should anyone question the truth of our stay, we will back you up 100%.

Hodder&Stoughton

BENRIK 1932-2005

Writers and Artists lived here in 1978 for a week or so

Monday 21 March

8	14
9	15
10	16
11	17
12	18
13	19

Teenage

Day Today act like a teenager

Blah blah blah this is like such a boring idea for a day. It sucks bigtime, I mean why am I doing this Diary? It's sooooo

patronising to assume that teens are all the same for one thing, like, attention-span-deficited, spotty, moaning hormones on legs. AAAA-AA-A-A-RRRRGGGHHH! It makes me wanna vom! It's like what Sartre said: "We're all free to be what we want to be." Or something. Don't Benrik get it?!!! Tragic... The world is a funny place. Who said that? Bah, this isn't worth writing about, I dunno why I get so wound up. Sometimes I do not think my opinions and insights into matters of the world significant enough to merit recording for posterity. My life is so empty. The universe is doomed. And I hate school, specially math. Gotta do homework man. Later.

Tuesday 22 March	
8	14
9	15
10	16
11	17
12	18
13	19

Teenage

Day Today act like a teenager

Blah blah blah this is like such a boring idea for a day. It sucks bigtime, I mean why am I doing this Diary? It's sooooo

patronising to assume that teens are all the same for one thing, like, attention-span-deficited, spotty, moaning hormones on legs. AAAA-AA-A-A-RRRRGGGHHH! It makes me wanna vom! It's like what Sartre said: "We're all free to be what we want to be." Or something. Don't Benrik get it?!!! Tragic... The world is a funny place. Who said that? Bah, this isn't worth writing about, I dunno why I get so wound up. Sometimes I do not think my opinions and insights into matters of the world significant enough to merit recording for posterity. My life is so empty. The universe is doomed. And I hate school, specially math.Gotta do homework man. Later.

Wednesday 23 March		
8		14
9		15
10		16
11		17
12		18
13		19

Join the Benrik T-shirt Club

Every month Benrik design an exclusive T-shirt that is sent to ambassadors of taste all around the world. This is your chance to feature on some of the world's most prominent chests. Send us your idea via the website and you may see it happen. At Benrik Limited, we can guarantee that all our T-shirts are made by 12-year-old children in Guatemala. Each T-shirt comes with a smiling photo of the 12-year-old who made it. All profits go to Benrik Limited. Some particularly successful past examples:

Thursday 24 March

8	14
9	15
10	16
11	17
12	18
13	19

Easter Weekend Treasure Hunt! This weekend, find the hidden Benrik Treasure on the internet and win a prize.

WWW.THISWEBSITEWILLCHANGEYOURLIFE.COM

Friday, Saturday, Sunday & Monday 25-28 March

Sing Wagner's Ring Cycle in the shower today

Genuine life-changing achievement is possible even in the most innocuous places, like the bathroom. Who doesn't want to tell the grandchildren how they once held the whole neighbourhood spellbound every morning with their Siegfried or Brunnhilde. Start today, and at 10 minutes a day you should have completed the cycle within 3 or 4 months. We've even attached the first sheet. Casting: gifted singers may wish to apply for a part in Benrik's interpretation of the Ring at the Royal Opera House in 2007, which will of course be set entirely in a power shower, that Rhine of the modern age. Contact us via our website for details of casting.

And if you really want to make Bayreuth, spin around in circles and play this bagpipe while you sing. Hahahahahahahahahahahahahahahahaha.

Tuesday 29 March

8		14	
9		15	
10		16	
11		17	
12		18	
13		19	

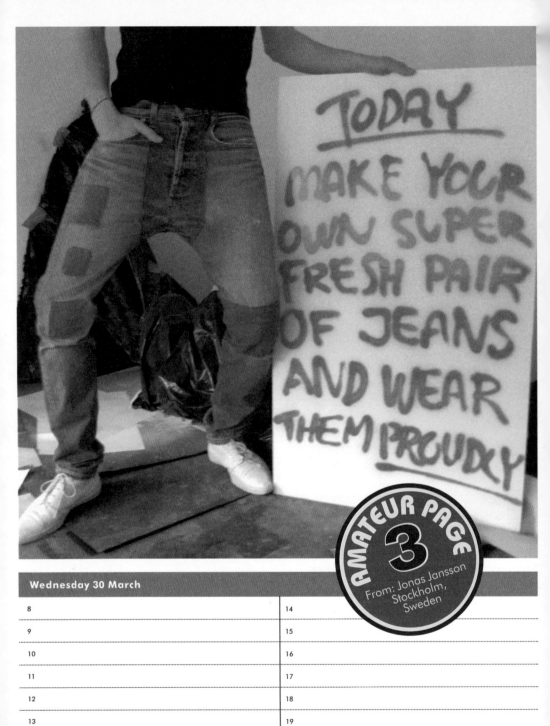

TODAY

MAKE YOUR OWN SUPER FRESH PAIR OF JEANS AND WEAR THEM PROUDLY

AMATEUR PAGE 3

From: Jonas Jansson
Stockholm,
Sweden

Wednesday 30 March

8	14
9	15
10	16
11	17
12	18
13	19

Ada Searle was born in Deptford, South East London, on the 7th of April 1913. Her mother died giving birth to her, so she was mostly brought up by her grandmother. Ada's father Fred lived with them, but worked night shifts on the tramways, and so saw less of her and her three older brothers than he might have done. The First World War didn't really affect her childhood, but alas in 1925 her grandmother died, which meant she had to leave school to stay at home and cook and clean for the rest of the family. Deptford suffered during the Depression in the thirties, but Ada still managed a busy life, joining the Salvation Army, working in the laundry business by day, and running with rather a dapper crowd by night. It was during this time that she met the man she was to marry, one Frederick George Thomas Peach, formerly of the Merchant Navy. Fred Peach JR was a charmer, who whisked Ada around in his dashing open top sports car, took her on darts team outings, and eventually married her in 1939. They moved in together in Barnhurst, on the eve of World War II. Their flat was meant to be luxurious as it was fitted with electricity. Soon afterwards though, Fred decided that they needed a garden, so they moved to a house in Woolwich, where she lives to this day. Although it did have a garden, it didn't have hot water, electricity or a bath, and only acquired an inside toilet in 1987. The main room was 12 square foot, and served as living room and kitchen. The food was bought every day as they didn't have a fridge of course. All the washing was done by hand. And every Friday night the tin bath would come out for the weekly bath, with water boiled on the stove. (This was a routine Ada was to follow until she was well over 80!)

Now, Woolwich was a military base and so was too dangerous to live in during the war. And thus in 1943, Ada was packed off to Northampton to have her first child, Barry.

The idea was to move expectant mothers away from big cities. Heavily pregnant, Ada had to cart her heavy suitcase on and off the

train and over to the house where she had been billeted. Once there, she was turfed out every morning and had to walk around Northampton all day until allowed back in at teatime. That at least gave her time to contemplate pregnancy; until she actually gave birth, she supposed the baby would emerge from her belly button. In the event things went smoothly and she was sent back to London a mere two weeks later with baby Barry in tow. Meanwhile the war was still raging. In March 1944, Ada and Barry were hiding under an iron table in the front room during an air raid, when a German bomb landed next door with a deafening boom. After the blast, Ada discovered she'd been blown out of the house and ended up at the bottom of the back garden still cradling Barry in her arms... The front of the house had been completely destroyed.

Fred spent the war in the Home Guard, repairing water mains that had burst during the air raids. He also did a stint fire-watching from Shooters Hill water tower. When the high drama of the war ended, Ada and Fred settled down to the reality of marriage. In 1947, Bernard was born, followed by Sylvia two years later. Ada would work in a high street launderette in the morning, and as a petrol pump attendant in the afternoon and evening, but not without coming home at lunchtime to cook her husband a meal. Fred wasn't always an easy man to get on with, and his initial charm seemed to wear off with the years. He used to grow dahlias at the end of the garden, and sell them for a bit of cash. However, when the weather ruined them, he used to pick what was left for his wife, but charge her 2 bob for it out of her already meagre allowance... Fred had had a tough upbringing, and so believed in authority: nobody was allowed to make even the slightest noise while he was trying to sleep, or they could get a belting. And so the rest of the family spoke in whispers, and had to listen to the Marconi radio with their ears pressed against the speakers. Ada retired from her final job as dinner lady at Shooters Hill Grammar School in 1973, aged 60. In 1979, Fred Peach died, to mixed feelings from Ada; when the doctor turned up too late and apologized, she told him not to worry about it. Since then Ada has had a vigorous retirement, with family trips to Paris and a healthy daily dose of Coronation St. She is not overly concerned with fame, but will celebrate her 15 minutes in the limelight today by reading the showbiz gossip in all the papers and seeing if she's made it.

Thursday 31 March		
8		14
9		15
10		16
11		17
12		18
13		19

Benrik April Fool

Every reader must claim to have been abducted by aliens.

Today, as all of you wake up all over the world, call your local authorities and tell them the same story, sticking to these exact details. They may deny the testimony of one, but not of millions.

Last night, you heard a whistling noise outside your window and looked out. A huge flash blinded you, and you felt your body dissolve through the window and zoom up towards the light source. About 30 seconds later, as you zipped through the stratosphere in a semi-transparent oxygenated pouch, you saw the mothership, which, contrary to much recent "sci-fi" propaganda, is shaped like a cup and saucer. You flew upwards and then down into a milky tea-substance, where the aliens live in their millions-strong city. The aliens greeted you (and thousands of others) with open tentacles, ripping some of you apart in the process in their clumsy childlike attempts at human affection. They are an octopus-shaped people. Indeed, for millions of years they have been abducting octopi, whom they initially thought were by far earth's most promising candidates for fraternization. They are not green but a tasteful khaki. They herded you into their great hall for a feast. There the leader, Kyrrtghyffiithorrr, made a speech which none of you understood as it was in Chinese, again an understandable mistake. However it seemed friendly, and the earth-octopus pie tasted pretty good. Your brain was then hooked up to some kind of pump, you fell asleep, and woke up peacefully in your bed with a strange craving for plankton. You're sorry it's a bit vague, but that's all you remember, kytdcfjkuvbadsfgndrtgfm.

Friday 1 April	
8	14
9	15
10	16
11	17
12	18
13	19

Fast all weekend **And force others around you to fast as well**

Fasting is an invaluable physical and spiritual discipline that leaves you feeling uplifted and renewed. A weekend without food and water will help you and those around you to cleanse your systems of toxins and reach inner peace. Your loved ones may not realize this immediately, but you are doing them a good turn by including them in your two-day fast. Empty the house of food, turn off all taps at the mains with the help of a qualified plumber and lock everyone in at dawn on Saturday morning. Then join hands and meditate together until midnight on Sunday.

Saturday & Sunday 2–3 April

Today: give back what you borrowed

There's a fine line between borrowing and stealing. Protect your reputation by returning any borrowed goods today. To jolt your memory, here is a list of items that frequently go missing:

LAWNMOWERS

SCISSORS

MONEY

CUPS

POWER

DRILLS

CONDOMS

PERIODICALS

RULERS

MATCHES

CDS

VASES

CARS

LADDERS

T-SHIRTS

PENS

BOOKS

DVDS

SUGAR

WHEELBARROWS

FLOUR

STAPLERS

UMBRELLAS

LOVERS

Borrowing the Diary

It is expressly forbidden to borrow this book. Last year 4,564 Diaries went AWOL from their owners as a direct result of this practice. Anyone who tells you they will return it (even if they use such words as "I promise") is a bare-faced liar. If you have borrowed this Diary or last year's "by mistake", today is your amnesty day. You have until midnight to return it to its rightful owner.

Monday 4 April

8	14
9	15
10	16
11	17
12	18
13	19

Don't forget to return that smurfette you borrowed on the 10th February!

EXORCISM DAY

Drive the Devil out of a loved one.

The Devil is all around us, more treacherous than ever. It is an inexcusable sin to realize that someone is in His fateful grip and yet fail to help them. A common misconception (the Devil's work!) is that only priests can perform exorcisms. In fact lay people may as well, as long as they are holy. A simple exorcism is provided below, which may be used at home or in the office.

The following is a simple exorcism prayer that can be said by priests or laity. The term 'exorcism' does NOT always denote a solemn exorcism involving a person possessed by the devil. In general, the term denotes prayers to 'curb the power of the devil and prevent him from doing harm.' As St. Peter had written in Holy Scripture, 'your adversary the devil, as a roaring lion, goeth about seeking whom he may devour.' (1 St.Peter 5,8)

The Holy Father exhorts priests to say this prayer as often as possible, as a simple exorcism to curb the power of the devil and prevent him from doing harm. The faithful also may say it in their own name, for the same purpose, as any approved prayer. Its use is recommended whenever action of the devil is suspected, causing malice in men, violent temptations and even storms and various calamities. It could be used as a solemn exorcism (an official and public ceremony, in Latin), to expel the devil. It would then be said by a priest, in the name of the Church and only with a Bishop's permission.

Prayer to St. Michael the Archangel: In the Name of the Father, and of the Son, and of the Holy Ghost. Amen.

Most glorious Prince of the Heavenly Armies, Saint Michael the Archangel, defend us in 'our battle against principalities and powers, against the rulers of this world of darkness, against the spirits of wickedness in the high places' (Eph., 6,12). Come to the assistance of men whom God has created to His likeness and whom He has redeemed at a great price from the tyranny of the devil. Holy Church venerates thee as her guardian and protector; to thee, the Lord has entrusted the souls of the redeemed to be led into heaven. Pray therefore the God of Peace to crush Satan beneath our feet, that he may no longer retain men captive and do injury to the Church. Offer our prayers to the Most High, that without delay they may draw His mercy down upon us; take hold of 'the dragon, the old serpent, which is the devil and Satan', bind him and cast him into the bottomless pit ... 'that he may no longer seduce the nations' (Apoc. 20, 2-3).

Exorcism: In the Name of Jesus Christ, our God and Lord, strengthened by the intercession of the Immaculate Virgin Mary, Mother of God, of Blessed Michael the Archangel, of the Blessed Apostles Peter and Paul and all the Saints (and powerful in the holy authority of our ministry)*, we confidently undertake to repulse the attacks and deceits of the devil. * Lay people omit the parenthesis above.

Psalm 67

God arises; His enemies are scattered and those who hate Him flee before Him. As smoke is driven away, so are they driven; as wax

A Simple Exorcism for Priests or Laity

Prayer Against Satan and the Rebellious Angels
Published by Order of His Holiness Pope Leo XIII

melts before the fire, so the wicked perish at the presence of God.

> V. Behold the Cross of the Lord, flee bands of enemies.
> R. The Lion of the tribe of Juda, the offspring of David, hath conquered.
> V. May Thy mercy, Lord, descend upon us.
> R. As great as our hope in Thee.

(The crosses below indicate a blessing to be given if a priest recites the Exorcism; if a lay person recites it, they indicate the Sign of the Cross to be made silently by that person.)

We drive you from us, whoever you may be, unclean spirits, all satanic powers, all infernal invaders, all wicked legions, assemblies and sects. In the Name and by the power of Our Lord Jesus Christ, + may you be snatched away and driven from the Church of God and from the souls made to the image and likeness of God and redeemed by the Precious Blood of the Divine Lamb. + Most cunning serpent, you shall no more dare to deceive the human race, persecute the Church, torment God's elect and sift them as wheat. + The Most High God commands you, + He with whom, in your great insolence, you still claim to be equal. 'God who wants all men to be saved and to come to the knowledge of the truth' (I Tim. 2,4). God the Father commands you. + God the Son commands you. + God the Holy Ghost commands you. + Christ, God's Word made flesh, commands you; + He who to save our race outdone through your envy, 'humbled Himself, becoming obedient even unto death' (Phil.2,8); He who has built His Church on the firm rock and declared that the gates of hell shall not prevail against Her, because He will dwell with Her 'all days even to the end of the world' (Matt. 28,20). The sacred Sign of the Cross commands you, + as does also the power of the mysteries of the Christian Faith. + The glorious Mother of God, the Virgin Mary, commands you; + she who by her humility and from the first moment of her Immaculate Conception crushed your proud head. The faith of the holy Apostles Peter and Paul, and of the other Apostles commands you. + The blood of the Martyrs and the pious intercession of all the Saints command you. +

Thus, cursed dragon, and you, diabolical legions, we adjure you

by the living God, + by the true God, + by the holy God, + by the God 'who so loved the world that He gave up His only Son, that every soul believing in Him might not perish but have life everlasting' (St.John 3, 16); stop deceiving human creatures and pouring out to them the poison of eternal damnation; stop harming the Church and hindering her liberty. Begone, Satan, inventor and master of all deceit, enemy of man's salvation. Give place to Christ in Whom you have found none of your works; give place to the One, Holy, Catholic and Apostolic Church acquired by Christ at the price of His Blood. Stoop beneath the all-powerful Hand of God; tremble and flee when we invoke the Holy and terrible Name of Jesus, this Name which causes hell to tremble, this Name to which the Virtues, Powers and Dominations of heaven are humbly submissive, this Name which the Cherubim and Seraphim praise unceasingly repeating: Holy, Holy, Holy is the Lord, the God of Hosts.

> V. O Lord, hear my prayer.
> R. And let my cry come unto Thee.
> V. May the Lord be with thee.
> R. And with thy spirit.

Let us pray.

God of heaven, God of earth, God of Angels, God of Archangels, God of Patriarchs, God of Prophets, God of Apostles, God of Martyrs, God of Confessors, God of Virgins, God who has power to give life after death and rest after work: because there is no other God than Thee and there can be no other, for Thou art the Creator of all things, visible and invisible, of Whose reign there shall be no end, we humbly prostrate ourselves before Thy glorious Majesty and we beseech Thee to deliver us by Thy power from all the tyranny of the infernal spirits, from their snares, their lies and their furious wickedness. Deign, O Lord, to grant us Thy powerful protection and to keep us safe and sound. We beseech Thee through Jesus Christ Our Lord. Amen.

> V. From the snares of the devil,
> R. Deliver us, O Lord.
> V. That Thy Church may serve Thee in peace and liberty:
> R. We beseech Thee to hear us.
> V. That Thou may crush down all enemies of Thy Church:
> R. We beseech Thee to hear us.
> (Holy water is sprinkled in the place where we may be.)

To learn more, visit
www.truecatholic.org and
www.truecatholic.org/pope.

Tuesday 5 April

8		14	
9		15	
10		16	
11		17	
12		18	
13		19	

Visit someone in hospital The sick need to be comforted. Today walk into your nearest hospital and cheer up an ailing stranger with a surprise hug. Here are some suggestions of people who, according to NHS Trust timetables, are due to be in hospital recovering today. Just ask for their bed number at reception.

Cardiff
Henrietta Evans, 49
Hip replacement
Cardiff Royal
Infirmary

London
Jack Trewin, 11
Broken leg
Royal Free Hospital

Sign Jack's plaster!

Brighton
Paul Burns, 34
Triple bypass
Royal Sussex
County Hospital

Birmingham
Liz Aldiss, 22
Kidney transplant
City Hospital

Manchester
Julian Bell, 29
Appendicitis
Manchester
Royal Infirmary

Dublin
Scott Evans, 31
Concussion
Beaumont Hospital

Edinburgh
Miriam Blake, 32
Dislocated ankle
Royal Victoria
Hospital

Liverpool
Anouk Baufurt, 23
Osteoporosis
Liverpool Women's
Hospital

Bristol
Jim Taylor, 48
Tonsillectomy
Nuffield Hospital

Wednesday 6 April

8	14
9	15
10	16
11	17
12	18
13	19

Become a hermit today

Who can be a hermit? Anyone! The hermit lifestyle is due for a serious comeback: it's the perfect antidote to modern clutter and materialism. This is what you need to get started.

A GROTTO
We're not talking Hugh Hefner here: any hole in the ground you can hide in will do. Consult Ordnance Survey to find grottos in your area.

A BLANKET
The hermit look is simply not complete without one. It also has practical applications, like stopping you from freezing to death.

A DOG
Purists may quibble over this one, but an animal companion is within the rules, provided it too becomes a hermit and does not fraternize with other dogs.

SCISSORS
To trim your great long grey straggly beard (women may dispense with this until the age of 70).

A STICK
To beat away the other dogs, and to threaten pesky kids whose idea of fun is to try and set you on fire.

A RAKE
To gather moss and lichen from the forest floor for food and for selling to local florists.

BROADBAND
To record your hermit experiences in a blog and share tips with other hermits.

Subscribe to Raven's Bread, the quarterly newsletter for hermits ("Food for those in solitude"). For a year, send a US bank draft for $10 to editors Paul and Karen Fredette at Raven's Bread, 18065 Hwy. 209, Hot Springs, North Carolina NC 28743, USA. Any extra donations are used to subsidise subscriptions for hermits who cannot afford the cost. Thank you.

Thursday 7 April

8	14
9	15
10	16
11	17
12	18
13	19

HOW TO PROTECT THE HOLE.
When it comes to the security of your hole, shoot first, ask later. Everyone is a potential threat to your ownership status. Even people that you may not distrust to begin with, for example friends and family, will eventually fall under the pressure and get all territorial and try to battle you for it.

Friday 8 April

8	14
9	15
10	16
11	17
12	18
13	19

Radical Spring Clean Weekend

Anyone can get rid of non-essential clutter. But doing without essential items is more of a challenge. This weekend see if your life really suffers without some of the so-called 'basics'.

Bed
Man managed for millions of years without the bed. Sleep on the floor for a few nights and you'll never look back.

Couch
No couch, no couch potatoes. Stand up to watch television and you'll be far more attentive to the programming.

Taps
Taps are fundamentally ugly, and a hazard to young children who might easily poke an eye out. Get your water from the local well like most of the world.

WC
What's wrong with the old chamber pot? Squatting is better for you, and it can even help prevent haemorrhoids.

Oven
Raw food contains more nutrients. This is true of vegetables and fruit, but also of meat, which many people fail to realize.

TV
No, you'd better keep this one.

Sell your unwanted items at the Benrik Car Boot Sale!!!

Start: 6am Sunday

Directions: turn off the M1 between Sheffield and Leeds (exit 36) and head for Broom Hill. Turn left onto the A633 towards Barnsley. At Shafton, go through the town centre and turn right past the superstore. The road ends after 100m and turns into a dirt track. After 5 minutes, turn left into a field which will be signposted 'Benrik Car Boot Extravaganza!' You have arrived. Report to us to get allocated a spot.

Saturday & Sunday 9–10 April

Today help destroy an ugly building

When Keble College Oxford was built in the late 19th century, it was judged so monstrous by some that a society was formed to destroy it by removing one brick a year. Today all Benrik readers are to pick a local eyesore and kickstart its demolition by stealing a small portion of it.

Monday 11 April

8	14
9	15
10	16
11	17
12	18
13	19

Today, praise an unsung achievement

Dear Sir,

I would like to say how much I enjoyed your review of Driving Miss Daisy in today's TV Weekly. 'Funny in parts but disappointing ending, watch if you're in' is as succinct and perspicuous a critique as one could wish to read. Thank you.

Dear Madam,

I was very taken by your weather update this morning on television. The way you explained the anticyclone's movements across the British Isles was pure poetry in motion and brought meteorology to life for me.

Dear Sir/Madam,

I purchased a pack of your toothpicks yesterday and I must confess I have never come across such marvellously crafted specimens! My mouth has not felt this clean for 65 years! Keep up the good work.

Gentlemen!

Please pass on my congratulations to the receptionist who transferred my call to your sales department this afternoon at 3.43pm; she did it so smoothly and in such a friendly manner that I hardly noticed the wait!

Dear neighbour,

Sorry for bothering you with this note, but I can no longer keep quiet. The way you deal with your rubbish never fails to inspire me. Your bags are beautifully tied yet quite hermetic and resistant to squirrels. You have all my respect.

Officer,

I live at 34B and watch you patrolling the street every day. Your posture is magnificent. You strike the perfect balance between scaring off the criminal mind, and reassuring the householder. Bravo! (I have sent a copy of this letter to your superiors.)

Tuesday 12 April

8	14
9	15
10	16
11	17
12	18
13	19

START A RELATIONSHIP WITH A FELLOW DIARY OWNER

Anyone following Benrik will necessarily have drifted away from their boring old non-Benrikian partner, still stuck in their gloomy miserable boring old everyday rut. Here is your chance to find somebody more suited to the new you. Today visit www.thiswebsitewillchangeyourlife.com and you will be able to chat live to dozens of like-minded individuals, one of whom might prove to be the love of your life.

Testimonial **John&Cindy**

John, 48, had been single for an unhealthy nine years when he met Cindy, 24, via a Benrik reading group. One year later, they are married with a gorgeous little boy, who they've called...Benrik! Cute. Says John: "Until I read the Diary, I was a complete schmuck. Women wouldn't give me the time of day, particularly supermodel-types like Cindy here. But we just hit it off. The Diary made me much more confident and witty, and it made her realize there was rather more to life than dating conventionally good-looking millionaires." John and Cindy married on 16 June, which in the 2004 Diary was "Today trust your gut instincts no matter how much those you thought were your friends laugh at you." Quips Cindy: "Benrik really did change our lives! That book was definitely worth the money, maybe even £1 or £2 more who knows."

BENRIK ARRANGED MARRIAGES

Such is the degree of compatibility between Diary followers that Benrik are bringing back arranged marriages. Who needs the messy rigmarole of dating, cohabiting and proposing when Benrik can take care of matters for you? Simply register on the website, answer a few simple questions, and within two weeks, Benrik will find a match for you, and give you a date for the wedding! What could be easier?

Benrik decisions on the suitability of partners for Benrik Arranged Marriages are final. The partners' legal and/or religious consent is superseded by their consent to the terms and conditions of the Benrik Arranged Marriages Programme. No correspondence will be entered into. Benrik reserve the right to attend the wedding as guests of honour and take photos for promotional purposes. At Benrik Ltd, we make every effort to find suitable matches, but this is not guaranteed. Benrik collect a fee based on the value of the partners' property and the likelihood they would have found love without Benrik's intervention. No refunds will be given, nor will divorce lawyers' fees be paid.

Wednesday 13 April

8	14
9	15
10	16
11	17
12	18
13	19

TODAY COMMIT TREASON

Under English law, it is still technically a treasonable offence to call for the end of the monarchy, punishable by exile and life imprisonment. Today test this law by walking up to Buckingham Palace and telling the guards you have come to remove H.M. the Queen from the throne which she has usurped from the people.

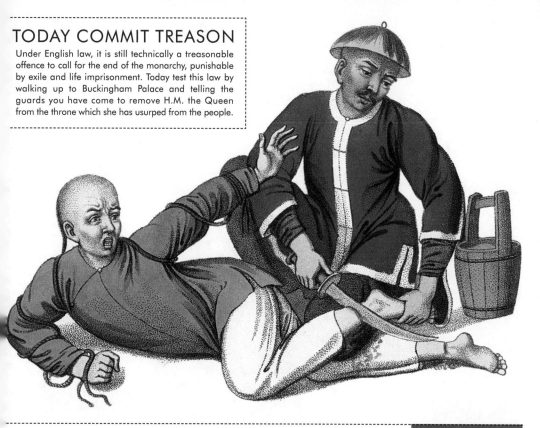

TREASON FELONY ACT 1848

3. Offences herein mentioned declared to be felonies ...If any person whatsoever shall, within the United Kingdom or without, compass, imagine, invent, devise or intend to deprive or depose our Most Gracious Lady the Queen, ...from the style, honour, or royal name of the imperial crown of the United Kingdom, or of any other of her Majesty's dominions and countries, or to levy war against her Majesty, ...within any part of the United Kingdom, in order by force or constraint to compel her... to change her...measures of counsels, or in order to put any force or constraint upon her or in order to intimidate or overawe both Houses or either House of Parliament, or to move or stir any foreigner or stranger with force to invade the United Kingdom or any other of her Majesty's dominions or countries under the obeisance of her Majesty...and such compassings, imaginations, inventions, devices, or intentions, or any of them, shall express, utter, or declare, by publishing any printing or writing...or by any overt act or deed, every person so offending shall be guilty of felony, and being convicted thereof shall be liable...to be transported beyond the seas for the term of their natural life.

Thursday 14 April

8	14
9	15
10	16
11	17
12	18
13	19

STALK AN ANIMAL!

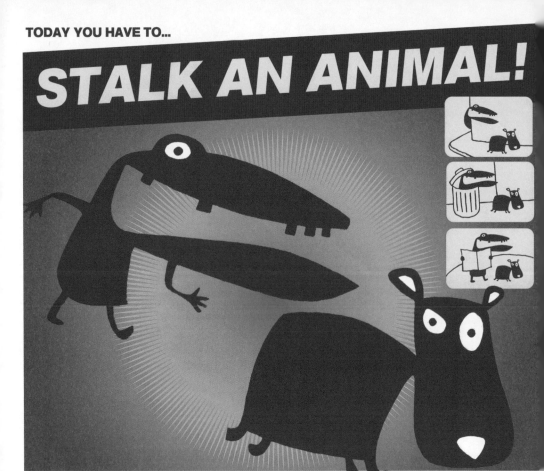

HEY LASSIE I'M GOING TO EAT YOU ALIVE YOU LITTLE BITCH.

It is only recently that humans have pulled ahead of the pack and started considering ourselves superior to other species. Today return to your animal roots by stalking another creature. It may take you a while to get the hang of it, so start with something simple, like a cat. Sniff its urine. Scan its tracks. Study its behaviour. Scare the hell out of it when you catch the damn thing. If it denounces you to the animal protection people, remind them that technically you too are an animal and therefore covered by statutory dog-eat-dog legislation. If all else fails either howl at the moon or roll over and play dead.

Friday 15 April	
8	14
9	15
10	16
11	17
12	18
13	19

This weekend, act suspiciously

Loiter outside MI5's headquarters and sketch them from all angles

Set all the alarm clocks on display in a department store to ring at the same time

We must be vigilant at all times, surrounded as we are by terrorists and other evil-doers. Help keep society on its toes today with your suspicious behaviour. This may cause some short-term inconvenience for you and for those around you, but in the long-term, you'll have done society a good turn, even if it doesn't appreciate it just today.

Walk past police sniffer dogs with a suitcase full of sausages

Call 10 Downing St and breathe dirty down the line

Page 'Osama' at the airport information desk

Avoid eye contact with everyone

Turn and walk the other way whenever a bobby comes near

"The only rational response to our über-rational society is to deny rationality itself. That is to say, we must divest ourselves of the language (language as praxis, pace Wittgenstein) of logical discourse in order to deny society's grip on our behaviour and practices. We must embrace the vicious circle of the irrational in order to re-emerge reborn free, on the other side of the black hole that is instrumental rationality such as it has been appropriated by the global post-capitalist technocracy. The 'retarded' constitute in actual fact the new avant-garde of our decadent times." (G. Klage, "Spazzing: the art of inarticulacy", Heidelberg Press, 2004)

Monday 18 April

8	14
9	15
10	16
11	17
12	18
13	19

INSIST ON SPEAKING TO THE MEDIA TODAY

The media isn't a circus, it's a club: same old faces, same old views, same old grudges. Today, demand to have your voice heard for a change! Speak out on what matters to you, whether it's how to run a good war, or about the strange way light sometimes shimmies on puddles, in country lanes, at the crack of dawn. Barge in and have your say! How to trick the media into giving you airtime Good: I have slept with the PM (and can prove it!); I have valuable information regarding a plot; I have swallowed a grenade and wish to say goodbye; I'm the replacement weatherman today. Bad: I am the foremost expert on country lane puddle lighting.

You aren't anyone if you haven't been on tv. And you're only a little someone if you've been on radio. And you're only a tiny teenie weenie of a somebody if you've been in the newspaper. But barely worth mentioning!

Tuesday 19 April

8	14
9	15
10	16
11	17
12	18
13	19

Today, tip abnormally

The arbitrary rule of tipping is to leave 10 to 15%, but this is an old-fashioned and lazy approach. Tipping is an art form, expressive of your personality and potentially a force for social disruption. Today explore its potential starting with our random guidelines. Begin with the tediously conventional 10% and add or subtract as follows

−£1 The tippee has green or greenish eyes	**+£1** The tippee has a visible tattoo on his or her chest	**+£1.⁵⁰** The sky is blue with fewer than three clouds	**+£1.⁵⁰** The tippee has used a word beginning with "R"
+£7 The sum of your bill is a primary number	**−£8** You can't figure out if it is a primary number	**+£1** The tippee has offered sex as part of the service	**−£6** The world's geo-political prospects look negative
−£1 The tippee resembles someone on TV	**−£4** Yesterday you went to bed drunk	**+£0.⁵⁰** The service provided was good	**NB.** In some cases you will end up with a negative sum, which is known as reverse tipping. Here the tippee owes you money, which you may collect in cash or through extra service. Show them this book if they query your claim.

Wednesday 20 April

8	14
9	15
10	16
11	17
12	18
13	19

PILGRIMAGE DAY

Today pay homage to Marco Polo by symbolically retracing his epic journey in your local area.

This map shows Marco's actual travels.

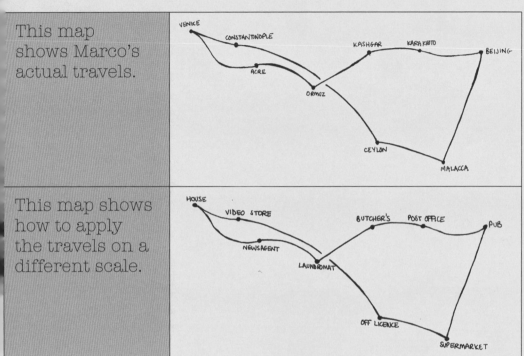

This map shows how to apply the travels on a different scale.

What Marco Polo learnt from his journey: "When a man is riding through this desert by night and for some reason – falling asleep or anything else – he gets separated from his companions and wants to rejoin them, he hears spirit voices talking to him as if they were his companions, sometimes even calling him by name. Often these voices lure him away from the path and he never finds it again, and many travellers have got lost and died because of this."

What *you* learnt from *your* journey:..
....
....
....
....
....
....
....
....

Thursday 21 April

8	14
9	15
10	16
11	17
12	18
13	19

Today, pour cocaine down an anthill

Recreate the feverish atmosphere of a financial trading floor by feeding the little workers a few grams of Columbian marching powder. Watch them zap that termite colony into oblivion. Watch them blitz that forest into wasteland. Just don't stand too close: their conversation will get very boring.

YARIBA!

Friday 22 April	
8	14
9	15
10	16
11	17
12	18
13	19

Naturism Weekend

There's nothing natural about clothes. We are born naked, but soon thrust into the straitjacket of clothing and taught that the naked body is sinful. In the future, no doubt, people will laugh at our prejudiced ways. Don't wait! Stop being a 'textile', at least for two days. Spend this weekend naked, and feel nature refresh your body, mind and soul.

PLEASE EXTINGUISH CIGARETTES HERE

THIS IS A NO SMOKING BUILDING AND NON-NATURIST

These photographs from the future are proof of systematic and horrific discrimination against Naturists. Do something, right now!

PROHIBITED
NO CYCLING OR SKATE BOARDING OR NATURISMING

DIY WARNING!

Watch out if you're going to do some DIY! Those power tools aren't very body-friendly... Be careful, and take out some special insurance through British Naturism on 01604 620361.

CAR PARK FOR TEXTILES ONLY

No naturist persons allowed beyond this point

Don't worry about getting arrested, thousands of other Diary owners will be running around naked too!

Saturday & Sunday 23–24 April

TODAY YOU ARE A COWBOY

There is much to be learnt from cowboy lore. Today follow these well-known cowboy precepts, dressed of course in the appropriate attire.

Don't squat with your spurs on. * Timing has a lot to do with the outcome of a rain dance. * Don't interfere with something that ain't botherin' you none. * If it don't seem like it's worth the effort, it probably ain't. * If you get to thinkin' you're a person of some influence, try orderin' somebody else's dog around. * Generally, you ain't learnin' nothing when your mouth's a-jawin'. * When you're throwin' your weight around, be ready to have it thrown around by somebody else. * If you're ridin' ahead of the herd, take a look back every now and then to make sure it's still there with ya. * Always take a good look at what you're about to eat. It's not so important to know what it is, but it's sure crucial to know what it was. * If you find yourself in a hole, the first thing to do is stop diggin'. * Tellin' a man to git lost and makin' him do it are two entirely different propositions. * The biggest troublemaker you'll probably ever have to deal with watches you shave his face in the mirror every morning. * When you give a personal lesson in meanness to a critter or to a person, don't be surprised if they learn their lesson. * Lettin' the cat outta the bag is a whole lot easier than puttin' it back in. * Never miss a good chance to shut up. * Always drink upstream from the herd. * It don't take a genius to

spot a goat in a flock of sheep. * Don't worry about bitin' off more than you can chew; your mouth is probably a whole lot bigger'n you think. * The quickest way to double your money is to fold it over and put it back into your pocket. * Good judgment comes from experience, and a lotta that comes from bad judgment. * Never ask a barber if you need a haircut.

Monday 25 April

8	14
9	15
10	16
11	17
12	18
13	19

PETITION DAY Submit your name on www.thiswebsitewillchangeyourlife.com and Benrik will automatically put your name to any petition of interest that comes our way. Here are just a few of the worthy causes you will support, free of charge.

U IS FOR UNFAIR!
ARTISTS WHOSE NAMES BEGIN IN U ARE NOT PROPERLY REPRESENTED IN OUR MUSEUMS. INCREASE THEIR PROPORTION TO 1/26TH NOW!

END THE FALKLANDS WAR NOW
THE WAR HAS BEEN GOING ON OVER 20 YEARS NOW, AT HUGE COST IN LIVES TO BOTH SIDES. WE ASK THE GOVERNMENT TO COME TO ITS SENSES.

NO TO WIDESCREEN
WIDESCREEN TV IS FLATTER AND THEREFORE DISCRIMINATES AGAINST THE TALLER ACTOR. WE THE UNDERSIGNED DEMAND ITS IMMEDIATE BAN NOW!

EVERY YEAR 7 DOGS ARE EATEN BY THEIR OWNERS
STOP THE MASSACRE! SIGNED BY:

DON'T CHOP DOWN THE BENRIK TREE!
TREE NEAR BENRIK HEADQUARTERS THREATENED BY COUNCIL GESTAPO.

FREE [TO BE CONFIRMED]!!!
[TO BE CONFIRMED] HAS BEEN WRONGLY ARRESTED! WE CALL ON THE PM TO RECTIFY THIS OUTRAGE IMMEDIATELY!

Tuesday 26 April

8		14	
9		15	
10		16	
11		17	
12		18	
13		19	

Wednesday 27 April

8	14
9	15
10	16
11	17
12	18
13	19

TODAY, PUT YOURSELF FORWARD FOR CLONING

NAME LAST.............................
NAME FIRST............................
DATE OF BIRTH.........................
PLACE OF BIRTH........................
WEIGHT AT BIRTH.......................
SEX MALE FEMALE.......................
BLOOD TYPE:
A ☐ B ☐ AB ☐ O ☐ RH FACTOR......
CURRENT HEIGHT........................
CURRENT WEIGHT........................
COLOUR EYES:
BROWN ☐   BLUE ☐   BLUE-GREEN ☐
HAZEL ☐ HAZEL-GREEN ☐ GREEN ☐
BODY BUILD: LARGER ☐   MEDIUM ☐   SLENDER ☐
IQ...
MARRIED ☐   SINGLE ☐   LIVING WITH PARTNER ☐
ETHNIC BACKGROUND: WHITE ☐ BLACK CARIBBEAN ☐
BLACK AFRICAN ☐   BLACK OTHER ☐   INDIAN ☐
PAKISTANI ☐ BANGLADESHI ☐ CHINESE ☐ ANY OTHER ☐
EDUCATION.............................
OCCUPATION............................
KNOWN ALLERGIES.......................
HEALTH PROBLEMS.......................
CURRENT MEDICATION....................
GP (NAME ADDRESS PHONE NUMBER).........................
....

ATTACH
PHOTO
HERE

I THINK I WOULD MAKE GOOD CLONING MATERIAL BECAUSE:
I'M TOLD I'M PRETTY GOOD-LOOKING......☐
I GET ON WITH MOST FOLK....................☐
I WANT TO MEET ME............................☐
I HAD THIS WEIRD DREAM ABOUT IT.......☐
I COULD USE MY CLONES TO SECRETLY CHEAT ON MY PARTNER........................☐
IT WOULD FURTHER MY PLANS FOR WORLD DOMINATION......................................☐
IT'D BE MORE INTERESTING THAN CLONING SOME DUMB SHEEP................................☐

CONTACT DETAILS:
ADDRESS...
....
....
....
PHONE NUMBER.................................
NEXT OF KIN.....................................
ADDRESS...
PHONE NUMBER.................................
I AM AVAILABLE FOR THE OPERATION:
MORNINGS ☐   AFTERNOONS ☐   EITHER ☐

I AUTHORISE CLONEX INC. TO SEDATE ME AND COLLECT SAMPLE TISSUE FROM MY BODY FOR THE PURPOSE OF PRODUCING CLONES OF ME, UP TO 100,000. I HEREBY WAIVE COPYRIGHT ON MY CLONES. I UNDERSTAND THAT THEY ARE THE PROPERTY OF CLONEX INC. AND CLONEX INC. ARE FREE TO USE THEM FOR ANY PURPOSE, INCLUDING MILITARY. I UNDERTAKE NOT TO TRY AND ARRANGE CONTACT WITH MY CLONES OTHER THAN THROUGH THE APPOINTED REPRESENTATIVES OF CLONEX INC. IN RETURN I WILL BE ALLOWED TO KEEP ANY DEFECTIVE CLONES (INCLUDING BUT NOT LIMITED TO BRAIN-DAMAGED, MALFORMED OR PSYCHOTIC CLONES). I FULLY UNDERSTAND THAT THE CLONING PROCEDURE IS STILL EXPERIMENTAL AND RESULTS ARE NOT GUARANTEED. I ACKNOWLEDGE THAT THERE IS A NON-NEGLIGIBLE CHANCE THE PROCEDURE WILL FAIL AND I MAY BE LEFT WITH IRREVERSIBLE PERSONALITY DISORDERS, OR MAY EVEN REQUIRE A LOBOTOMY. I ACCEPT THESE RISKS AND HEREBY WAIVE ANY CLAIM FOR DAMAGES.

SIGNED AND DATED ....

SEND TO: CLONEX INC. R&D, PO BOX 23342, FORT LAUDERDALE, FL 33304, USA.

Thursday 28 April

8	14
9	15
10	16
11	17
12	18
13	19

ICONOCLASM DAY: DEFACE A POWERFUL IMAGE

EVER SINCE OUR CAVEMEN ANCESTORS THOUGHT PAINTING MAMMOTHS WOULD HELP THEM CATCH THE REAL THING, WE HAVE BEEN IN THRALL TO IMAGES. EVEN THESE DAYS WE CAN SCARCELY BRING OURSELVES TO THROW AWAY PHOTOS OF LOVED ONES, SUCH IS OUR ATTACHMENT TO THE QUASI-VOODOO NOTION THAT WHAT WE DO TO THE PHOTO SOMEHOW AFFECTS THE PERSON. SHATTER THIS SELF-IMPOSED TABOO TODAY BY DEFACING A POTENT IMAGE, BE IT A PHOTO OF YOUR PARENTS, OR THE ONE WE PROVIDE.

Friday 29 April

8	14
9	15
10	16
11	17
12	18
13	19

BENRIK WEEKEND BREAK

Spend this weekend at Benrikland, Benrik's fun new theme park in Kent.

- ✚ First Aid
- ⓘ Information
- 🅿 Parking
- ♿ Disabled
- ☎ Telephone
- 🍺 Beer Hall
- ⛳ Mini Golf
- 🛏 Baby Care
- ✕ Diner

5% off! Show this Diary at the entrance and get 5% off the price of a day-ticket.

Top attractions!

BENRIK SPACE SHOOTER Kids shoot up into space! For good! ❶
ROLLERCOASTER RESTAURANT The world's only vomit-proof rollercoaster! ❷
HANSEL AND GRETEL SLEEPOVER Don't worry parents, that oven only heats up to 40 degrees! ❸
CRASHMANIA JG Ballard-inspired bumper cars ❹

❺ BENRIK CASTLE We kidnap three guests a day and see if the family pays the ransom
❻ A&E 3000 A concrete-lined bouncy castle
❼ "SHARK-A-LARK" The pool that's also an aquarium!
❽ SPLAT TOWERS Learn the trapeze in 10 minutes flat

DIRECTIONS: M20 to Maidstone, A229 to Staplehurst, second left towards Frittenden, third track into the forest (leave car here), box office past the police lines.

Saturday 30 April & Sunday 1 May

Monday 2 May   BANK HOLIDAY (UK)

8		14	
9		15	
10		16	
11		17	
12		18	
13		19	

Today be a Good Spouse

Historical Interest
At precisely 13.24 GMT today, Western civilization will reach its apex. From then

The spousal relationship is unfashionable in some quarters, but can provide the bedrock of a happy and emotionally fulfilled life. And in this day and age, you don't need to be married or even in a relationship to enjoy it! Simply pick someone at random, and follow these seven easy steps. ① Keep their dinner warm in the oven. ② Ask them about their day. ③ Call them "dear". ④ Do the dishes together. ⑤ Give them a useful domestic gadget. ⑥ Sit together in silence. ⑦ Spoon.

Tuesday 3 May	
8	14
9	15
10	16
11	17
12	18
13	19

Hunter-gatherer day

Hunting-gathering is in our genes, but we could all do with a refresher course. Today practise your prehistorical skills with the help of our chart. When civilization collapses overnight, you'll kick yourself if you didn't prepare.

HUNTINGS								
	EDIBLE	NON-EDIBLE	EDIBLE	NON-EDIBLE	EDIBLE	EDIBLE	EDIBLE	EDIBLE
NON-EDIBLE	NON-EDIBLE	EDIBLE	EDIBLE	NON-EDIBLE	EDIBLE	EDIBLE	NON-EDIBLE	NON-EDIBLE
NON-EDIBLE	NON-EDIBLE	EDIBLE	EDIBLE	EDIBLE	EDIBLE	EDIBLE	NON-EDIBLE	EDIBLE
EDIBLE	EDIBLE	EDIBLE	NON-EDIBLE	NON-EDIBLE	NON-EDIBLE	EDIBLE	NON-EDIBLE	NON-EDIBLE
NON-EDIBLE	NON-EDIBLE	NON-EDIBLE	NON-EDIBLE	NON-EDIBLE	EDIBLE	NON-EDIBLE	EDIBLE	NON-EDIBLE
GATHERINGS								
	EDIBLE	POISONOUS	DEADLY	POISONOUS	EDIBLE	DEADLY	EDIBLE	DEADLY

Wednesday 4 May

8	14
9	15
10	16
11	17
12	18
13	19

YOU CAN BE A MOVIE EXTRA

This may be your ticket to fame and fortune. Anyone can become a movie extra, as it does not require any particular acting talent. Ideally you should choose one of these two main looks.

ANONYMOUS

If you are of average height and build, are neither exceptionally ugly nor attractive, and have no distinctive scars, tattoos or other unusual features, this is for you. Directors mostly require extras to blend into the crowd, not distract the audience's attention from the special effects and highly-paid stars.

WEIRD

Occasionally, the producers will require someone of a particular physical type, a bald dwarf say, or an obese Japanese teenager. This specialized market is better paid and more exclusive. On the downside, however, parts are more limited in their availability.

The best way to find a part is to get an agent. Look on the internet for a reputable agency in your area and send in a photo with your CV. Optional: include a list of films you think would have been better with you in them (and why).

HOW TO BEHAVE ON SET

Traditional advice is to take a good book, listen to instructions carefully, and keep a low profile. This of course will not change your life much. What you really want is to impress by your sheer magnetism. You want to make love to the camera. You want to get spotted. You will not achieve this by lurking quietly in the background. Take every little opportunity to get in the director's eyeline. Exchange showbiz gossip with the stars during the lunch and tea breaks. Accidentally "stumble" into a scene when the camera is rolling and deliver some hilarious repartee that the scriptwriter will kick himself for not having thought of. Ignore the petty-minded orders of junior crew members and thrust yourself into the limelight. Film history is packed with examples of extras who have made it big in exactly this way. Good luck luvvie! Mwah!

–Darling, I'm seeing your pain, now I want to feel it myself! This is your final glorious death rattle! Exude!

–Fabulous! Now just take it down 10%. We need to see your little soul fluttering away like an autumn leaf. Action!

–CUT!

Thursday 5 May	
8	14
9	15
10	16
11	17
12	18
13	19

Tonight,
watch the sun set, and reflect on your insignificance in the cosmic order.

You have fewer than 30,000 chances to watch a sunset. Make sure you take that chance today.
Sunset time Paris: 9.32pm

Friday 6 May

8	14
9	15
10	16
11	17
12	18
13	19

If this is your DNA sequence, you've won $100,000,000,000!

LUCKY PERSON !!!!

We collected this DNA sample off a discarded toothbrush. Could it be yours? Visit your local GP to get a free DNA reading, and match it to this one. The closest match... walk away with the cash! Good luck.

Saturday & Sunday 7–8 May

FLASHMOB DAY

Every month Benrik organize a global flashmob. Some notable ones in 2004 included everyone throwing paper planes past airport security; and converging on your local Accident and Emergency with a strange disease whose only symptoms are a painful left eye and a constant urge to urinate. Today, however, will be in a different league. Consult www.thiswebsitewillchangeyourlife.com for the confidential details today, but be prepared to meet at 7pm wherever you are in the world.

Photos: take your camera. At least one photo of each event should be sent to Benrik.

Monday 9 May

8	14
9	15
10	16
11	17
12	18
13	19

Today, impress your librarian

Walk into your local library and borrow something thick, preferably by Sartre, preferably in the original French. Return it with a satisfied smile 27 minutes later. Check their reaction as you saunter out, full of your new learning. You now have a local reputation as a savant.

Tuesday 10 May

8	14
9	15
10	16
11	17
12	18
13	19

Today, mess up your kid so they turn into Picasso

Early deprivation of affection and the subsequent inner conviction that you are worthless fuel the compulsive ambition that drives the artist. By namby-pamby standards, it may seem that you are being cruel to your children, but really you are doing them a favour. 'They fuck you up, your Mum and Dad' is not therapeutical babbling, but the poet's grateful acknowledgement of his two-headed Muse. As Proust said, 'everything we think of as great comes from neurotics. They alone have founded religions and composed masterpieces' He knew this first hand: when he didn't get his customary goodnight kiss from his mother one night at the age of seven, he concluded that love was doomed and was plunged into the lifelong despondency that produced his magnum opus. As his example shows, nothing heavy-handed is required; a forgotten kiss, a strange look, or a rash word are all it takes to spice up a life.

MY NAME IS ADOLF. AT LEAST THATS WHAT MY DADDY CALLS ME. MY REAL NAME IS BILLY. BUT DADDY SAYS ADOLF IS BETER FOR ME. HE SAYS I WILL UNDERSTAND WHEN I GROW UP. IT MAKES THE OTHER KIDS AT SKOOL LAUGH. I DONT KNOW WHY. MUMMY IS A PAINTER. SHE PAINTS WITH ME. I LIKE PAINTING BUT I DONT LIKE BLAK. BLAK IS THE ONLY COLOR MUMMY SAYS I CAN USE UNTIL I AM 9. THEN I CAN USE PINK. I DONT LIKE PINK. ON SUNDAYS DADDY AND MUMMY TAKE ME TO THE MUSEUM. I SIT IN FRONT OF THE PAINTINGS. THEN THEY GO TO THEY GO TO THE PUB. CAN'T GO BECAUS I AM 8. DADDY SAYS THE PAINTINGS WILBE MY MUMMY AND DADDY FOR 2 HOURS. BUT SOMETIMES ITS 3. I KNOW BECAUS I COUNT THE SEKUNDS IN MY HEAD. I CAN COUNT UP TO 14858. THAT WAS THE MOST THEY WERE IN THE PUB AND i WERE LOOKING AT THE PAINTING. SOMETIMES I DREAM THEY ARE DEAD. DADDY SAID GOOD BOY ADOLF AND GAVE ME RED PAINT FOR MY BIRTHDAY.

ME AND MY MUMMY AND MY DADDY

Wednesday 11 May

8	14
9	15
10	16
11	17
12	18
13	19

Today plant marijuana outside a government building and report them to the local newspaper.

Where to plant? Picking a good location to plant your seed is crucial. Ideally you are looking for grass interspersed with trees and small bushes, and available water (bear in mind official lawns are often automatically watered). If the soil is very poor, consider adding a layer of organic topsoil with lime to make it more fertile. Sunlight is a definite plus; four hours a day is a minimum, preferably in the morning. Mid-May is a good time to plant. Plant your seeds about one half-inch deep, with two inches between seeds. To guarantee a decent harvest that will photograph well, allow for 200+ seeds. Planting at night is advisable to ensure an element of surprise.

SOME GOOD OUTDOOR SEEDS | EARLY GIRL: EASY TO GROW, NOT TOO POTENT | MASTER KUSH: STRONG EARTHY SMELL

AFGHAN: STRONG AROMA, HEAVY SMOKE | SNOW WHITE: NICE SMOOTH TASTE | CHRYSTAL: GOOD YIELDS, QUICK HIGH

Thursday 12 May

8	14
9	15
10	16
11	17
12	18
13	19

Friday 13 May

8	14
9	15
10	16
11	17
12	18
13	19

This weekend, self-medicate

Don't just obey medical prejudices: trust your instinct to find the medicine that works for you. Plenty of modern cures were discovered by doctors administering the wrong drugs by mistake. These are Benrik's own medical guidelines, but feel free to experiment and come up with your own.

	Yellow and blue Diseases of the knee		Blue and red Heavy diarrhoea
	Yellow and red Cures swollen arteries		Red and white When you find yourself on fire
	Yellow and brown For sex-related headaches		Black Brings on sudden death
	Dark green and light green Club foot		Orange and green To put you in a bad mood
	Yellow and green Prevents bad dreams		Pink and green Women's troubles
	Red and blue Heavy constipation		Grey and white Against boredom
	Red and pink If your hair is too long		Purple Discharges of all kinds
	Dark red and brown Loss of limb		White These have no effect, avoid

Advanced: medical cocktails. When you have mastered the basics of self-medication, you may progress to combining. It is advisable to try the combinations on a small animal beforehand, as even the most modern drugs can have serious negative side effects when mixed. In truth, not even Benrik have tried all combinations of the above; this will take a lifetime. But yellow/blue with red/pink is definitely best avoided.

Saturday & Sunday 14–15 May

WEEK OF REVOLUTION!
UNDERGROUND

DOWN WITH THE POST CAPITALIST ORDER!

COMRADES UNITE IN OVERTHROWING THE GOVERNMENT! USE ANY MEANS NECESSARY!

WHY FIGHT FAIR WHEN THE STATE APPARATUS DOES NOT?

REPRESSION BEGETS REACTION! ANARCHY IS TOO TIMID!

RISE AGAINST THE RULING CLASS AND ITS LAPDOG THE MIDDLE CLASS

THEY MAY SPEND MONEY BUT WE WILL SPEND BLOOD! AND LOTS OF IT!!!!!!

WHO IS THE ENEMY? THEY KNOW WHO THEY ARE! AND SO DO WE!

IF YOU ARE A BOURGEOIS JUST SHOOT YOURSELF AND SAVE US TIME

Print your own samizdat

Revolution is made in the mind. Plant its seeds with your very own samizdat pamphlet. Samizdat rules: no pictures or colours are allowed, it's not meant to be enjoyed. Avoid margins, a waste of scarce paper. Simple words are best, in capitals for emphasis. Logic may be shaky, as long as the main thrust is clear.

Monday 16 May	
8	14
9	15
10	16
11	17
12	18
13	19

Foment
unrest away
from home

Dear Benrikians

Following yesterday's outburst, you will have been banished. Use this time wisely to make contacts in the revolutionary diaspora. Distribute pamphlets outside offices, speak at covert meetings, rouse the rabble! If you do not come to the attention of the local authorities, you are not fomenting hard enough.

Tuesday 17 May

8		14	
9		15	
10		16	
11		17	
12		18	
13		19	

WEEK OF REVOLUTION!
PROPAGANDA

Develop your own revolutionary brand today

With so many things to oppose, it's important to give your revolution some individuality. It could be out-of-control facial hair, an unusual scapegoat (the weather?) or a rhetorical device, like starting all your sentences with "But!"

REMINDER: THE STATUS QUO If your revolution is simply a generic one against the status quo, here is a reminder of its basics: our world is dominated by a global elite based on interlocking military economic social and cultural networks, organised to exploit the rest of us as workers and consumers, and configured to exclude even the possibility of serious dissent.

Wednesday 18 May	
8	14
9	15
10	16
11	17
12	18
13	19

WEEK OF REVOLUTION!

REVOLUTION

Hijack a train to the scene of your coup

No revolution is complete without the spectacular arrival from the hills of the bearded revolutionaries. Today board a train and demand that it divert to the government HQ, or better still, the TV station, where you will take over the country, using force of some description.

Thursday 19 May

8	14
9	15
10	16
11	17
12	18
13	19

WEEK OF REVOLUTION!
NEW DAWN

Impose your new society

The hardest part is done. Now we must change society. Form neighbourhood committees, headed by the local Diary reader. Pool all your salaries (including bonuses and benefits in kind) and divide them equally. Put all the houses in a hat and just reallocate them at random. Enforce equality of opportunity. Then take the rest of the day off as a national holiday.

I CAN'T SEE

8	New Job tod	14	
9		15	
10		16	
11		17	
12		18	
13		19	

Now liquidate absolutely everyone you've met this week

"DON'T THINK. IF YOU THINK, DON'T SPEAK. IF YOU SPEAK, DON'T WRITE. IF YOU WRITE, DON'T SIGN. IF YOU THINK, SPEAK, WRITE AND SIGN – DON'T BE SURPRISED!!!"

Saturday & Sunday 21–22 May

TODAY CONFUSE FUTURE ARCHAEOLOGISTS BY DATING THINGS WRONGL

The historian of tomorrow has it too easy. Complicate matters slightly by picking an item of consume electronics, dating it 23/05/1778 in marker pen, and burying it in your back garden. Thousands c years from now, you could be the cause of a major re-evaluation of Late Second Millennium history

8	14
9	15
10	16
11	17
12	18
13	19

Slapstick Day

SLIP ON A BANANA PEEL

SOASH

THROW A CUSTARD PIE

SPLASH

WALK INTO A LAMP POST

PAKOFF!

HIT SOMEONE WITH A FRYING PAN

SAFFA!

DROP YOUR ICE CREAM BALL

FOFF

LEAVE A WATER BUCKET ABOVE THE DOOR

BAFF!

FALL INTO AN OPEN MANHOLE

POING

STEP ON SOMEONE'S TOE

PWEF!

GET STUCK IN REVOLVING DOORS

SUSHI

Tuesday 24 May	**DROP THIS BOOK ON SOMEONE'S FOOT!**
8	14
9	15
10	16
11	17
12	18
13	19

TODAY BE A MODEL CONSUMER

Help the economy by spending exactly £37. Economists have determined that £37 is the optimal figure for everyone to spend at this point in the business cycle. Do your duty for the world economy by purchasing £37 of goods and services during business hours today.

HOW THE £37 SHOULD BE SPENT

£37 EFFECT ON THE EURO/DOLLAR RATIO

£37 EFFECT ON INFLATION

£37 EFFECT ON BOND FUTURES

Wednesday 25 May

8	14
9	15
10	16
11	17
12	18
13	19

HOLD HANDS ALL DAY TODAY

WHILE CROSSING THE STREET

WHILE MAKING LOVE TO SOMEONE

WHILE WALKING IN THE PARK

WHILE DRIVING YOUR CAR

WHILE GOING TO THE TOILET

WHILE SINGING IN THE RAIN

WHILE SWIMMING

WHILE SHOOTING SPEED BALLS

Thursday 26 May

8	14
9	15
10	16
11	17
12	18
13	19

Muzak!

Carry your own desired musical ambience around with you today. Make a tape of songs appropriate to the mood you wish to convey to those around you, and play it on a beatbox all day long. For instance

ANGRY

Fight The Power Public Enemy
The Prisoner Iron Maiden
White America Eminem
Fifth Symphony Beethoven
Fuck The Pain Away Peaches
Mutter Ramstein
Injustice For All Metallica
Smells Like Teen Spirit Nirvana
Won't Get Fooled Again The Who
Two Tribes Frankie Goes To Hollywood

Good for: asking for a pay rise, complaining in shops.

SAD

Everybody Hurts REM
Yesterday The Beatles
So Far Away Carole King
Last Christmas Wham!
Moonlight Sonata Beethoven
Crying Roy Orbison
Crying Primal Scream
Tears In Heaven Eric Clapton
Send In The Clowns Frank Sinatra
Do They Know It's Xmas? Band Aid

Good for: dumping partner, telling someone they have a parking ticket.

HUNGRY

Strawberry Fields Forever The Beatles
Candy And A Currant Bun Pink Floyd
Sugar And Spice The Searchers
Vindaloo Fat Les
Rock Lobster B-52s
Hungry Like The Wolf Duran Duran
Soup Is Good Food Dead Kennedys
Mashed Potatoes The Smashing Pumpkins
Cinnamon Girl Neil Young
Crème Brulee Sonic Youth

Good for: restaurant settings, supermarkets.

Lustful

Horny Mousse T
You Sexy Thing Hot Chocolate
Sex Machine James Brown
Erotica Madonna
Push It Salt'n'Pepa
I Touch Myself The Divinyls
Touch Me Samantha Fox
Suck My Dick Lil' Kim
Can't Get Enough... Barry White
I Want Your Sex George Michael

Good for: first date, public masturbation.

HAPPY

Dancing Queen Abba
Shiny Happy People REM
Beautiful Day U2
Freedom Aretha Franklin
Holiday Madonna
It's Raining Men Weather girls
Celebration Kool And The Gang
Club Tropicana Wham!
Don't Worry Be Happy Bobby McFerrin
La Bamba Los Lobos

Good for: winning the lottery, delivering babies.

MAD

Freak Radiohead
Rambling On Procol Harum
Livin' La Vida Loca Ricky Martin
I Talk To The Trees Tony Bavaar
Party Out Of Bounds B-52s
Rock Me Amadeus Falco
Who Let The Dogs Out? Baha Men
O Superman Laurie Anderson
Can We Fix It Bob The Builder
Ring Cycle Wagner

Good for: scaring away muggers, scaring away loved ones.

Friday 27 May

8	14
9	15
10	16
11	17
12	18
13	19

Dirty
Weekend

™

This weekend all readers are to take filthy pics of their exploits and post them on www.thiswebsitewillchangeyourlife.com

Go on!
You know
you want it!

Imagine you, naked, on the internet. Doesn't it give you a great feeling?

Caught at it!

Ooo errr!

Great feeling! Being naked on the internet is perfect!

Naughty!

Being naked on the internet is a great feeling!

Sex!
Sex!
Sex!

Lots of sex here!

Saucy
Readers behaving BADLY!

Saturday, Sunday & Monday 28–30 May

BANK HOLIDAY (UK)

IT'S GREAT!

You scratch mine!
I really needed to itch my back, right where the shoulder blade is (which is ungettable, unless you have dislocating arms) and I thought I should ask a stranger to scratch it, and then offer to scratch theirs in return. Wadda ya think?

(no pix: needs photos of objects "I did think that the page could be made up of various implements of different kinds that could be used to scratch ones back. A bamboo stick, a piece of spaghetti, a fork a CD etc.")

Tuesday 31 May

8		14	
9		15	
10		16	
11		17	
12		18	
13		19	

Optional: Then kill them, chop them up and stuff them under the floorboards

8	14
9	15
10	16
11	17
12	18
13	19

CLOUDS

THERE ARE PROBLEMS AHEAD AT WORK, GO ON HOLIDAY.

MOUNTAINS

SYMBOLS OF SPIRITUAL AWARENESS. GO SKIING IMMEDIATELY

LADDERS

YOU ARE CLIMBING TOWARDS YOUR GOAL. HURRY UP BEFORE SOMEONE BEATS YOU TO IT

CATS

YOU NEED MORE INDEPENDENCE, QUIT YOUR JOB AND DUMP YOUR PARTNER.

FALLING

YOU FEAR FAILURE. DON'T DO ANYTHING AT ALL TODAY

FIRE

SOMEONE HATES YOU: HATE THEM BACK.

Dream analysis
Work out what your dreams are telling you to do and do it!

TREES

YOU NEED EMOTIONAL SUPPORT. HUG A TREE

ROPES

YOU FEEL ALL TIED UP. NOT MUCH YOU CAN DO HERE

ANGELS

YOUR END IS NEAR, GET LIFE INSURANCE.

DESERT

YOU ARE LONELY. WAKE UP AND TALK TO SOMEONE.

SERPENTS

YOU ARE BEING DECEIVED BY A PERSON WHO LOOKS A BIT LIKE A SERPENT. KILL THEM

WEB

YOU ARE TRAPPED! RUN AWAY NOW.

SEX

YOU WANT SEX. HAVE SEX.

DEATH

YOU ARE AFRAID OF DYING, GO TO YOUR GP FOR A CHECK-UP.

MIRRORS

YOUR SELF IS DIVIDED, PULL YOURSELF TOGETHER.

CASTRATION

YOU ARE HAVING A CLICHÉD DREAM. WAKE UP IMMEDIATELY!

KEYS

THE SOLUTION TO YOUR PROBLEM IS IN THE CUPBOARD THAT OPENS WITH THOSE KEYS.

Thursday 2 June

8	14
9	15
10	16
11	17
12	18
13	19

Send a drink over to someone today

Do not send it to someone
if they are with their partner.

It is traditional to send over
drinks with alcoholic content only.

Wait until they raise their glass at
you, then nod at them knowingly.

Do not send a drink over to
someone already visibly drunk.

If they raise their glass at someone
else, have the waiter fired.

If they send it back, they probably
wouldn't have slept with you anyway.

8	14
9	15
10	16
11	17
12	18
13	19

JUDGEMENT DAY

Judgement Day is looming! Prepare for it ahead of time with our "Judgement Day Self-Assessment" form below. On the day itself simply hand it in to God, who will appreciate your time-saving efforts and award you a bonus point!

MY GOOD DEEDS	MY SINS	OTHER
Helped blind person across street	Fornicated with strangers	Drank semi-skimmed milk
Comforted crying child	Lied to my own mother	Knitted green jumper
Returned lost wallet	Murdered my father	Tried to repair toaster to no avail
Gave to worthwhile charity	Stole ice cream from a child	Kept CDs in alphabetical order
Loved my neighbour	Engaged in sodomy (repeatedly)	Always sat in front row at movies
Cured the sick	Padded out my expense claims	Preferred pepper to salt
Fed the hungry	Envied everyone I ever met	Holidayed in the Bahamas twice
Did a good turn	Lied about my age to lover	Enjoyed chess as a hobby
Helped the aged	Was gluttonous as a baby	Had a friend named Toby
Saved a cat from up a tree	Chronically undertipped hookers	Kept a goldfish for 4 years
Rewound videos before returning them	Made greed my true religion	Worked in a bar whilst travelling
Planted a tree	Sacrificed goats to Satan	Visited long-lost cousin in Scotland
Forgave an enemy	Talked behind backs	Read mostly non-fiction
Went to church	Secretly despised my children	Broke a leg skiing
Have been a good listener	"Borrowed" library book forever	Went to Jon Bon Jovi concert
Was faithful to my spouse	Shoplifted pornography	Played the lottery regularly
Dried the dishes without being asked	Masturbated uncontrollably	Never really had favourite film
Rescued family from house on fire	Listened to Alice Cooper backwards	Redecorated spare bedroom in fuchsia
Adopted a stray dog	Stole from the cookie jar	Sent total of 658 postcards
Prayed in earnest	Skipped Sunday school	Rose to senior manager position
Found a family for ugly orphan	Told orphan they were ugly	Saw documentary about orphanage once
Total	Total	Total ....

If your sins exceed your good deeds, you're going to hell buddy! Unless you make up the deficit between now and midnight. If your other deeds preponderate, God will decide your fate on a passing whim, or maybe even by tossing a coin, who knows.

Monday 6 June

8	14
9	15
10	16
11	17
12	18
13	19

Today rearrange your local supermarket according to your own preferences

2 Dairy section
Milk is always at the back so everyone has to trek through the whole store. Put it by the cash tills instead of the sweets and save everyone an unnecessary walk.

1 Bread smells
Smell machines are used to awaken the consumer's appetite. Ask them to feature your other favourite products, like beer or tuna chunks.

3 Adjacencies
Supermarkets try to display complementary products next to each other to increase sales, like tomato sauce near pasta. Create your own, like vodka and tranquillizers.

4 Swapping
As soon as you get to know the store's layout, they swap things around so you walk through the whole place again. Ask the security guards to wipe out this practice.

5 Aisles
Traditionally aisles are wide because most people don't like touching and being touched by other shoppers. But you certainly do, so squeeze them close together.

My! This modified-atmosphere-processed, irradiated, ethyl butyrate, osoamyl acetate, menthyl benzoate, cis-3 hexenol, isoamyl isovalerate, ethyl decanoate-flavoured melon smells simply delicious! I'll take two dozen.

Tuesday 7 June

8	14
9	15
10	16
11	17
12	18
13	19

Guest Day

Today,

imagine that everything made by humans
could be different to the way it currently is -
and could be changed again

Signed...... *Alain de Botton*

Wednesday 8 June		
8		14
9		15
10		16
11		17
12		18
13		19

Today make people believe you're a billion-dollar cyborg

People believe what they've seen on TV, so stick to this storyline, maybe changing a small detail like your name, and you won't be challenged: you were test piloting a NASA experimental craft when it spun out of control and crashed. In the crash you lost your left arm, your right eye and both legs. You would have died had the government not fitted you with cybernetic body parts that are much more effective than the originals, at a cost of billions. They were going to make you do all sorts of fancy missions on their behalf, but you got a good lawyer and now you're suing them.

BIONIC NEURO LEG
REFERENCE ++XD45678
BIONIC NEURO HAND
REFERENCE ++XD78654-5643A
POWER SUPPLY: PLUTONIUM 0-678 RE:
12KW >SURGE> 50KW
CONFIDENTIAL
CLASS 56/US/UK/AW
BIONIC NEURO LEG
REFERENCE ++XD45678
BIONIC NEURO HAND
REFERENCE ++XD78654-5643A
POWER SUPPLY: PLUTONIUM 0-678 RE:

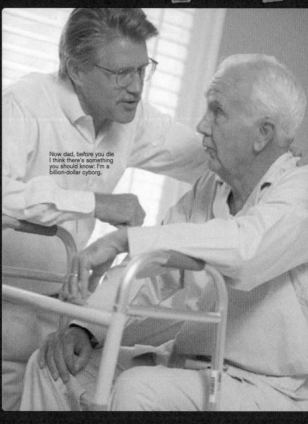

Now dad, before you die I think there's something you should know: I'm a billion-dollar cyborg.

Thursday 9 June

8	14
9	15
10	16
11	17
12	18
13	19

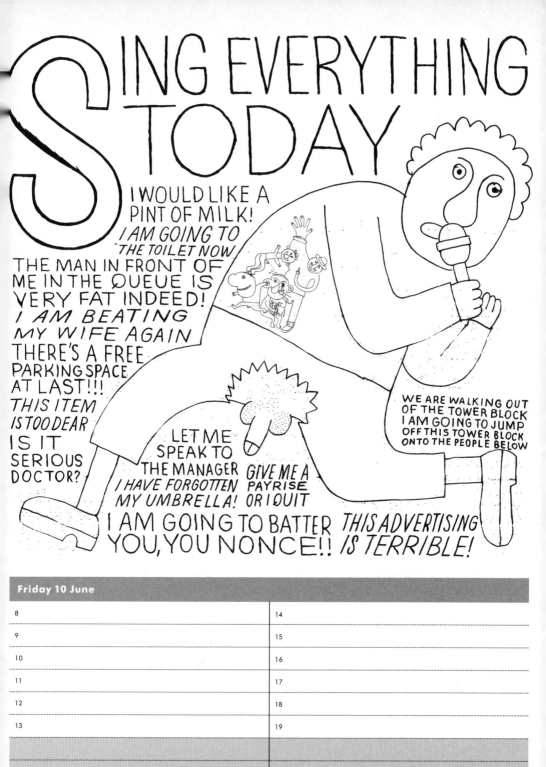

8	14
9	15
10	16
11	17
12	18
13	19

Saturday & Sunday 11–12 June

MICRONS OF AMPLIFIED MAXIMUM GROUND MOTION

10^9

RICHTER SCALE

GRAPHIC REPRESENTATION

Benrik jump, today

8.9

Largest Recorded
(Offshore Chile, 1960)

Alaska, 1964

GREAT

San Francisco, 1906

10^8

8

MAJOR

Great Devastation
and Many
Fatalities Possible

10^7

7

Loma Prieta, CA, 1989

STRONG

10^6
10^5

6
MODERATE

10^4
10^2

5
SMALL

4

Damage Begins
Fatalities Rare

10^{-1}

3

2

MINOR

10^{-1}

-1 0 1

NOT FELT

-1 0 1 2 3 4 5 6 7 8 9

Today at 10.46 everyone jump to cause an earthquake

In 2001, a million British children jumped simultaneously in their school playgrounds, releasing two billion joules of energy and causing a seismic shock that registered 3 on the Richter scale. Because they all jumped in geologically irrelevant spots, no major earthquake was caused. Today, however, Diary readers are to jump at key epicentres, triggering massive tectonic movement across the globe. They are: San Francisco (California), Kansu (China), Banos (Ecuador), King's Lynn (UK). DANGER! Today's task is potentially dangerous: to avoid straining your ankle whilst jumping, make sure you bend your knees and spring up with both feet off the ground at the same time. Wear suitable footwear, and hold your arms out for balance. If you are over 70, or have a medical condition, check with your doctor before joining in.

Monday 13 June	
8	14
9	15
10	16
11	17
12	18
13	19

Today leave a trail behind you, Hansel & Gretel style...

■ GOOD THINGS TO USE
■ BAD THINGS TO USE

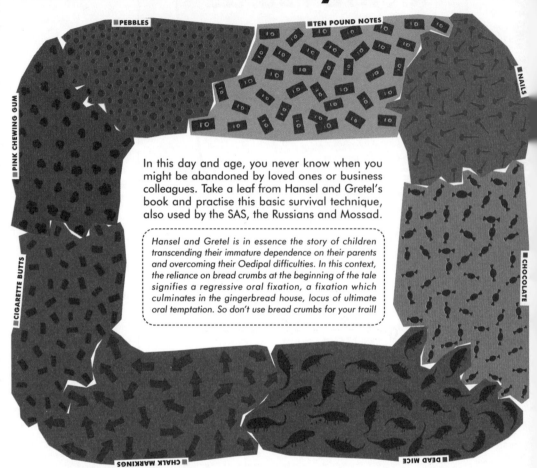

PEBBLES

TEN POUND NOTES

NAILS

PINK CHEWING GUM

CIGARETTE BUTTS

CHOCOLATE

In this day and age, you never know when you might be abandoned by loved ones or business colleagues. Take a leaf from Hansel and Gretel's book and practise this basic survival technique, also used by the SAS, the Russians and Mossad.

Hansel and Gretel is in essence the story of children transcending their immature dependence on their parents and overcoming their Oedipal difficulties. In this context, the reliance on bread crumbs at the beginning of the tale signifies a regressive oral fixation, a fixation which culminates in the gingerbread house, locus of ultimate oral temptation. So don't use bread crumbs for your trail!

CHALK MARKINGS

DEAD MICE

Tuesday 14 June	
8	14
9	15
10	16
11	17
12	18
13	19

MASS CHEATING DAY

It's Anna Bourne's final exam today, and she needs all the support she can get. Everybody help her by reading out the tricky bits she can't remember from her textbooks out loud outside the exam building with a megaphone.

Go to: Examination Schools, 75-81 High Street, Oxford, from 10.15am to 11.45am.

"On the day of the accession of James the First, England descended from the rank which she had hitherto held, and began to be regarded as a power hardly of the second order. During many years the great British monarchy, under four successive princes of the House of Stuart, was scarcely a more important member of the European system than the little kingdom of Scotland had previously been. This, however, is little to be regretted. Of James the First, as of John, it may be said that, if his administration had been able and splendid, it would probably have been fatal to our country, and that we owe more to his weakness and meanness than to the wisdom and courage of much better sovereigns. He came to the throne at a critical moment. The time was fast approaching when either the King must become absolute, or the parliament must control the whole executive administration. Had James been, like Henry the Fourth, like Maurice of Nassau, or like Gustavus Adolphus, a valiant, active, and politic ruler, had he put himself at the head of the Protestants of Europe, had he gained great victories over Tilly and Spinola, had he adorned Westminster with the spoils of Bavarian monasteries and Flemish cathedrals, had he hung Austrian and Castilian banners in Saint Paul's, and had he found himself after great achievements, at the head of fifty thousand troops, brave, well disciplined, and devotedly attached to his person, the English Parliament would soon have been nothing more than a name. Happily he was not a man to play such a part. He began his administration by putting an end to the war which had raged during many years between England and Spain; and from that time he shunned hostilities with a caution which was proof against the insults of his neighbours and the clamours of his subjects. Not till the last year of his life could the influence of his son, his favourite, his Parliament, and his people combined, induce him to strike one feeble blow in defence of his family and of his religion. It was well for those whom he governed that he in this matter disregarded their wishes. The effect of his pacific policy was that, in his time, no regular troops were needed, and that, while France, Spain, Italy, Belgium, and Germany swarmed with mercenary soldiers, the defence of our island was still confided to the militia. As the King had no standing army, and did not even attempt to form one, it would have been wise in him to avoid any conflict with his people. But such was his indiscretion that, while he altogether neglected the means which alone could make him really absolute, he constantly put forward, in the most offensive form, claims of which none of his predecessors had ever dreamed. It was at this time that those strange theories which Filmer afterwards formed into a system and which became the badge of the most violent class of Tories and high churchmen first emerged into notice. It was gravely maintained that the Supreme Being regarded hereditary monarchy, as opposed to other forms of government, with peculiar favour; that the rule of succession in order of primogeniture was a divine institution, anterior to the Christian, and even to the Mosaic dispensation; that no human power, not even that of the whole legislature, no length of adverse possession, though it extended to ten centuries, could deprive a legitimate prince of his rights, that the authority of such a prince was necessarily always despotic; that the laws, by which, in England and in other countries, the prerogative was limited, were to be regarded merely as concessions which the sovereign had freely made and might at his pleasure resume; and that any treaty which a king might conclude with his people was merely a declaration of his present intentions, and not a contract of which the performance could be demanded. It is evident that this theory, though intended to strengthen the foundations of government, altogether unsettles them. Does the divine and immutable law of primogeniture admit females, or exclude them? On either supposition half the sovereigns of Europe must be usurpers, reigning in defiance of the law of God, and liable to be dispossessed by the rightful heirs. The doctrine that kingly government is peculiarly favoured by Heaven receives no countenance from the Old Testament; for in the Old Testament we read that the chosen people were blamed and punished for desiring a king, and that they were afterwards commanded to withdraw their allegiance from him. Their whole history, far from countenancing the notion that succession in order of primogeniture is of divine institution, would rather seem to indicate that younger brothers are under the especial protection of heaven. Isaac was not the eldest son of Abraham, nor Jacob of Isaac, nor Judah of Jacob, nor David of Jesse nor Solomon of David. Nor does the system of Filmer receive any countenance from those passages of the New Testament which describe government as an ordinance of God: for the government under which the writers of the New Testament lived was not a hereditary monarchy. The Roman Emperors were republican magistrates, named by the senate. None of them pretended to rule by right of birth; and, in fact, both Tiberius, to whom Christ commanded that tribute should be given, and Nero, whom Paul directed the Romans to obey, were, according to the patriarchal theory of government, usurpers. In the middle ages the doctrine of indefeasible hereditary right would have been regarded as heretical: for it was altogether incompatible with the high pretensions of the Church of Rome. It was a doctrine unknown to the founders of the Church of England. The Homily on Wilful Rebellion had strongly, and indeed too strongly, inculcated submission to constituted authority, but had made no distinction between hereditary end elective monarchies, or between monarchies and republics. Indeed most of the predecessors of James would, from personal motives, have regarded the patriarchal theory of government with aversion. William Rufus, Henry the First, Stephen, John, Henry the Fourth, Henry the Fifth, Henry the Sixth, Richard the Third, and Henry the Seventh, had all reigned in defiance of the strict rule of descent. A grave doubt hung over the legitimacy both of Mary and of Elizabeth. It was impossible that both Catharine of Aragon and Anne Boleyn could have been lawfully married to Henry the Eighth; and the highest authority in the realm had pronounced that neither was so. The Tudors, far from considering the law of succession as a divine and unchangeable institution, were constantly tampering with it. Henry the Eighth obtained an act of parliament, giving him power to leave the crown by will, and actually made a will to the prejudice of the royal family of Scotland. Edward the Sixth, unauthorised by Parliament, assumed a similar power, with the full approbation of the most eminent Reformers. Elizabeth, conscious that her own title was open to much objection, and unwilling to admit even a reversionary right in her rival and enemy the Queen of Scots, induced the Parliament to pass a law, enacting that whoever should deny the competency of the reigning sovereign, with the assent of the Estates of the realm, to alter the succession, should suffer death as a traitor. But the situation of James was widely different from that of Elizabeth. Far inferior to her in abilities and in popularity, regarded by the English as an alien, and excluded from the throne by the testament of Henry the Eighth, the King of Scots was yet the undoubted heir of William the Conqueror and of Egbert. He had, therefore, an obvious interest in inculcating the superstitious notion that birth confers rights anterior to law, and unalterable by law. It was a notion, moreover, well suited to his intellect and temper. It soon found many advocates among those who aspired to his favour, and made rapid progress among the clergy of the Established Church. Thus, at the very moment at which a republican spirit began to manifest itself strongly in the Parliament and in the country, the claims of the monarch took a monstrous form which would have disgusted the proudest and most arbitrary of those who had preceded him on the throne."

Wednesday 15 June

8	14
9	15
10	16
11	17
12	18
13	19

BECOME A SUPERHERO TODAY

Don't remain Clark Kent all your life. It only takes a little effort to acquire potentially useful superhero powers. Here's how.

SUPER GM — Get a job in a corporate genetic modification lab. Late one night, "accidentally" fall into the experimental seeds centrifuge. Powers: can clone himself at the drop of a hat.

WASPGIRL — In the course of a stroll outside Sellafield, get stung by a nestful of unusually large wasps... Powers: each of her fingertips contains a radioactive sting!

Snakeboy — Steal an Amazonian tribe's prized medicinal plant for the pharmaceutical industry and be cursed for 1000 years as a result. Powers: with his forked tongue, can lie his way out of any situation.

MEATMAN — Fall into the vat of "unfit for human consumption" meat during a guided tour of an abattoir. Powers: can antagonize vegetarian villains.

PUNK WOMAN — Listen to Sex Pistols album repeatedly until timewarp projects you back to the late seventies. Powers: her anger can cause any society to implode.

MONSTER MAN — This one was just born this way, you can't become one. Powers: turns into a scary monster.

Thursday 16 June

8	Last day work at Tuglex!	14	
9		15	
10		16	
11		17	
12		18	
13		19	

BENRIK
SUPERHERO
NECKLACES
ON THE WEB FROM TODAY!

Today, write and thank your most influential teacher

You've been very naughty by not doing this much earlier though, so you have to write it 100 times!

....
....
....
....
....
....
....
....
....
....
....
....
....
....
....
....
....
....
....
....
....
....

Friday 17 June

8	14
9	15
10	16
11	17
12	18
13	19

Father's Day Weekend!

Assess your Dad's performance so far

Father's name...

Father's age...

Father's age when he met my mother..............................

Father's age when he had me..

Degree of certainty that he is my father............................/10

What I call my father

Dad ☐   Daddy ☐   Father ☐   Papa ☐   Pop ☐   Bastard ☐

Other..

....

....

GENERAL

	YES	NO	DON'T KNOW
My father has provided me with a sense of stability	☐	☐	☐
My father has provided me with a sense of security	☐	☐	☐
My father has provided me with a sense of purpose	☐	☐	☐
My father's relationship with my mother has made me feel that loving relationships are:.........the norm	☐	☐	☐
....hard work	☐	☐	☐
....a bitter illusion	☐	☐	☐

In your own words, write your assessment of your father so far, along with suggestions as to how he might improve. *Cut it out and paste it into his Father's Day card.*

....
....
....
....
....
....
....
....
....
....
....
....
....
....
....
....

MEN *My father's relationship with me:*

...has been that of a positive role model which has enabled me to identify with him and develop into a well-balanced male ☐

...has been that of an overpowering tyrant, nipping my confidence in the bud and leading to repressed violence and depression ☐

...has been absent, leaving me with an unresolved Oedipal conflict and a confused sexual identity ☐

WOMEN *My father's relationship with me:*

...has allowed me to deal with the Electra complex to the point where I can enjoy fulfilling relationships with men ☐

...has fostered a dependency on overtly callous men whom I normally expect to leave me after a few months at best ☐

...has turned me into a distrustful shrew who avoids men and indeed close relationships in general ☐

Saturday & Sunday 18–19 June

Bite animals back today

Here's where to bite those animals that dare to bite humans!

Dog
Bite their tail!

Cat
Bite their whiskers!

Lion
Bite their mane!

Weasel
Bite their snout!

Rat
Bite their tummy!

Tiger
Bite their stripes!

Horse
Bite their hoof!

Bat
Bite their wing! (don't bite their head off no matter what you may have read)

Shark
Bite their fin!

Mosquito
Bite their proboscis!

Monday 20 June

New job starting today!

	14
	15
0	16
1	17
2	18
3	19

My Tattoo

This is Frankie Easton. He's tattooed in all kinds of places, but for years he's left his back free for "the big one". Problem is, getting it is such a big step in life that he doesn't know good from bad anymore... Therefore he's asking the Diary readers for help.

Help him! He's only getting it done to look cool to you anyway. Out of the following fifteen motifs, which one should he choose? The final design will be printed on his back for all to see three months from now, on September 21. Voting starts now.

a)
b)
c)
d)
e)
f)
g)
h)
i)
j)
k)
l)
m)
n)
o)

Tattoo Area

Vote at www.thiswebsitewillchangeyourlife.com

Tuesday 21 June

8	14
9	15
10	16
11	17
12	18
13	19

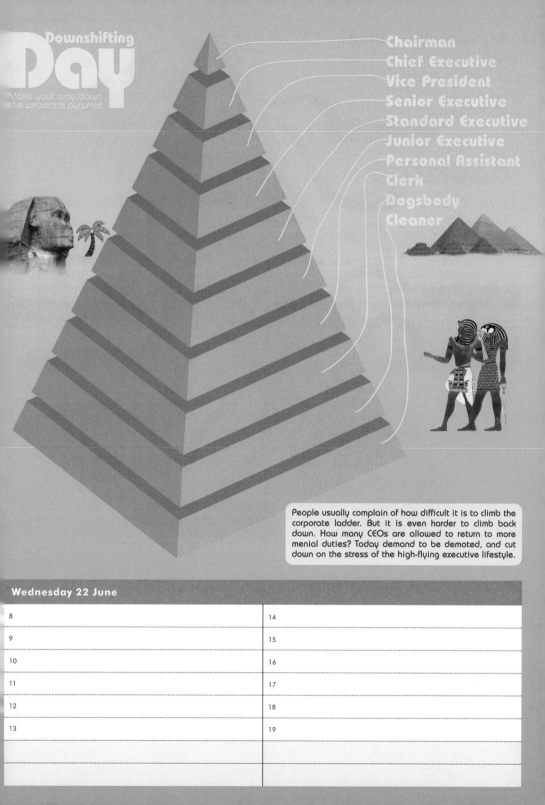

Downshifting Day

Make your way down the corporate pyramid

Chairman
Chief Executive
Vice President
Senior Executive
Standard Executive
Junior Executive
Personal Assistant
Clerk
Dogsbody
Cleaner

People usually complain of how difficult it is to climb the corporate ladder. But it is even harder to climb back down. How many CEOs are allowed to return to more menial duties? Today demand to be demoted, and cut down on the stress of the high-flying executive lifestyle.

Wednesday 22 June

8	14
9	15
10	16
11	17
12	18
13	19

Today use your remote control for evil purposes

Don't just point it at the TV! Instead try these functions:

Turns traffic lights green

Activates dark side of people

Restarts supercomputers

Remote Nuclear War Button

Triggers immediate orgasm

Makes cats vomit

Disables incoming missiles

Jams other people's mobiles

Makes aeroplanes go faster

Pauses pacemakers

Even its maker has forgotten what this one does

Thursday 23 June

8	14
9	15
10	16
11	17
12	18
13	19

Do not attempt this with taxi drivers. In this instance, go straight for sexual favours, no messing about. They like it.

STROKE A BUS OR TRAIN CONDUCTOR AS PAYMENT FOR THE FARE When a bus conductor or other custodian of public transport asks for a fare, admit that you have no money, but offer to stroke him/her in an affectionate but non-sexual manner. It might be interesting to find out exactly how many strokes are equivalent to the appropriate fare.

Friday 24 June

8	14
9	15
10	16
11	17
12	18
13	19

Fastest cricket streaker

Most own goals in single football match

Shortest basketball player

Longest involuntary ski jump

Unusual sporting achievement weekend

Sport has become the preserve of a drug-fuelled sponsorship-addled elite. An ordinary person today stands no chance of breaking a world record. So why bother playing by the rules? This weekend come up with your own way of making an imprint on sport history.

First marathon run backwards

Only tennis match played entirely from the net

Longest distance swum holding a rubber duck for buoyancy

First barefoot ice hockey match

Saturday & Sunday 25–26 June

Benrik Stamp Day

Benrik are exasperated by the tacky selection of stamps available from the postal authorities, and so are launching their very own range. Today circulate these vibrant new design masterpieces and brighten up your correspondence.

Included in the price of the Diary!!!

Monday 27 June

8	14
9	15
10	16
11	17
12	18
13	19

HELP COBBLER PIOTR SAVE HIS BUSINESS TODAY

Piotr is putting on a brave face and known to his (few) clients as a good humoured worker, but as you can see he is deeply troubled by the business cycle

in Wimbledon, and helped him find a home, premises, and, last but not least, a catchy name. Until the late nineties, business was pretty good, if not exactly booming. But then trainers became all the rage, and turnover took a hit. Piotr has never liked trainers ("shoes fit for a lazy peasant") but he has to face the new reality. Benrik are looking for suggestions of how Piotr might reengineer his cobblering skills to the trainers market. Here are some of the services he might offer to the more discerning customer. Go to his shop and ask for them, and prevent him from sliding into bankruptcy.

Fit your trainers with crampons for muddy roads

Sew on a personalized logo to stand out from the crowd

Ladies! Get heels fitted for that ladylike look

NEW! The retro clog

Piotr Jareski has been running his business "A Load of Cobblers" in the leafy London suburb of Wood Green since 1991. He learnt his trade in his native Poland, where he was apprentice to the famous Konrad Grudzinski of Krakow. He moved over with his family after Grudzinski's death in 1989. His brother was already established as a painter-decorator

Piotr's 17-year-old son Wojtek keeps him in touch with the word on the street. "Retro" is all the rage, which gave Piotr an idea. He called up his old buddy Janusz who took over the Grudzinski business, and ordered a shipment of Janusz's lifelong speciality, the "Krakow clog". Never has anyone seen such a fine clog, from the Baltic to the Ukraine. But Piotr's idea was to adapt it to the Western market. How? By customizing it with the names of all the churches in Pomerania with a simple marker pen. Can you do better?

Tuesday 28 June

8	14
9	15
10	16
11	17
12	18
13	19

Today *hijack a public performance*. In the time-honoured tradition of the avant-garde, add your twist to a public event. Contemporary composers and playwrights almost expect the audience to erupt at some point, and the dead ones won't mind anyway. If anyone queries your right to shout out FIRE! as a postmodern performative construct, ridicule their philistine literalism and accuse them of disrupting your narrative. BUT! Avoid these clichés, unless you possess superhuman powers of irony:

Wednesday 29 June

8	14
9	15
10	16
11	17
12	18
13	19

Today presell your memoirs based on your spectacular future achievements

12a Shrubland Rd
Sutton SN1 1WB
London, England

Dear Mister/Madam Publisher,

This is a once-in-a-lifetime opportunity for you to buy my memoirs.

I am Bert Brown, and if you haven't heard of me yet, you sure will! At the present moment I am 29 years of age. In the next ten years, it is my intention to: climb Mt Everest naked, marry a Hollywood actress (identity to be confirmed), interview the head of the Chinese secret police, and become a chess champion.

After that, in my forties, my plan is to regroup Van Halen with me as drummer, cure cancer of the pancreas (I know someone who had it) and enter the political arena.

My plans for my fifties are a little hazy as it's still a while to go, but I reckon something to do with the Moon (we will live in space by then don't forget), divorce the famous actress (identity to be confirmed), and become a champion of the oppressed, possibly within the UN if that august international body still exists.

So you see my life will make a GREAT book of memoirs, which I am offering to YOU now. I want $100,000 for it, not a penny less. You have 24 hours or I'm off to your rivals.

Yours
Bert Brown
(Author)

8		14	
9		15	
10		16	
11		17	
12		18	
13		19	

From the Borgias to JFK, poisoning has claimed thousands of victims. Yet few take the necessary precautions against it. Today ask a family member or a waiter to taste your food before you ingest it. Then observe them for 20 minutes for the slightest sign of illness, like vomiting, convulsions or massive internal haemorrhaging. Only then may you relax and enjoy your meal.

Have all your food tasted for poison today

Tell-tale signs that your food is poisoned

Roast chicken
Wings look slightly shrunken

Cod and chips
Chips break in two very easily

Cheeseburger
Cheese has greenish tinge

Steak
Veins bulging (with the poison)

Ham and cheese sandwich
Ham and cheese stuck together

Apple crumble
No visible signs, avoid

Rasputin's top tip: the "mad monk" was the target of many assassination attempts, including one to poison him with huge doses of cyanide. Amazingly, he survived, having deliberately exposed himself to increasing amounts of poison over the years to build up some immunity. Of course he was eventually shot and dumped in a frozen river. Not much you can do about that.

Friday 1 July

8	14
9	15
10	16
11	17
12	18
13	19

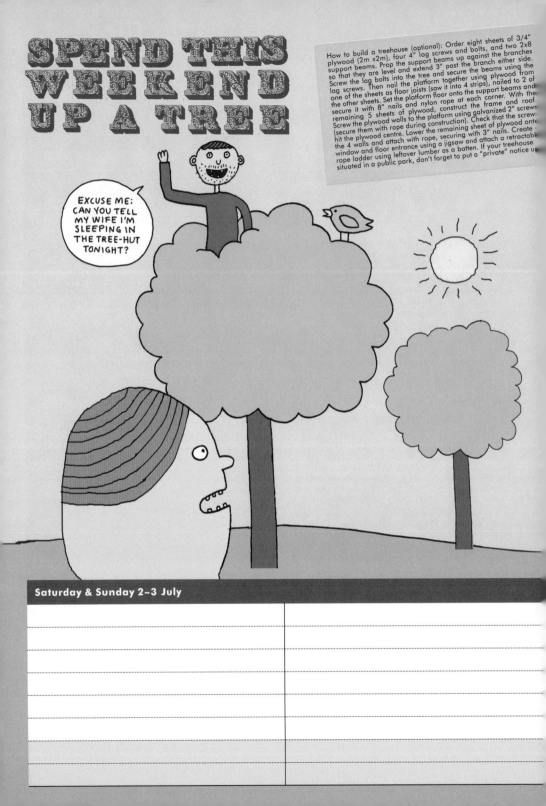

SPEND THIS WEEKEND UP A TREE

How to build a treehouse (optional): Order eight sheets of 3/4"
plywood (2m x2m), four 4" lag screws and bolts, and two 2x8
support beams. Prop the support beams up against the branches
so that they are level and extend 3" past the branch either side.
Screw the lag bolts into the tree and secure the beams using the
lag screws. Then nail the platform together using plywood from
one of the sheets as floor joists (saw it into 4 strips), nailed to 2 of
the other sheets. Set the platform floor onto the support beams and
secure it with 8" nails and nylon rope at each corner. With the
remaining 5 sheets of plywood, construct the frame and roof.
Screw the plywood walls to the platform using galvanized 2" screws
(secure them with rope during construction). Check that the screws
hit the plywood centre. Lower the remaining sheet of plywood onto
the 4 walls and attach with rope, securing with 3" nails. Create a
window and floor entrance using a jigsaw and attach a retractable
rope ladder using leftover lumber as a batten. If your treehouse is
situated in a public park, don't forget to put a "private" notice up.

EXCUSE ME:
CAN YOU TELL
MY WIFE I'M
SLEEPING IN
THE TREE-HUT
TONIGHT?

Saturday & Sunday 2–3 July

US Independence Day: today help reconquer America

Clearly the decision to allow the USA to acquire independence was a historical booboo. Benrik are today taking charge of the military reconquest and recolonization of America. Here is how you can help.

Stage 1: Invasion
Meet at 7.30am at Dover, where we shall commandeer ferries to ship our thousands of volunteers to the East Coast. By 2.30pm (local time), we shall reach Manhattan, Boston, Washington, Miami, Detroit and Chicago, where we shall disembark disguised as tourists and overpower local security forces with our command of the English language.

Stage 2: Reconquest
The President shall be presented with newly-uncovered legal evidence that the Declaration of Independence was a fake. In the spirit of the great new era, however, an amnesty shall be granted to all who have served in the spurious US 'governments' of the past 200+ years. Control of the US military and the CIA shall revert to Whitehall forthwith.

Stage 3: Recolonization
This two-part process shall begin at midnight. 1) One million British shall be relocated to Middle America over the next year. Their task shall be to wipe out the American accent. 2) The 200 million Americans shall be 'retrained' to prefer cricket to baseball, and books to TV. On the Fourth of July 2006, they shall celebrate "Dependence Day".

Monday 4 July

8		14	
9		15	
10		16	
11		17	
12		18	
13		19	

HIDDEN PROMISE DAY

You never know who around you might shoot to fame overnight these days, so collect their autographs now before they're too important to talk to you.

FATHER	NEWSAGENT	LOVER
MOTHER	DRYCLEANER	MISTRESS
BROTHER 1	SUPERMARKET CHECKOUT GIRL	FIRST LOVE
BROTHER 2	GAS STATION ATTENDANT	FRIEND 1
SISTER 1	BUILDER	FRIEND 2
SISTER 2	CAB DRIVER	FRIEND 3
SON	BANK TELLER	FRIEND 4
DAUGHTER	FISHMONGER	ACQUAINTANCE 1
GRANDFATHER 1	GARDENER	ACQUAINTANCE 2
GRANDFATHER 2	CLEANER	ACQUAINTANCE 3
GRANDMOTHER 1	HOOKER	ACQUAINTANCE 4
GRANDMOTHER 2	PSYCHOTHERAPIST	COLLEAGUE 1
AUNT	PERSONAL TRAINER	COLLEAGUE 2
UNCLE	TAX INSPECTOR	COLLEAGUE 3
COUSIN 1	LOCAL VICAR	COLLEAGUE 4
COUSIN 2	LOCAL POLICEMAN	COLLEAGUE 5
NEIGHBOUR 1	LOCAL TRAMP	BOSS
NEIGHBOUR 2	LOCAL PAEDOPHILE	EMPLOYEE 1
TEACHER	LOLLIPOP LADY	EMPLOYEE 2
BUTCHER	VILLAGE IDIOT	EMPLOYEE 3
GREENGROCER	SPOUSE	GIRL NEXT DOOR*

*MOST LIKELY TO SHOOT TO FAME: MAKE SURE YOU GET HER AUTOGRAPH

Tuesday 5 July

8	14
9	15
10	16
11	17
12	18
13	19

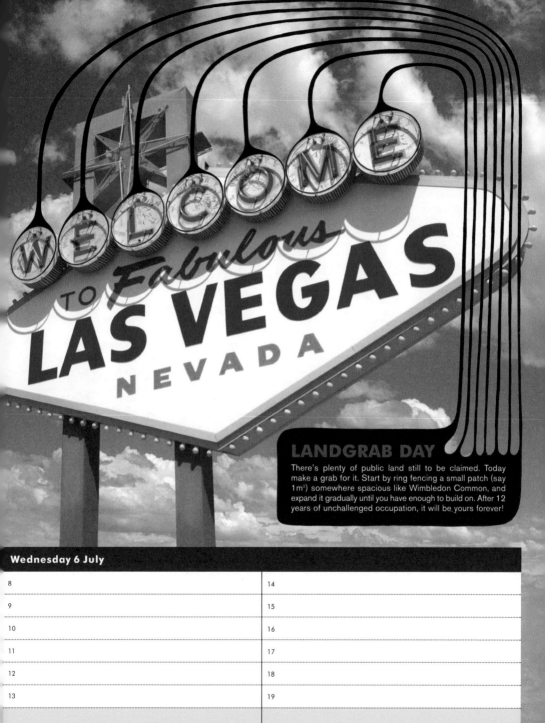

LANDGRAB DAY

There's plenty of public land still to be claimed. Today make a grab for it. Start by ring fencing a small patch (say 1m²) somewhere spacious like Wimbledon Common, and expand it gradually until you have enough to build on. After 12 years of unchallenged occupation, it will be yours forever!

Wednesday 6 July

8	14
9	15
10	16
11	17
12	18
13	19

Today write a letter to your future self

Hello future me.
I'm glad we're still around to read this in the year 2035. What's happened to us in the last 30 years? Obviously I can't speculate too much, but from where I'm standing now, we'll have done well to avoid personal and global annihilation! So if im reading this, things have gone pretty good already. What are my hopes for the future me? I hoped we've lived up to my promise and become a race car driver. I imagine we've married and have kids (2 or 3) though I'll understand if we've become gay. It's because of that Martha bitch isn't it? We never liked her. Anyway, have we gone around the world as planned? I'd have to say I'd be really pissed off if we hadn't as I've just started saving. Also it's my life dream, so if we haven't got a good excuse that makes us a big fat loser in my book. Did we ever get caught for that tax scam? I'm pretty nervous about it now. I don't imagine we can get away with that in 2035, when computers probably monitor your every move. Maybe we're a famous astronaut? In which case schoolchildren will be reading this and learning about our life! But probably not. Anyway gotta go and live our life, so that's all from 2005.

Your 2005 self

To: Year 2035 self

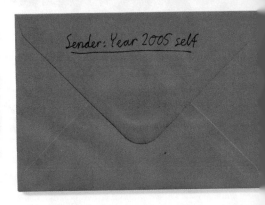

Sender: Year 2005 self

Thursday 7 July

8	14
9	15
10	16
11	17
12	18
13	19

TODAY SPEAK THE
UNSPEAKABLE

In our verbally incontinent society, recover the power of words by finding something you cannot actually bring yourself to say out loud in public.

Friday 8 July

8	14
9	15
10	16
11	17
12	18
13	19

This weekend, go round the world

For the first time in the history of humanity, we can circumnavigate the Earth in a day or two. To previous generations, this would have been as unthinkable as going to the moon. And yet anyone can do it. Book a round-the-world flight leaving today Saturday, and by tomorrow evening you'll have circled our tiny planet

Saturday & Sunday 9–10 July

Sell your sperm today
Sell your eggs today

As a Diary reader, you are at the very top of the gene pool. Share some of your lucky gametes with those less fortunate in Nature's great lottery. Go to your local clinic and volunteer your services. You will undergo medical and psychological tests and be placed on their books. Men may contribute as much sperm as possible, as often as once a week. Women have fewer eggs, and so their compensation is higher, although they may donate no more than three times. Try to negotiate more than the standard payment as you are a Diary reader and therefore of desirable genetic stock. Your long-term goal is to be responsible for over ten pregnancies, at which point you will begin to impact the local gene pool significantly. You will earn money, your Benrik-reader genes will spread, and the world will become a better place all round.

Monday 11 July

8	14
9	15
10	16
11	17
12	18
13	19

Today: impulse buy!

Tuesday 12 July

8		14	
9		15	
10		16	
11		17	
12		18	
13		19	

Instructions: leave the Diary open on your knees at this page and gather two or three friends round to begin the seance. It is crucial that you only invite people who treat the board with the appropriate respect, otherwise it will not work. Hold the oracle in your hand, get your friends to put their hands on top of yours and let it drift over the board. Ask a pertinent question to rouse the spirits, like "is anyone there" or "can you hear me Beelzebub". You will sense the board's pull when you reach the appropriate letter. It is perfectly permissible to write down the board's replies, particularly if you are a beginner. Once you have established communication with the other realm, start to conjure up a malevolent spirit with teasers such as "Archatapias, hear my call" or "Lucifer, it is time!" When you are bored of toying with the evil spirit, simply place the oracle on GOOD BYE.

Wednesday 13 July

8	14
9	15
10	16
11	17
12	18
13	19

HANDS FREE DAY

We are constantly burdened with accessories, from handbags to mobile phones. Today leave them all at home and see how you much freer you feel without all these supposedly essential items.

Thursday 14 July

8	14
9	15
10	16
11	17
12	18
13	19

TODAY STARE INTO OTHER PEOPLE'S HOMES

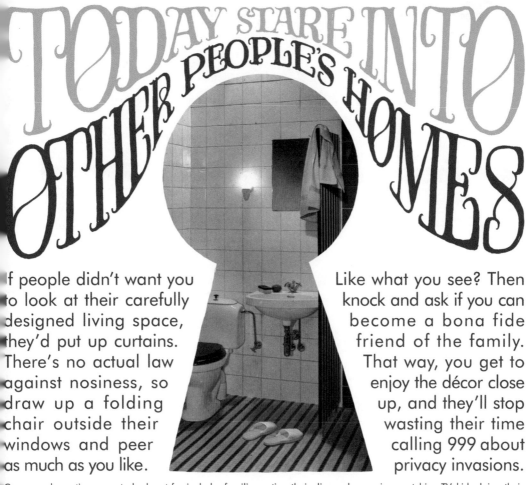

If people didn't want you to look at their carefully designed living space, they'd put up curtains. There's no actual law against nosiness, so draw up a folding chair outside their windows and peer as much as you like.

Like what you see? Then knock and ask if you can become a bona fide friend of the family. That way, you get to enjoy the décor close up, and they'll stop wasting their time calling 999 about privacy invasions.

Common domestic scenes to look out for include: families eating their dinner, housewives watching TV, kids doing their homework, clocks ticking, babies crying, neighbours borrowing cups of sugar, teenagers picking up the phone, salesmen doing their spiel, dogs fouling the carpet, wives cheating on their husbands, husbands cheating on their wives, lovers hiding in cupboards, bailiffs repossessing the fridge, grannies beating their cats, sadomasochistic suburban orgies, cockroaches jumping in the soup, instances of spontaneous combustion, plots being hatched against civilization itself. Don't get caught peeking!

Friday 15 July

8	14
9	15
10	16
11	17
12	18
13	19

This weekend, speedread War & Peace

Everyone means to read War & Peace, but few actually do. Don't be daunted by its length, it's a quick read if you put your mind to it and follow a few basic time-saving guidelines

Time yourself
Let's say you have 26 hours of reading time this weekend. At 1200 pages, that means you can devote 78 seconds to each page. Remind yourself of this deadline every time you turn the page.

78

Skip the descriptions
Yadda yadda yadda. Sometimes even the greatest novelist can go on a bit. Dialogue is more important, plus it's fun to imagine what the characters are wearing yourself.

Pick out key words
No one knows how this works, but if you squint at the page, your subconscious self somehow spots the key words that really matter to comprehension.

Read only the right-hand pages
This was Marshall McLuhan's method. You'll still pick up most of the plot, but you'll halve your reading time. If the book ends on a left-hand page though, you may break the rule.

Rename the characters
Work out who the characters remind you of amongst your friends and rename them all accordingly. This provides a useful psychological shortcut.

Already read War & Peace? Then just pick another masterpiece from the following list: Remembrance of Things Past, Ulysses, the Bible, David Copperfield, Anna Karenina, Don Quixote, Moby Dick

---

CHAPTER I

"Well, Prince, so Genoa and Lucca are now just family estates of the Buonapartes. But I warn you, if you don't tell me that this means war, if you still try to defend the infamies and horrors perpetrated by that Antichrist- I really believe he is Antichrist- I will have nothing more to do with you and you are no longer my friend, no longer my 'faithful slave,' as you call yourself! But how do you do? I see I have frightened you- sit down and tell me all the news."

It was in July, 1805, and the speaker was the well-known Anna Pavlovna Scherer, maid of honour and favourite of the Empress Marya Fedorovna. With these words she greeted Prince Vasili Kuragin, a man of high rank and importance, who was the first to arrive at her reception. Anna Pavlovna had had a cough for some days. She was, as she said, suffering from la grippe; grippe being then a new word in St. Petersburg, used only by the elite.

All her invitations without exception, written in French, and delivered by a scarlet-liveried footman that morning, ran as follows:

"If you have nothing better to do, Count (or Prince), and if the prospect of spending an evening with a poor invalid is not

too terrible, I shall be very charmed to see you tonight between 7 and 10– Annette Scherer."
"Heavens! what a virulent attack!" replied the prince, not in the least disconcerted by this reception. He had just entered, wearing an embroidered court uniform, knee breeches, and shoes, and had stars on his breast and a serene expression on his flat face. He spoke in that refined French in which our grandfathers not only spoke but thought, and with the gentle, patronizing intonation natural to a man of importance who had grown old in society and at court. He went up to Anna Pavlovna, kissed her hand, presenting to her his bald, scented, and shining head, and complacently seated himself on the sofa.

"First of all, dear friend, tell me how you are. Set your friend's mind at rest," said he without altering his tone, beneath the politeness and affected sympathy of which indifference and even irony could be discerned.

"Can one be well while suffering morally? Can one be calm in times like these if one has any feeling?" said Anna Pavlovna. "You are staying the whole evening, I hope?"

"And the fete at the English ambassador's? Today is Wednesday. I must put in an appearance there," said the prince. "My daughter is coming for me to take me there."

"I thought today's fete had been cancelled. I confess all these festivities and fireworks are becoming wearisome."

Anna Pavlovna = Tracy Baker

Saturday & Sunday 16–17 July

TODAY DO EVERYTHING IN SLOW MOTION

The reason movies show dramatic events in slow motion isn't just to let us see the details. Accidents and other high-stress situations are actually experienced in slow motion. Scientists speculate that the rush of adrenalin alters our brain's perception of time – what the Greeks called tachypsychia or distortion of the 'speed of the mind'. Those Greeks!

6.23 PM:

Monday 18 July	
8	14
9	15
10	16
11	17
12	18
13	19

Today, discover...
The Dark Side of the Rainbow

You will need:

An audio copy of Pink Floyd's 'Dark Side of the Moon', a copy of 'The Wizard Of Oz on DVD or video.

Now, begin DSotM just as the MGM lion (at the very beginning of WoO) roars for the third time. You know you're right if the title 'Produced by **MERVIN LE ROY**' appears just as 'Speak to Me' fades into 'Breathe'.

You may have heard that pink floyd's 'dark side of the moon' album acts as a sort of soundtrack to 'the wizard of oz'. I tried this the other day and the results are quite exciting if you get it in sync properly. http://members.cox.net/stegokitty/dsotr_pages/dsotr.htm will tell you everything you need to know and includes a list of things to look out for.

Tuesday 19 July

8	14
9	15
10	16
11	17
12	18
13	19

Attempt to be noticed from space today

There are hundreds of spy satellites orbiting the earth with cameras that can pick out objects a few inches wide. Do something unusual enough to spark their attention. Arrange 100 of your friends into the shape of a giant caterpillar. Dig a nuclear-style crater on the beach. Send a message like 'EMPEROR XORG WE ARE READY FOR YOUR ARRIVAL' in Morse with a giant arc-lamp. CIA analysts too need something to lighten up their day.

Wednesday 20 July

8		14
9		15
10		16
11		17
12		18
13		19

Dumbing Down Day

Today see if you can reduce your IQ by at least 30 points

IQ at 8am:

Watch TV for 6 hours, though nothing that contains evidence of thinking

Listen to heavy metal through your headphones at maximum volume

Read the tabloids from A to Z, paying particular attention to the astrology section

Drink a bottle of Scotch whilst watching TV and chase it with some vodka shots

Smoke a couple of joints, take a couple of pills, snort a quick line

Tailor your diet to exclude brain-friendly substances such as fish, avocados, spinach or water

Avoid using human language: instead grunt when people speak to you

Bang your head against a hard surface for a minute

I'M TAKING TODAY OFF; I AM ALREADY STUPID.

IQ at 8pm:

Thursday 21 July		
8		14
9		15
10		16
11		17
12		18
13		19

Today mislead a tourist

The world would be a brighter place if tourists got lost more regularly. When an inquisitive foreigner asks his way today, send him off in an unexpected direction. He's read about all the obvious landmarks in his guidebook anyway.

Friday 22 July	
8	14
9	15
10	16
11	17
12	18
13	19

WEEKEND CANCELLED: GO TO WORK

ATTENTION

DUE TO AN UNFORESEEN ECONOMIC SLOWDOWN, THIS WEEKEND HAS BEEN CANCELLED. PLEASE GO TO WORK AS YOU WOULD DURING THE WEEK. ANYONE WHO DOES NOT REPORT TO WORK WILL BE CHARGED WITH ABSENTEEISM AND RISKS BEING DISMISSED.

SPECIAL NOTE: CHURCH-GOERS MAY ATTEND MASS ON SUNDAY MORNING, BUT ONLY IF THEIR PRIEST CERTIFIES IN WRITING THAT THEY ARE REGULARS.

Saturday & Sunday 23–24 July

TODAY TAKE PART IN THE GREAT CYCLE OF LIFE

We humans stand too aloof from the basic processes of our planet.
And yet we are as crucial a part of the Earth's ecosystem as fruitflies or plankton.
Today make a conscious effort to play your part in the cycle of life.

Let a mosquito bite you
Shit in the vegetable patch
Feed your hair to the dust mites
Carry pollen from one flower to another
Discard fruit seeds in a park
Help worms find the cemetery
Let yourself be eaten by a lion

Monday 25 July

8	14
9	15
10	16
11	17
12	18
13	19

Today keep an eye out for subtle body language

Students of psychology know that hands on hips signifies confrontation, or that touching your nose means lying. But the truly significant emotions are more deeply repressed, and thus are revealed in extremely subtle ways. Today learn to look out for these and many others.

EYES FOCUSING 4M AWAY
Person is plotting against your country

LEFT EAR FULLY OPEN
Signifies desire for urgent sexual congress

LITTLE FINGER BENT 45°
Betrays lying, deception on a colossal scale

NOSTRILS FLARED
Person will physically attack you within 20 seconds

BLINKING 5% MORE THAN USUAL
Person is questioning your sexual orientation

BUTTOCKS CLENCHED
Shows desire to evacuate bowels

NIPPLES ERECT
Indicates love at first sight

LEG HAIR RAISED
Appreciates your sense of humour

STOMACH MUSCLES TWITCHING
Signifies deep discomfort with your clothing

FOOT TILTED TOWARDS MECCA
Indicates person will agree with you just so as to go home

Tuesday 26 July

8	14
9	15
10	16
11	17
12	18
13	19

TODAY FIGHT FOR YOUR COUNTRY!

Today the world's major countries battle it out for supremacy on our website. Click on yours to help it triumph over its rivals! At midnight tonight GMT, the winner will be revealed.

MAY THE BEST MAN WIN!

WWW.THISWEBSITEWILL
CHANGEYOURLIFE.COM

8	14
9	15
10	16
11	17
12	18
13	19

Today, appear on TV!

Benrik have arranged for one lucky reader to appear on TV today live. Meet us at 8am outside the Post Office at 193 Cricklewood High Street, London, where we will select the individual to appear.

Criteria for immediate disqualification:

Stark nakedness

Tourette's syndrome

Possession of a weapon

Family link with Benrik

Aged over 39

Previous appearance on Big Brother

Wearing of visible sponsorship

Wearing of motorcycle helmet

Hidden agenda

Thursday 28 July	
8	14
9	15
10	16
11	17
12	18
13	19

Today, ask everyone you meet to jump

Life photographer Philippe Halsman invented 'jumpology', a simple technique to reveal people's true personality to the camera: he'd ask them to jump. 'In a jump the subject, in a sudden burst of energy, overcomes gravity. He cannot simultaneously control his expressions, his facial and his limb muscles. The mask falls. The real self becomes visible.' Today ask everyone you meet to jump and reveal their true selves.

Friday 29 July

8	14
9	15
10	16
11	17
12	18
13	19

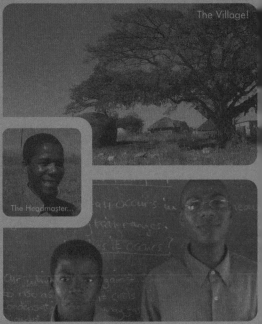

The Village!

The Headmaster...

Learning maths!

SWAZILAND WEEKEND

Benrik have a small but loyal fanbase in Swaziland. The children of Kaphunga are all doing their best to follow it, though it is sometimes difficult for them as they have limited resources. But they appreciate encouragement and visits from other Diary fans worldwide. Write to them c/o Myxo, Box 2455, Manzini, Swaziland, and donate £17.99 to help them purchase the latest edition.

TOP TIP! *When in Swaziland, stay at Myxo's!* Myxo's Place is set in a beautiful location in central Swaziland and is run by Swazis. Learn siSwati, enjoy traditional food, chat with laid back owner Myxo, and visit all the children at school! DIRECTIONS: 6km outside Manzini on the Big Bend Road, Pass the Imphilo clinic. Turn left at the Big Surprise Bottle Store and follow the signs. Call 268 505 8363 for reservations.

Saturday & Sunday 30–31 July

SWAZILAND

Swaziland is the jewel at the heart of South Africa. Its 1.1 million people are known for their hospitality. It is ruled by King Msawti III, member of the Dlamini dynasty. Its inhabitants depend mostly on agriculture, although tourism is booming. Foreigners come for the unspoilt nature reserve of Malolotja and the whitewater rafting on the wild Usutu river, as well as to meet the people! Business hours are 08h00 - 13h00 and 14h00 - 17h00 Mondays to Fridays. Bank hours are 18h30 - 14h30 Mondays to Fridays and some banks, 08h30 - 11h00 on Saturdays. Post offices are open 08h00 - 16h00 Mondays to Fridays and 08h00 - 11h00 on Saturdays.

Today grimace as the wind changes and sue the weather bureau if your face freezes forever

Origins of the myth

Like many a myth, this one has some basis in reality. It originated with the Arctic people, who lived much of the year in gale-force winds. The myth evolved to serve a very practical purpose: if an Arctic papoose ventured out into the glacial conditions of the tundra with his or her face scrunched up for too long, sometimes frostbite would set in between the wrinkles and lead to painful cramping. Thus the children were instructed to keep their faces as smooth as possible. The tale was magically illustrated for generations of Arctic kids by famous artist Tornarsuk. He told the story of Little Nootaikok, who made a grotesque face in the storm and had to live with the penguins ever after as no one else could look at him. To this day 'Beware the fate of Nootaikok!' is a phrase that inspires dread in the heart of many an Inuit.

Monday 1 August

8	14
9	15
10	16
11	17
12	18
13	19

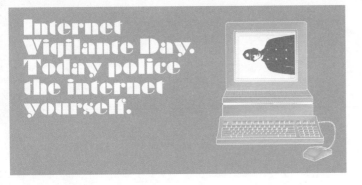

Internet Vigilante Day. Today police the internet yourself.

<cutie69er> asl
<cutie69er> im 13
<LuvinBoy> 16,m,malaysia
<Ready> hello cutie
<cutie69er> hi
<LuvinBoy> 3 years older]
<LuvinBoy> hehe
<Vigilante> Hey you two are underage!
<LuvinBoy> hi
<hottiewithabody> no freedom im am too! haha
cassandra sets mode: +b *!*@26E1AC.EBA119B.7903A39D.IP
<MasterYoda> bored bored bored bored
aziz is now known as SwEeT_BoY_MsN
<cutie69er> hi
<Vigilante> cutie69er isn't it past your bedtime?
<LuvinBoy> wazzup...
*some^boy thinks freedom2fight4 is wrong
<handsomeboy_932> 18,mmalaysia
<cutie69er> nm
<sexypip> any m wnt chat, 15 f uk
<Freedom2Fight4> sure u are hottie
<LuvinBoy> nm?
<Freedom2Fight4> whys that some boy
<CKY_17> hi

<hottiewithabody> i am if you knew me you would agree too
<Vigilante> enough of this lechery let's talk about something else guys and girls
*some^boy isnt too coward to state facts that are insulting... freedom2fight4 u suck.... (an insulting fact)
<cutie69er> hi any hot guys?
gangsta_18 is now known as Wolf_King
<some^boy> :)
<some^boy> lol
<DrPel_6931> Any girl who wants to have a real talk pvt me (Spanish,German.Italian,French, language iis not a problem-)
<Vigilante> Dr? You don't sound like a teen, get out of our chatroom
<Freedom2Fight4> well i dont and thats why im neutral at the moment
<DrPel_6931> Any girl who wants to have a real talk pvt me (Spanish,German.Italian,French, language iis not a problem-)
<hottiewithabody> im in this HUGE fight right now with a few ppl just b/c i stated the facts
<Freedom2Fight4> sure u are someboy
<some^boy> lol

l_6931> and u r a moron who's only a man behind a computer 8-)
<Vigilante> cutie69er pvt me and I'll help you fight these degenerates
*SEXYIRISHGIRL sits on the arms chair
*SHAZ hey some^boyyyyyyyyyyyyyyyyyyyyyyyyyyyyyyyyyy
<DrPel_6931> and u r a moron who's only a man behind a computer 8-)
<nurse> hiya everyone
<Vigilante> a nurse? Whatever next?
cassandra sets mode: +b *!*sweet_gi*@*
nurse is now known as nurse_538
*Web_Cam_BoY please Àù want WEB CAM girls
<Baby_Bunny> ANY1 FOUND ANY PERVES 2NI
<Vigilante> it's full of perverts raaaaaghhhhhh
DrPel_6931> :S damn it
<DrPel_6931> someone dropped me :S
<hobby> where are hot girls ?
<Vigilante> where are they those dripping hot ones?????????!!!!!!
*SHAZ hb some^boy
<scrpion1> hiiiiiiiiiiiiiiiiiiiiiiiiiiiiiiiiiiiiiii
<nurse_538> he wants a three some y u not up 4 that
cassandra sets mode: +b *!*araCroft@*
<hobby> any girl wanna chat
<LuvinBoy> anybody want to tok dirty pvt me
<Vigilante> DIRTY LITTLE WHORES OF BABYLON!!!!!!!
<beachgirl> hi room
<samiekins_3469> here!
*SEXYIRISHGIRL sneezes
<hobby> hi beach girl
<samiekins_3469> yeah n e fit guys wntin sommat gooooood pvt me
<Vigilante> that's better. Bye for now.
*some^boy is back... again
<samiekins_3469> :P

Tuesday 2 August

8	14
9	15
10	16
11	17
12	18
13	19

Today try Prozac and increase your level of happiness

Prozac works by boosting levels of serotonin, the chemical that determines our mood levels. So far, it has mostly been used by the clinically depressed. But there is a much wider market. However happy you are, surely you could be happier? Visit your doctor today and demand that little extra bit of bliss.

Wednesday 3 August

8	14
9	15
10	16
11	17
12	18
13	19
	NO:
	YES:

KIDNAP A WORM DAY

There's no law against it!

THE WORM'S COUSIN CRYING:

THE WORM'S UNCLE CRYING:

THE WORM'S BROTHER CRYING:

THE WORM'S MOTHER CRYING:

Thursday 4 August

8	14
9	15
10	16
11	17
12	18
13	19

On the face of it, this well-known work by Algerian-born painter Khaled Reghine presents us with a straightforward narrative. Entitled *Number 12*, it weaves the tale of two boys who have (just?) competed in a wheelchair race. One has won and is holding the trophy. The other (the eponymous Number 12) has lost, one of his wheels lying on the ground. Also he seems to be a werewolf. The locus is a simple one: we as spectators are enjoined to feel sympathy for No12, who holds us in his tearful gaze.

Yet this deceptively simple scene conceals a web of conflicting narratives which a closer textual/pictorial interpretation will reveal.

Consider the winning boy more closely. Even though he has won, he is still angry with the werewolf. Indeed, he is not only holding the trophy, but also threatening or preparing to throw it. Next to him, his mother or lover congratulates and kisses him (she is dichotomous). They stand as one pictorial mass, conjoined also to the forest, symbol of motherhood and refuge. No12, by contrast, sits alone. He is triply isolated: from the forest, from the other two, and last but not least, from us the viewers – he is stranded in the foreground of the canvas, floating in the perspectival abyss between the field of our gaze and the "grounded" plane of conifers behind him.

This is a quintessentially Freudian mise-en-scene. The second boy has crossed the Oedipal bridge to the point where he is at one both with his mother (he has conquered her affection and respect) and with his lover. It is no coincidence that the pine trees in the background stretch to the sky, erect. He brandishes his trophy/penis, keen to hurt his rival with it in a display of brute testosterone-filled caveman machismo.

Yet this is only one strand in this many-faceted masterpiece. For the wheelchairs provide a second key (clef) to the text. Both competitors are it seems disabled. They are formally similar too in

Stare at a single work of art for hours until you understand it fully

Number 12, by Khaled Reghine (1921-1984) (Musee De L'Art Populaire Algerien, Wahran)

that their wheels are perfectly aligned – save of course for the werewolf boy's left wheel which has come off. Many critics have sought to explain this in strictly narrative terms. Was it an accident? Did the winner push him right off the road, or even sabotage the wheelchair? Post-Marxist aficionados of Reghine in particular have found this a rich vein of analysis, positing the broken wheel as a symbol of the internal contradictions of our technocapitalist society literally coming off their axis, leaving us bereft of escape routes. All that is left to us is self-defeating faceless (numbered) struggle in a dog-eat-dog world.

But this is simplistic. The true import of the wheels is to be divined at a more formal level. For the broken wheel disrupts the picture's visual field, shattering the perspective both in its positioning and through its (abnormally small) size.

And this is where we intuit the force of "Number 12". The werewolf boy is doubly other: he is disabled, indeed, but beyond that he is in radical rupture with the dimensions (three) of the rest of his world, the world of the canvas. Two corresponding circles signify this, both lying flat against the viewer's eye: his lost wheel, and his moony face, grotesquely malformed by the transformation *unter* werewolf, that archetypal Other of our culture. He is alienated from his world, from his body, from his condition. He can no longer condone the dread illusion. He faces us directly, not merely as representation, but as mirror to our lost selves ("mon semblable, mon frère" indeed). We, like him, are pure form. He cries not at the other boy but at us and for us, for we are he, and he is us...

KHALED REGHINE IS IN TOWN REALLY IS HE SHOWING NUMBER 12?

Friday 5 August

8	14
9	15
10	16
11	17
12	18
13	19

Living History Weekend

This weekend, live the life of a 13th century peasant.

Wake at dawn as the pig you share your straw bed with relieves himself on your foot. Shake off the fleas, flies and lice, and prepare to meet the day! Skip your bath as usual, you had one last year. Wake your spouse and your eight (or is it nine?) children, and enjoy a breakfast of tasty dry bread, washed down with ale (you don't drink the water from the river - it tastes foul as a result of being used as a sewer). You notice your ox in its wisdom has decided to bash in part of the house's wall. Make a mental note to patch it up with mud when you have two seconds, or maybe with some of the copious manure the ox produced overnight. But for now, off to the fields you go, not to your own strip, but to work on your lord's. It's harvesting time, so grab your sickle, a rusty bit of metal as likely to land you with a tetanus cut as to help you harvest. The crop this year is pretty weak, because it rained for two weeks continuously in June. So you don't want to tire yourself out completely, since there might be little food to help you recuperate. On the other hand if you don't work hard, there'll be no food at all and you'll starve to death. In any case the lord's reeve will be keeping an eye on you and you'll get

Don't forget
the shoes.

fined or beaten if you don't pull your weight. Time for lunch, not a moment too soon as you're hungry. You're hungry most of the time anyway though, so it's nothing to complain about. Lunch is more dark bread, with a bit of rat-nibbled cheese if you're lucky. And ale. More work, maybe on the church's land this time. There are other peasants working nearby, but there's not much time for gossip with Hans, Will or Sal (they have no surnames and neither do you. You don't need a surname as there's only a few dozen of you in the village you were born in and which you'll probably never leave in your 13th century life in any case. Not that you know what century you're living in.) Anyway as the sun sets you down tools and head home. Tonight's supper is pottage, a stew of oats with the odd turnip. You're exhausted but you might attempt some rather clumsy intercourse with your spouse, never mind the kids and animals. They've seen and heard it all before. Repeat tomorrow. And every day for the rest of your life, which will probably end around age 45 if you're lucky.

You will need: ❶ Mud ❷ Rats ❸ A straw bed ❹ A pig ❺ Cloth ❻ An ox ❼ A field ❽ Leprosy ❾ Ale ❿ Turnips ⓫ Manure

---

Saturday & Sunday 6–7 August

☼	☼
☼	☼
☼	☼
☼	☼
☼	☼
☼	☾

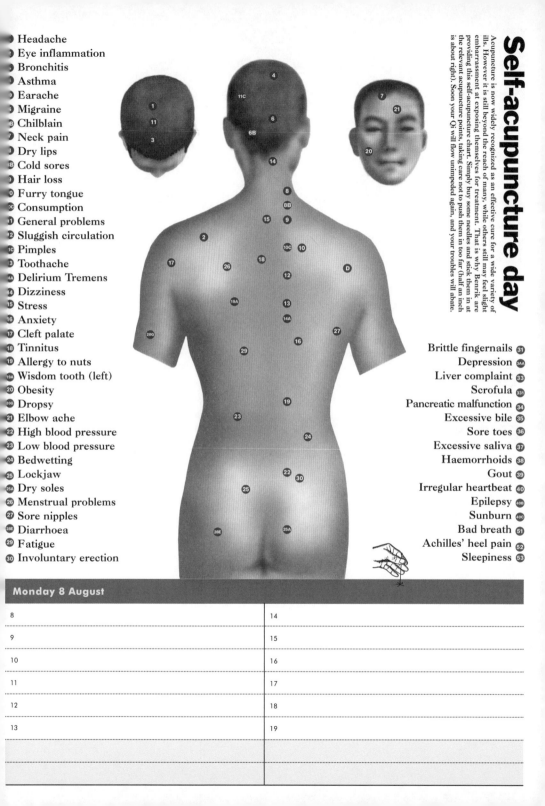

Self-acupuncture day

Acupuncture is now widely recognized as an effective cure for a wide variety of ills. However it is still beyond the reach of many, while others still may feel slight embarrassment at exposing themselves for treatment. That is why Benrik are providing this self-acupuncture chart. Simply buy some needles and stick them in at the relevant acupuncture points, taking care not to push them in too far (half an inch is about right). Soon your Qi will flow unimpeded again, and your troubles will abate.

1. Headache
2. Eye inflammation
3. Bronchitis
4. Asthma
5. Earache
6. Migraine
7. Chilblain
8. Neck pain
9. Dry lips
10. Cold sores
11. Hair loss
12. Furry tongue
13. Consumption
14. General problems
15. Sluggish circulation
16. Pimples
17. Toothache
18. Delirium Tremens
19. Dizziness
20. Stress
21. Anxiety
22. Cleft palate
23. Tinnitus
24. Allergy to nuts
25. Wisdom tooth (left)
26. Obesity
27. Dropsy
28. Elbow ache
29. High blood pressure
30. Low blood pressure
31. Bedwetting
32. Lockjaw
33. Dry soles
34. Menstrual problems
35. Sore nipples
36. Diarrhoea
37. Fatigue
38. Involuntary erection

Brittle fingernails 31
Depression 3AA
Liver complaint 33
Scrofula 33I
Pancreatic malfunction 34
Excessive bile 35
Sore toes 36
Excessive saliva 37
Haemorrhoids 38
Gout 39
Irregular heartbeat 40
Epilepsy 40B
Sunburn 40C
Bad breath 51
Achilles' heel pain 52
Sleepiness 53

Monday 8 August

8	14
9	15
10	16
11	17
12	18
13	19

TODAY CARRY A HIDDEN WEAPON

With street crime allegedly rife, perhaps you should go armed. Today conceal some means of defending yourself, like scissors or a hammer. Do you feel safer? Or does it merely ramp up your insecurity?

NOTE TO THE POLICE
This fine gentleman/lady/child is carrying a dangerous weapon as part of a Benrik mind experiment into the psychosociology of crime. Please do not arrest them. Benrik vouches for their peaceful nature.

LÖDPASTA

Tuesday 9 August

8	14
9	15
10	16
11	17
12	18
13	19

Today,

YOU MUST STOP HORSING AROUND.

YOUR LIFE UP UNTIL TODAY HAS

BEEN NOTHING BUT HORSE PLAY

AND NOW IT'S TIME TO STOP IT,

YOU IDIOT.

Signed...

DAVID SHRIGLEY

8	14
9	15
10	16
11	17
12	18
13	19

SORRY
MY BEAUTIFUL
BUSINESS PARTNER
SORRY
TO WAKE YOU
AT THIS HOUR
LISTEN TO MY VOICE
VIBRATING UNDER
YOUR WINDOWSILL
I AM DESPERATE TO
TALK TO YOU
OH MY BUSINESS PARTNER
I FEEL AS IF IN BUSINESS
WE ARE MAKING A SWEET MELODY
BUT WITH THIS SONG
I COME TO ANNOUNCE TO YOU
THAT WE HAVE REACHED
BANKRUPTCY OH MY BUSINESS
PARTNER I FEEL AS IF IN BU-
SINESS WE ARE MAKING
A SWEET MELODY
ALAS I OFFER YOU MY
APOLOGY
I WISH IT COULD
BE OTHERWISE
BUT WE ARE LIQUIDATED
I COULD NO LONGER
WAIT TO ANNOUNCE IT
AS THE BAILIFFS ARE
HERE BELOW YOUR
WINDOWSILL!!!
OH MY BUSINESS PARTNER
I FEEL AS IF IN
BUSINESS
WE ARE MAKING
A SWEET MELODY
ALAS
FORGIVE ME
SORRY
TO WAKE
YOU

SERENADE
SOMEONE
TODAY!

Thursday 11 August

8	14
9	15
10	16
11	17
12	18
13	19

Today have a sleep somewhere random

1) Beginner (somewhere else in your own bedroom e.g. under your bed)

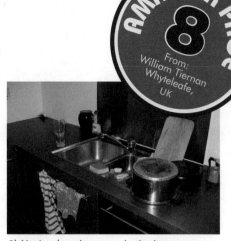

2) Novice (another room in the house e.g. kitchen)

3) Intermediate (somewhere within your own (or parents') property e.g. garden, garage or car)

4) Expert (anywhere else, e.g. on top of a bus shelter or up a tree in the park)

Friday 12 August

8	14
9	15
10	16
11	17
12	18
13	19

TODAY DRAW GOD

IT DOESN'T NEED TO BE A MAN. IT DOESN'T HAVE TO BE A WOMAN. IT DOESN'T EVEN HAVE TO BE A PERSON. BUT: IF YOU DRAW HIM/HER/IT BADLY YOU GO TO HELL!!

Monday 15 August

8	14
9	15
10	16
11	17
12	18
13	19

Nanonap Day

Scientists have discovered that the age-old tradition of sleeping for hours on end may not be the most efficient way to rest. Instead, 'nanonaps' are being mooted as the future of sleep. Astronauts first alerted the scientific community to the phenomenon, when they found they felt more energetic after many small naps than after one long one. A nanonap only lasts for 20 to 30 seconds, and may take place anywhere – at the office, on the train, at school. Napoleon is said to have prefigured them by sleeping upright on his horse during brief lulls in the battle. Test the theory today by taking up 100 thirty-second nanonaps at regular intervals. Rest your head on this page with your mouth over our waterproof 'dribble zone'. Dribbling only occurs during deep sleep, so you will have a reliable measure of how well you have slept. If your dribble spreads out beyond the box, nanonaps are for you.

DRIBBLE ZONE
DRIBBLE HERE

Tuesday 16 August

8	14
9	15
10	16
11	17
12	18
13	19

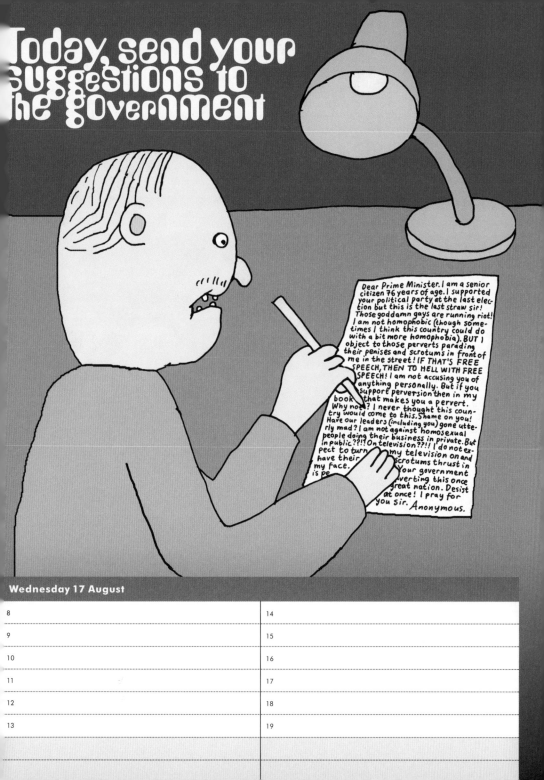

Wednesday 17 August

8	14
9	15
10	16
11	17
12	18
13	19

Today, price tag all your possessions

Everything has its price. Work it out and stick it on your possessions today with the understanding that anyone who meets that price can buy them. Factor in sentimental value; if an old tea towel was your first friend, then it's perfectly legitimate to value it in the thousands. Restrictions: human beings are legally impossible to buy or sell, but pets are fair game.

SALE PRICE

The coat in which I lost my virginity 1988. £6.99

Thursday 18 August

8		14	
9		15	
10		16	
11		17	
12		18	
13		19	

Make someone hate you today

Hatred is as mysterious and volatile an emotion as love. It is relatively easy to pinpoint why we dislike someone. Dislike is socially acceptable, one of the inevitable lubricants of our close-quarters living. Hatred is socially disruptive. Its intensity is pathological. It overrules rational argument and shreds the social fabric. What drives anyone to hate? Find out today by trying to make someone hate you. It can be someone who already dislikes you, or you can start from scratch with a stranger or a friend. Good luck, and don't forget to tell them it was a joke tomorrow!

Illustration taken from Hell's Angels rule-book under the headline "Tattoos that we accept you to have on your face in our club".

Ignore them

When your receptionist smiles and says hello as usual, pretend she's invisible, pause for a moment as if trying to locate the source of a particularly nasty smell, and stride on into the elevator.

Attack their family

Ask your neighbour over the garden fence if she minds that her husband sees the dominatrix in Pond St every other Monday evening on his way home. Say you assumed she knew as everyone else seems to.

Insult their beliefs

Your great aunt has been praying fervently all her life to get to heaven. Get her a free subscription to Science magazine with instructions to look out for articles on what actually happens after death.

Friday 19 August

8	14
9	15
10	16
11	17
12	18
13	19

ZAPPING WEEKEND

This weekend, we've picked the best programmes for you, so follow our TV-watching schedule to the minute and relax.

	CH1	CH2	CH3	CH4	CH5	CH6	CH7	CH8	CH9	CH10	CH11	CH12	CH13	CH14	CH15	CH16	CH17	CH18	CH20
SAT 6.00pm													■						
SAT 6.15pm						■													
SAT 6.40pm										■									
SAT 6.50pm															■				
SAT 7.00pm			■																
SAT 7.30pm													■						
SAT 7.45pm								■											
SAT 8.48pm																			■
SAT 8.49pm											■								
SAT 8.50pm	■																		
SAT 9.20¹²pm						■													
SAT 9.30pm																			
SAT 9.50pm				■															
SAT 10.00pm																	■		
SAT 10.40pm								■											
SAT 10.52pm			■																
SAT 11.10pm														■					
SAT 11.50pm																			■
SUN 12.18am						■													
SUN 1.20am											■								
SUN 6.00am		■																	
SUN 6.21pm																		■	
SUN 6.50pm				■															
SUN 7.00pm												■							
SUN 7.10pm																	■		
SUN 7.20pm	■																		
SUN 7.21pm						■													
SUN 7.59pm											■								
SUN 8.12pm										■									
SUN 8.29pm																		■	
SUN 8.50pm															■				
SUN 9.00pm			■																
SUN 9.05pm		■																	
SUN 10.05pm													■						
SUN 10.06pm								■											
SUN 10.07pm																		■	
SUN 11.01pm					■														
SUN 11.40pm											■								
SUN 11.58pm																			
SUN 11.59pm			■																■

Saturday & Sunday 20–21 August

Today, stick a message on a banknote

Banknotes are the ultimate media, circulating between millions every day free of charge. Benrik believe that their use for communication purposes would reinforce the social tissue and make the spending experience a lot more "fun".

POSSIBLE MESSAGES TO WRITE:
- Darling don't forget the milk
- Mistress Eva 07890 616 471
- Mickey ❤ Tracy
- Save the blue-crested grebe!
- Sorry about the herpes everyone

Caution:

The Bank Of England are not yet fully convinced by our plan. This is their current position: "We strongly discourage people from taking any action which will, even to a very limited extent, shorten the life of our banknotes. Clearly sticking labels to banknotes is likely to do this. As for making the notes "more fun" that is not the purpose of a banknote. You may also find yourself prosecuted if the portrait of the Queen is defaced in any way. May I suggest that you find another way to advertise your publication." Public Enquiries Group, Bank Of England

Monday 22 August

8	14
9	15
10	16
11	17
12	18
13	19

TODAY LET A DOG WALK YOU

WATCH OUT!
Dogs must clean up after their humans. Humans with a history of dangerous behaviour are prohibited. Humans must be licensed and vaccinated. Humans must be wearing a collar with identification at all times. Leaving humans unattended is prohibited. SCOOP THE POOP!

THE PEOPLE
(FOULING OF LAND) ACT 1996.

CLEAN IT UP!
MAXIMUM FINE £1000

Tuesday 23 August

8		14	
9		15	
10		16	
11		17	
12		18	
13		19	

Discover who you were in a past life

Our past lives are stored in our subconscious. It is said that Buddha remembered all 500 of his when he fully Awakened! You can't compete with that, but try and remember your last one, using this simple technique: close your eyes and move your finger around this page at random whilst chanting 'Nam-myohorenge-kyo' 10 times. Your finger will stop on your previous life, and the memories should start flooding back.

Which one of these were you?

Flower	Toad	Pharaoh Ramses II	Troll	Napoleon
Monk	Angel	Plankton	George Washington	Emperor Xorg
Dung beetle	Dung	Pope	Peasant	Other

Wednesday 24 August

8	14
9	15
10	16
11	17
12	18
13	19

YUMMY!*

Extreme Fruitarianism Day

Vegetarianism is murder! If you eat something that is alive, you kill it, whether meat, vegetable or fruit. Even the so-called enlightened diets are genocide on a grand scale. There are only two acceptable alternatives. 1) Breatharianism, which means surviving on love and fresh air, but which still needs some practical fine-tuning. 2) Extreme Fruitarianism, where you may only eat fruit that has fallen off the tree of its own accord. There are over 3000 extreme fruitarians worldwide, mostly living near orchards. The rules are strict: you may not shake the branch or even touch the tree in order to make the fruit fall. Eating fruit with worms is forbidden, of course. However, you may eat fruit that the wind has shaken off the tree. The benefits are manifold: clearer conscience, clearer skin, light-headedness and medically significant weight loss.

Thursday 25 August	
8	14
9	15
10	16
11	17
12	18
13	19

*(BUT YOU CAN'T HAVE IT UNTIL IT HAS FALLEN!)

Today fire your bank for the sake of it

This should be the easiest task in the book. But don't just send them a one-liner ending it. Explain in great detail why you are booting them out of your life, in small print.

Thank you for being my bank over the last few years. Now it's time for us to part and I'd like to explain why clearly and succinctly. When you raised 'first-time' buyer interest rates from 5.6%* to 6.1%** on 12/08/05 (7.56% APR), my overall ratio of debt to overdraft rose to 345%, adjusted for inflation (231% in real terms, based on 2004 Treasury figures). My salary dropped to 78% of my expenditure as a result, from a mid-2004 low of 94%. Over the last few years you have caused an increase in my blood pressure of 2.3% (1999), 2.7% (2000), 2.8% (2001), 4.6% (2002), 7.8% (2003), 9.9% (2004 estimated). This represents a cumulative rise of 23.5%, adjusted for natural ageing of the arteries. Typical example: £78,987 mortgage (87%): Purchase price £110,500, mortgage over 25 years, charged at a discounted 3.1% variable rate for 36 months, then 7.55% variable rate (standard plus account with Breakthru discount + 0.5%, exclusive of fees). 36 payments of £566.78 gross then 294 payments of £897.04 gross. Total amount payable over the term £234,879.56 excluding fees. Fees include: solicitor's fee £235, valuation fee £270 (standard valuation***), CHAPS transfer fee £34. APR (VARIABLE) 6.9% calculated over the term of the mortgage. If mortgage is redeemed within 16 months, a charge of £5,876 will apply, along with redemption charges of 1.4% of total value of the mortgage over the term. Redemption administrative fee £545. Redemption administrative fee if remortgaging with your current lender £445. Rates correct as of 13/04/03, subject to variation. Interest will be payable on the mortgage from the date on which the cheque (or telegraphic transfer) is issued until the following 31 December. In each succeeding year, interest will be charged on the balance of the whole debt outstanding at the end of the preceding year. In addition, if any further sums become owing during any year, interest will be charged from the date such sums become owing until the end of that year. In the year of repayment of the whole debt, interest will be charged on the whole debt outstanding at the end of the preceding year (and on any further sums becoming owing during that year) up to and including the date on which cleared funds are received by the society to repay the whole debt in full. Interest will accrue from day to day but will be payable partly in advance (if appropriate having a regard to the payment date) and partly in arrears by monthly instalments during the year (each month being treated for this purpose as a twelfth of the year). Your home is at risk if you do not keep up repayments on a mortgage or other loan secured on it. Payment holidays, overpayments and equity transfer are subject to status, terms and conditions. For interest only mortgages, you should arrange an appropriate repayment vehicle. It is strongly advised for any mortgage that you take out suitable life insurance cover. Written quotation available on request. Security required. Only available to UK residents aged between 21 and 68, subject to status and to terms and conditions. In this section, 'me', 'my' and 'I' refer to my person as a legal entity. 'You', 'my bank' and 'you evil bastards' refer to your plc, your holdings plc and any subsidiaries, associated and affiliated companies. If I have not delivered the standard of explanation you require, or if you think I have made a mistake, please let me know. I will then investigate the situation and, if appropriate, attempt to remedy the situation with steps to prevent you contacting me ever again. If you remain dissatisfied, there is precious little you can do about it. English law applies to this letter. Me and you submit to the non-exclusive jurisdiction of the courts of England and Wales.

Friday 26 August

8	14
9	15
10	16
11	17
12	18
13	19

*5.6% before deduction of tax **APR: gross rate compounded ***advanced valuation recommended £345 fee includes test for rising damp, dry rot, condensation, woodworm, electrical wiring, masonry and structural problems.

Censored page

After consultation with our editors, lawyers and the Metropolitan Police, we have no choice but to remove the task for the weekend of 27 & 28 August from the print edition of "This Diary Will Change Your Life 2005". Readers are invited to view it online on www.thiswebsitewillchangeyourlife.com. We have been asked to remind our readers that 'pranks' may well be in violation of the law, and that humour does not constitute a valid defence. In other words, have fun, yes, but responsible fun.

Thank you, Benrik Limited

Let children rule the world today

Children are pure and innocent. If we all do their bidding, the world can only become a better place. Do nothing today without first asking for instructions from the nearest available child.

Armies to be composed of pets.

Grrr. Grrr.

Beat up the fat kids.

Only cartoons on TV.

Detention for all teachers.

Naughty Boy

Lolly-mountain

Spend all money on candy.

Parents in bed by 8.

stories

Breakfast: Lunch: Dinner:

Burger and chips every meal.

Monday 29 August

8	14
9	15
10	16
11	17
12	18
13	19

Today make sure your body survives you

Upon death your soul and body will part ways, but that's no reason to abandon your corpse entirely. Your body is an integral part of you and deserves to survive to preserve your memory. Pick one of the three options below and make the necessary arrangements today.

- Boy, the scavenger termites did a really great job stuffing that human.
- Yeah it's scary how real it looks.

1) PLASTINATION Invented by celebrity professor Gunther Von Hagens, plastination impregnates the body with reactive polymers such as resin and silicone rubber. This is a marvellous way of preserving your body, although do note they remove the skin. You may volunteer your body for plastination by contacting the Bundesverband der Korperspender (Federal Association of Body Donors). Write c/o Institut fur Plastination, Rathausstrasse 11, D-69126, Heidelberg, Germany, or call the Body Donation Office direct on +49 6221 33 11 50.

2) TAXIDERMY Taxidermy has been around since the hunter-gatherers in one shape or another. Yet only in recent history has it reached a state of refinement where it is now possible to 'mount' human beings with any degree of artistic success. The main advantage over plastination is that your body retains its outer form. The disadvantage is that your innards go. Still, if you are less interested in what's under the skin, try calling a taxidermist in your area. To find one, look in the yellow pages, or write to: the International Guild of Taxidermy (President: Joe Boggs), 411 George Street, Aurora, IN 47001. Phone: (812) 926-4868.

3) STATUARY This is very much the old-fashioned option. Get a local sculptor to cast you in plaster. You will be covered in hot sticky goo for the best part of the day, and lose any body hair, probably for good. However, it's cheaper than the above two options, and will look decorative in your descendants' garden. Note: if you want the authentic 'lost an arm at Troy' look, get it chopped off from the final statue, and not prior to modelling.

Tuesday 30 August

8		14	
9		15	
10		16	
11		17	
12		18	
13		19	

TODAY, TOPPLE A DICTATOR USING ONLY THE INTERNET

The information revolution is a direct challenge to authoritarian states. With its many points of access and its decentralized, disembodied nature, the internet is the perfect rallying point for change. Yet it has still to claim its first direct dictator scalp. Diary readers can change that today by emailing them and convincing them to step down from power with a few well-chosen arguments.

Kim Jong Il (North Korea)
www.korea-dpr.com

Hu Jintao (China)
www.govonline.cn

Fidel Castro (Cuba)
www.cubagov.cu

Robert Mugabe (Zimbabwe)
www.gta.gov.zw

Than Shwe (Burma)
www.myatmyanmar.net

Omar Al-Bashir (Sudan)
www.sudan.gov.sd

Saparmurat Niyazov (Turkmenistan)
www.mct.gov.tm

Alexander Lukashenko
(Belarus)
www.president.gov.by

Crown Prince Abdullah (Saudi Arabia)
www.shura.gov.sa

Wednesday 31 August

8	14
9	15
10	16
11	17
12	18
13	19

GO BACK TO SCHOOL TODAY

Maybe you weren't well. Maybe you skipped it without realizing its importance. But through no real fault of your own, you missed a crucial lesson, undermining your life since then. Today, go back to your local school and insist on attending a class you missed.

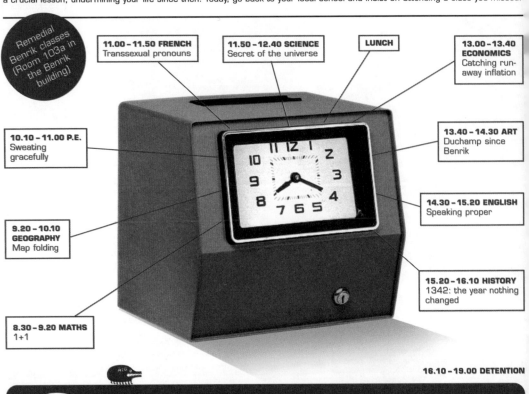

Remedial Benrik classes (Room 103a in the Benrik building)

11.00 – 11.50 FRENCH
Transsexual pronouns

11.50 – 12.40 SCIENCE
Secret of the universe

LUNCH

13.00 – 13.40 ECONOMICS
Catching run-away inflation

10.10 – 11.00 P.E.
Sweating gracefully

13.40 – 14.30 ART
Duchamp since Benrik

9.20 – 10.10 GEOGRAPHY
Map folding

14.30 – 15.20 ENGLISH
Speaking proper

8.30 – 9.20 MATHS
1+1

15.20 – 16.10 HISTORY
1342: the year nothing changed

16.10 – 19.00 DETENTION

HOMEWORK You're not allowed out to play with the others until you've finished your homework! Your assignment is to write a 1000-word essay answering any of the following questions. 1) To what extent did post-Kantian attempts to discover an all-encompassing first principle of philosophy succeed (with particular reference to Fichte and Schelling)? 2) "For Mallarmé, symbolism ultimately anticipated the synthesis of Christ and Thanatos". Discuss. 3) Describe how you spent your holiday. Use detail!!!

Thursday 1 September

8	14
9	15
10	16
11	17
12	18
13	19

MAKE AN INSECT'S DAY

THE LIFE OF AN INSECT IS GENERALLY NASTY BRUTISH AND SHORT. BRING A LITTLE WARMTH TO BEAR ON THIS MISERABLE EXISTENCE TODAY BY GIVING ONE OF THEM THE EXPERIENCE OF AN INSECT LIFETIME.

YOU ARE NUMBER ONE

YOU ARE TO INSECTS WHAT GANDHI WAS TO HUMANS

- POUR A PUDDLE OF HONEY IN THE PATH OF AN UNSUSPECTING ANT
- CAPTURE A BEE AND LET IT LOOSE IN A FLOWER SHOP
- CHASE A MOSQUITO INTO A PACKED SAUNA
- PLACE A GRASSHOPPER ON A TRAMPOLINE
- FURNISH A TERMITE COLONY WITH A LOUIS XIV COMMODE
- SMUGGLE A FLY INTO A MORTUARY

Friday 2 September

8	14
9	15
10	16
11	17
12	18
13	19

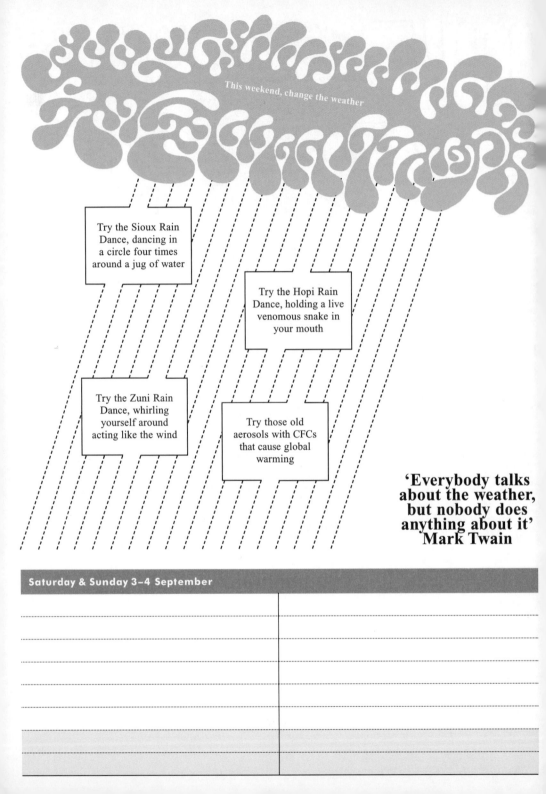

This weekend, change the weather

Try the Sioux Rain Dance, dancing in a circle four times around a jug of water

Try the Hopi Rain Dance, holding a live venomous snake in your mouth

Try the Zuni Rain Dance, whirling yourself around acting like the wind

Try those old aerosols with CFCs that cause global warming

'Everybody talks about the weather, but nobody does anything about it'
Mark Twain

Saturday & Sunday 3–4 September

Could you be the face of...

Today think of the brand you could be a great spokesperson for, and contact them to become rich.

Zappot Spot Cream!
IF YOU'RE BEAUTIFUL YET SPOTTY

Whitex Toothpaste!
If you have great teeth

Aunt Edna's Thick Soup
If you have a thick mustache

FOREVER BATTERIES
If you're unnaturally old

YUMYUM CHOCOLATE
IF YOU'RE FAT BUT HAPPY

SMOOTH CIGARETTES
IF YOU'RE DEAD

Monday 5 September

8	14
9	15
10	16
11	17
12	18
13	19

Save someone's life today

They will be eternally grateful. They will be your friend for life. They will talk about you to everyone they know. They will hug you often. They will dedicate their autobiography to you. They will name their children after you. They will include you in their will. Nothing but good can come of this day.

OH! I'M FALLING DOWN FROM THE DATE-BOX AND WILL SURELY BREAK MY FUCKING NECK.

DON'T WORRY BABE, THIS BLOCK OF TEXT HERE IS FAIRLY SOFT AND WILL CUSHION YOUR FALL.

Tuesday 6 September

8

9

10

11

12

13

14

15

16

17

18

19

Keep an eye out for genuine opportunities to save a life. Should one not arise, however, force your luck. Leave a flower pot teetering over a window ledge and push someone out of the way as it falls. Elbow someone discreetly on a crowded train platform and pull them back as they wobble. Jump on top of someone and claim a sniper had his laser sights trained on them. Don't worry how implausible your story is, no one wants to be ungrateful to their saviour.

EIGHT MILLION WAYS TO DIE

We all have to die of something. Today make your preference known by ranking this selection of ways to die from 1 to 100.

Hit by truck............................/100
Hit by car.............................../100
Hit by bus............................../100
Volcanic eruption....................../100
Earthquake.............................../100
Meteorite on head........................./100
Cancer................................../100
Burnt alive............................../100
Flower pot falls on head................/100
Fall under train........................./100
Pushed under train......................./100
Plane crash............................./100
Parachute jammed......................./100
Cocaine overdose......................../100
Heroin overdose........................./100
Painkiller overdose....................../100
Trampled at rock concert................/100
Struck by lightning....................../100
Ebola virus............................./100
Snake bite.............................../100
Snake constriction......................./100
Tarantula............................../100
Scorpion................................/100
Swallowed wasp........................../100
Broken heart............................/100
Nuclear bomb............................/100
Anthrax in mail........................../100
Friendly fire............................/100
Spontaneous combustion................./100
Eaten by sharks........................./100
Eaten by cannibals....................../100
Eaten by piranhas......................./100
Eaten by dinosaurs......................./100
Eaten by zombies ..../100
Eaten by flesh-eating bug............../100
Drowned................................../100
Hanged.................................../100
Lynched................................../100
Strangled.............................../100
Decapitated............................./100
Crucified................................/100
Sliced up.............................../100

Disembowelled.........................../100
Eviscerated............................./100
Microwaved............................../100
Vaporized............................../100
Shot in head............................/100
Shot in heart.........................../100
Shot in stomach........................./100
Shot in foot............................/100
Dropped on head........................./100
Gangrene................................/100
Choking................................./100
Choking on a bone......................./100
Choking on a nut......................../100
Unexpected nut allergy................../100
Lift brake failure......................./100
Spacesuit leak........................../100
Stabbed................................/100
Stabbed in the back..................../100
Bludgeoned with baseball bat...../100
Abducted by aliens for tests......../100
Gas...................................../100
Paper cut.............................../100
Lethal injection......................../100
Electric chair........................../100
Guillotine............................./100
Duel.................................../100
Suicide................................/100
Suicide-bombed........................./100
Suicide-bomber........................./100

Food-poisoned............................./100
Alcohol-poisoned........................./100
Poison-poisoned........................../100
Poisoned umbrella tip.................../100
In my sleep (N/A)......................../100
Machine-gunned........................../100
Hypothermia............................./100
Heart attack............................/100
Malaria................................./100
Measles................................/100
Mumps.................................../100
Smallpox................................/100
Cholera................................/100
Whooping cough........................./100
Black death............................./100
Car accident............................/100
Mafia................................../100
Buried alive............................/100
Prematurely cremated.................../100
Routine surgery gone wrong........./100
Bondage session gone wrong....../100
Superman impression gone wrong./100
Russian roulette........................./100
Murdered by serial killer................./100
Assassinated............................/100
Ransom unpaid by family.............../100
Caught in crossfire....................../100
Fall into vat of acid...................../100
Hara Kiri.............................../100

Supplementary information

If you have to be tortured
first, which would you prefer?
A Beatings
B Cigarette burns
C Psychological
D Water torture

Please hand
this to any
kidnappers.

Wednesday 7 September

8	14
9	15
10	16
11	17
12	18
13	19

Today learn a sex trick from an animal

Human sex lives are fairly boring compared to what goes on in other species. Observe what goes on in the animal and insect kingdoms today, and expand your copulatory range.

DO IT IN FLIGHT Many birds, such as the chimney swift, mate in mid-air. Don't forget your parachutes.

DO IT IN PUBLIC Humans are the only creatures to have sex in private. Break the taboo!

EAT THE MALE IMMEDIATELY AFTER COPULATION The praying mantis is famous for getting the munchies after sex. But girls, who doesn't?

DO IT HANGING FROM A TREE The orangutan's favourite position: you'll need strong arms, and a strong branch.

Advanced: caress an animal lasciviously. Beware: bestiality is illegal! Do not engage in actual sexual relations. The purpose of this experiment is solely to discover if the animal freaks out in horror at your perversion.

ANIMAL BESTIALITY
JUST SAY NO!!!

Thursday 8 September

8	14
9	15
10	16
11	17
12	18
13	19

TODAY GET A GREEN CARD

The American Dream is within your reach! Provided certain basic requirements are met, anyone can enter the Green Card lottery, otherwise known as the Diversity Immigrant Visa Program. There are 50,000 permanent resident visas up for grabs, with the winners drawn by computer. It's certainly easier than marrying an American, so apply now! For a small fee, Benrik will help process your application, with a personalized letter to the President on your behalf. Fill in this form and send with a $350 cheque to Benrik Ltd, c/o Hodder & Stoughton, 338 Euston Road, London, NW1 3BH, United Kingdom. Or you may apply online at www.dvlottery.state.gov. Entries for this year close December 31.

AMERICAN GREEN-CARD REGISTRATION FORM

1. FULL NAME - Last/Family Name, First Name, Middle Name
....

2. DATE OF BIRTH - Day, Month, Year
....

3. GENDER - Male or Female
....

4. CITY/TOWN OF BIRTH
....

5. COUNTRY OF BIRTH - The name of the country should be that which is currently in use for the place where the applicant was born.
....

6. PROFESSION
....

7. MAILING ADDRESS
....

8. PHONE NUMBER (optional)
....

9. E-MAIL ADDRESS (optional)
....

10. COUNTRY OF ELIGIBILITY IF THE APPLICANT'S NATIVE COUNTRY IS DIFFERENT FROM COUNTRY OF BIRTH
....

11. MARRIAGE STATUS
....

12. NUMBER OF CHILDREN THAT ARE UNMARRIED AND UNDER 21 YEARS OF AGE
....

Photograph of applicant

13. SPOUSE INFORMATION
Name.................
Date of Birth.................
Gender.................
City/Town of Birth.................
Country of Birth.................

Photograph of applicant's spouse

14. CHILDREN INFORMATION
Name.................
Date of Birth.................
Gender.................
City/Town of Birth.................
Country of Birth.................

Photograph of applicant's children

NOTE: Entries must include the name, date and place of birth of the applicant's spouse and all natural children, as well as all legally-adopted and stepchildren, who are unmarried and under the age of 21, excepting those children who are already U.S. citizens or Legal Permanent Residents, even if you are no longer legally married to the child's parent, and even if the spouse or child does not currently reside with you and/or will not immigrate with you. Note that married children and children 21 years or older will not qualify for the diversity visa. Failure to list all children will result in your disqualification for the visa.

REQUIREMENTS FOR ENTRY: Applicant must be a native of one of a list of approved countries. Native of a country whose natives qualify: In most cases this means the country in which the applicant was born. However, if a person was born in a country whose natives are ineligible but his/her spouse was born in a country whose natives are eligible, such person can claim the spouse's country of birth providing both the applicant and spouse are issued visas and enter the U.S. simultaneously. If a person was born in a country whose natives are ineligible, but neither of his/her parents was born there or resided there at the time of the birth, such person may be able to claim nativity in one of the parents' country of birth. Applicant must meet either the education or training requirement of the DV program. Education or Training: An applicant must have EITHER a high school education or its equivalent, defined as successful completion of a 12-year course of elementary and secondary education; OR two years of work experience within the past five years in an occupation requiring at least two years of training or experience to perform. Applicants will also find a link to a Labor Department list of qualifying occupations at the Consular Affairs website: www.travel.state.gov. If the applicant cannot meet these requirements, he or she should NOT submit an entry to the DV program.

Friday 9 September

8	14
9	15
10	16
11	17
12	18
13	19

TIME LAPSE WEEKEND

Shoot your typical weekend on video and speed it up from 48 hours to one hour. Then watch it and find out if you've accomplished anything useful.

TRY TO SELL YOUR USED KNICKERS TODAY

In Japan, schoolgirls make decent pocket money by selling their underwear. Why shouldn't you? Just make sure you've worn it for a full eight-hour day, otherwise it's not legally 'used'.

JFK's last Y-fronts
$189,765

Queen Victoria's bloomers
$67,970

Gandhi's prison G-string
$65,100

Virgin Mary's knickers
$12,657

Top ten most sought-after

Pope's shorts
$8,554

Sigourney Weaver slip in Alien
$38,939

David&Victoria Beckham Thong
$3,869

Churchill's D-Day Boxers
$59,655

Panties worn by Florence Nightingale in Crimea
$21,786

Catherine the Great's horse pants
$45,000

In 1993, three Japanese entrepreneurs set up 90 vending machines in Tokyo with used underwear "guaranteed to have been worn by a Japanese schoolgirl". The soiled underwear retailed for $29 apiece. Despite the outcry, nothing could be done as unsurprisingly there was no specific law against the practice. Eventually a creative prosecutor charged them under the Antique Dealings Act, which stipulates that dealers in second-hand items must obtain a licence from the local authorities. The business went bankrupt.

Monday 12 September

8	14
9	15
10	16
11	17
12	18
13	19

Change your name to Benrik by deed poll

YES! You can change your boring old name to a more exciting one for free with our legally valid deed poll! The only restrictions on name changes are that it mustn't be impossible to pronounce and it can't include numbers, symbols or punctuation marks (except apostrophes). So you are perfectly entitled to change your name to Clark Kent, Booty Licious or Bobby Charlton. "Benrik", however, is much more suitable.

A Deed Poll

THIS CHANGE OF NAME DEED *made this 13th day of September 2005 by me the undersigned* BENRIK *of* ....*now or lately known as* ....*(former name) a citizen of* ....*by birth.*

WITNESSES AND IT IS HEREBY DECLARED *as follows:*

1. I absolutely and entirely renounce relinquish and abandon the use of my said former name of................................... ....*(former name) and assume adopt and determine to take and use from the date hereof the name of* benrik *in substitution for my former name,*................................... ....*(former name).*

2. I shall at all times hereafter in all records deeds documents and other writings and in all actions and proceedings as well as in all dealings and transactions and on all occasions whatsoever use and subscribe the said name of BENRIK *as my name in substitution for my former name of*................................... ....*(former name) so relinquished as aforesaid to the intent that I may hereafter be called known or distinguished not by the former name but by the name of* BENRIK *only.*

3. I authorize and require all persons at all times to designate describe and address me by the adopted name of BENRIK.

IN WITNESS *hereof I have hereunto subscribed my adopted and substituted name of* BENRIK *and also my said former name of*...*(former name) and have affixed my seal the day and year first above written.*
Signed sealed and delivered by the above-named Benrik *in the presence of*

Witness 1...

Witness 2...

Seal (from stationer's shop)

Send it for safe keeping to the Enrolment Books of the Central Office of the Supreme Court of Deeds, at the Royal Courts of Justice (Strand, London WC2A2LL). Alternatively just show this deed poll to government departments and other organizations and ask them to change your records.

Tuesday 13 September

8	14
9	15
10	16
11	17
12	18
13	19

Egg&Spoon Day

Carry an egg in a spoon all day long without dropping it. You are not allowed to put it down. If you are going to be indoors, use a boiled egg for safety. If you drop it, start again tomorrow, and again until you complete a whole day. Don't rush! This isn't a race.

Wednesday 14 September

8	14
9	15
10	16
11	17
12	18
13	19

Discreetly give the finger to people all day today

FIG. A: What's in my eye?!

FIG. B: Just chilling out...

FIG. C: Hmmm... I wonder...

FIG. H: I like to stay informed

FIG. D: Everything's in order, officer

FIG. F: Rich pickings...

FIG. G: Is there something in my teeth?

FIG. E: Sure, take the last seat!

Thursday 15 September

8	14
9	15
10	16
11	17
12	18
13	19

GO TO PRISON TODAY!

Prison has proved a life-changing experience for many illustrious personalities, from Winston Churchill to Mahatma Gandhi. Nelson Mandela, the most famous prisoner of the 20th century, learnt to overcome his anger at the apartheid regime and forge a new path for South Africa as a result of his 27 years in prison. If it worked for Mandela, it could work for you! Experience prison for yourself today by committing a very minor offence and refusing to pay the fine (one-day sentences have been passed for the peaceful blockade of an arms fair, for instance, or the assaulting of a bollard).

Friday 16 September

8	14
9	15
10	16
11	17
12	18
13	19

Work out your alcohol tolerance level scientifically this Weekend

Everyone's reaction to alcohol is different. Today work out the exact levels at which you become drunk. Start on an empty stomach for accuracy. Procure a 700ml bottle of vodka. Drink it one measure every 5 minutes, and use our graph to work out how many minutes it takes you to become drunk (V). Now open a bottle of red wine and repeat. The red wine result is R. Repeat again with a gallon of beer (B). Your average number of drinks to get drunk is $(V+R+B) - age/1.15 + weight (kgs)/34.5$.

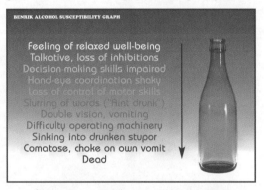

BENRIK ALCOHOL SUSCEPTIBILITY GRAPH

Feeling of relaxed well-being
Talkative, loss of inhibitions
Decision-making skills impaired
Hand-eye coordination shaky
Loss of control of motor skills
Slurring of words ("Aint drunk")
Double vision, vomiting
Difficulty operating machinery
Sinking into drunken stupor
Comatose, choke on own vomit
Dead

Saturday & Sunday 17–18 September

Today, Dance with Death

We are only ever one minute away from the er
Today, experience death's insane proximity
as to savour life all the more. Stand next to
running chainsaw. Stumble on the train platfor
Stare over the edge of the cliff. Run a red light. Ins
a skinhead. Just don't take anyone with you thoug

In 1976, installation artist Bruce Mercer created
"Untitled 22", which involved setting up a loaded
gun in a gallery, pointed at the audience and
primed to fire once at a random moment over
the following 20 years. The exhibition attracted
record numbers. The gun fired just after dawn on
October 6, 1993, nearly injuring a cleaner.

Monday 19 September

		14	
		15	
0		16	
1		17	
2		18	
3		19	

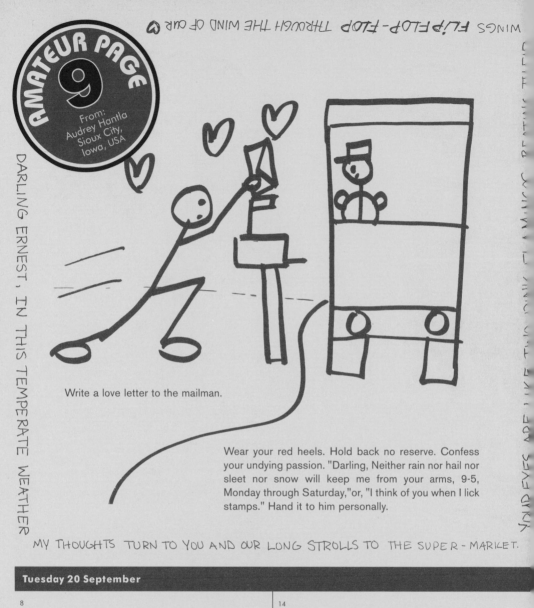

AMATEUR PAGE
9
From:
Audrey Hantla
Sioux City,
Iowa, USA

DARLING ERNEST, IN THIS TEMPERATE WEATHER

Write a love letter to the mailman.

Wear your red heels. Hold back no reserve. Confess your undying passion. "Darling, Neither rain nor hail nor sleet nor snow will keep me from your arms, 9-5, Monday through Saturday,"or, "I think of you when I lick stamps." Hand it to him personally.

MY THOUGHTS TURN TO YOU AND OUR LONG STROLLS TO THE SUPER - MARKET.

Tuesday 20 September

8		14	
9		15	
10		16	
11		17	
12		18	
13		19	

Dear Audrey, this was a good attempt. May we point out however, that your drawing skills are moderate. To highlight the topic of love in your concept you could have used a photograph, like this one for example, postman in his sexual prime):

Benrik Check-up

By accepting this Diary as a gift or purchasing it, you have legally committed yourself to following it. Today Benrik need to check on your progress. If you have been diligent, you have nothing to fear from this test. If you fail, however, we will know you have not been doing your daily tasks, and will have to ask you to return the Diary to the bookshop.

Answer this multiple choice test and send it to us. You will be notified of the results within 3 weeks.

NO PEEKING!

1. For how long were you asked to think about Ada Peach?
a)30 seconds b)15 minutes c)5 hours

2. What word terrifies the Arctic papoose?
a)Nootaikok b)Amaguq c)Nanootik

3. Who do Benrik suggest you draw on August 15?
a)Donald Duck b)God c)Benrik

4. Jonas Jansson's sexuality is best described as?
a)Mainstream b)Gay c)Confused

5. Which Benrik amateur wrote "Everybody scream today"?
a)Joel Moss Levinson b)Alex Nicholson c)Tracy Shiraishi

6. How many pounds did the model consumer need to spend?
a)36 b)37 c)38

7. Who is 19th in line to the throne of England?
a)Duke of Kent b)Earl of Ulster c)Prince Philip

8. How much money do Benrik suggest you transfer on February 3?
a)£17.99 b)£1000 c)All your money

9. Who wrote "Spazzing: the art of inarticulacy"?
a)D. Heisenger b)G. Klage c)S. Weissmarker

10. How does the winning genetic code on May 7 end?
a)ATTAGTA b)AAAGGTA c)GGGATTGG

11. Which small African country counts the most Benrik fans?
a)Lesotho b)Angola c)Swaziland

12. Which phone area code people are dark and mysterious?
a)01932 b)01588 c)01284

13. What is the Esperanto word for dominatrix?
a)Domino b)Dominati c)Seksmastrinon

14. How deep can the Drillmaster II dig?
a)10m b)50m c)200m

15. What is the going rate for Japanese schoolgirl soiled underwear?
a)$29 b)$56 c)$99

16. What is the name of Celine's baby?
a)Henri-Martin Dupre b) Rene-Charles Angelil c)Louis-Celine Dion

17. How much do Benrik's lawyers charge per hour?
a)$150 b)$350 c)$700

Send to: Benrik Limited
You should know the address by now!

Wednesday 21 September

8	14
9	15
10	16
11	17
12	18
13	19

PLEASE WEAR THIS STICKER ON YOUR BACK TODAY

If this sticker's message is not appropriate to your location, circumstances or personality, here are some others you may enlarge with a colour photocopier.

Thursday 22 September

8	14
9	15
10	16
11	17
12	18
13	19

CALL A CALL CENTRE IN INDIA AND GET THE STAFF TO TEACH YOU ABOUT THEIR CULTURE FOR A CHANGE

More and more companies are outsourcing their call centres to India, where the workforce is cheap and all speak perfect English. Staff are even made to watch *EastEnders* and Premier League football in order to understand English culture. But why should the cultural interchange be one-way only? Take this golden opportunity to ask questions and learn about everyday life in India. Don't worry how long the telephone call lasts, it's courtesy of some multinational corporation!

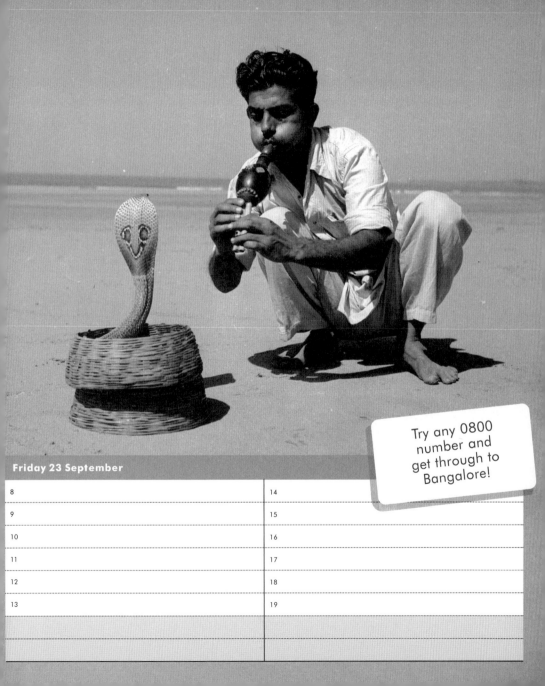

Try any 0800 number and get through to Bangalore!

Friday 23 September

8	14
9	15
10	16
11	17
12	18
13	19

HELP THE HOMELESS!

**Thousands on our streets!
Please give generously!
Winter is coming!**

AFRICA ACTION
MILLIONS ARE AT RISK.
MILLIONS FACE DROUGHT.
MILLIONS LOOK TO YOU...

THIS WEEKEND, DO SOME GOOD FOR A CHANGE: WALK THE STREETS RAISING MONEY FOR CHARITY. THERE'S NO NEED TO REGISTER, JUST FIND A TIN AND A RATTLE AND GLUE ONE OF THESE FINE HANDY CUT-OUTS AROUND IT.

EVERY YEAR 100's OF ELDERLY DIE. PLEASE HELP US SAVE THEM

BENRiK

THESE AUTHORS BADLY NEED YOUR CASH TO FUND THEIR UNHEALTHY LIFESTYLE CHOICES

Saturday & Sunday 24–25 September

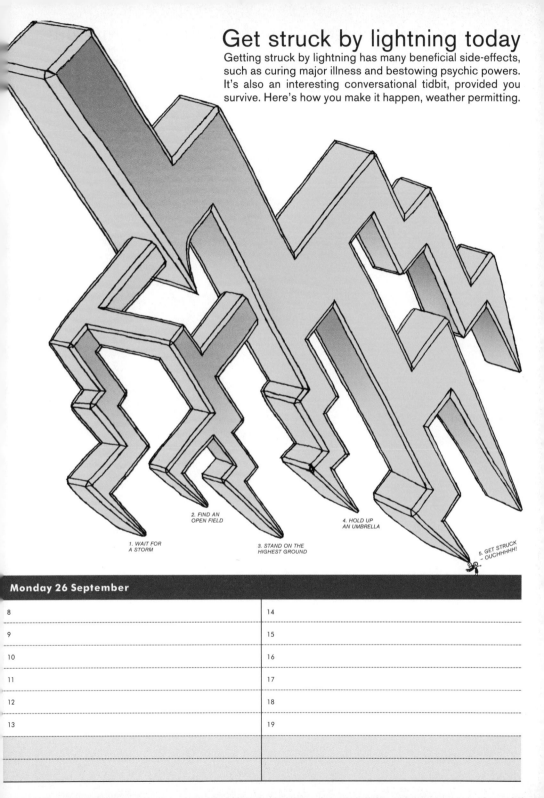

Get struck by lightning today

Getting struck by lightning has many beneficial side-effects, such as curing major illness and bestowing psychic powers. It's also an interesting conversational tidbit, provided you survive. Here's how you make it happen, weather permitting.

2. FIND AN OPEN FIELD

4. HOLD UP AN UMBRELLA

1. WAIT FOR A STORM

3. STAND ON THE HIGHEST GROUND

5. GET STRUCK – OUCHHHHH!

Monday 26 September

8		14
9		15
10		16
11		17
12		18
13		19

TODAY LIST ALL YOUR FRIENDS AND ACQUAINTANCES AND PRUNE THEM

According to anthropologist Robin Dunbar, the part of the human brain that deals with social interaction is only wired to cope with 150 people. Beyond that, alienation and aggression rear their ugly heads. List everyone you know below, and cut the dead weight

FRIENDS	ACQUAINTANCES		GET RID OF THESE GUYS
1	51	101	151
2	52	102	152
3	53	103	153
4	54	104	154
5	55	105	155
6	56	106	156
7	57	107	157
8	58	108	158
9	59	109	159
10	60	110	160
11	61	111	161
12	62	112	162
13	63	113	163
14	64	114	164
15	65	115	165
16	66	116	166
17	67	117	167
18	68	118	168
19	69	119	169
20	70	120	170
21	71	121	171
22	72	122	172
23	73	123	173
24	74	124	174
25	75	125	175
26	76	126	176
27	77	127	177
28	78	128	178
29	79	129	179
30	80	130	180
31	81	131	182
32	82	132	183
33	83	133	184
34	84	134	185
35	85	135	186
36	86	136	187
37	87	137	188
38	88	138	189
39	89	139	190
40	90	140	NOW YOU'RE JUST LYING
41	91	141	191
42	92	142	192
43	93	143	193
44	94	144	194
45	95	145	195
46	96	146	196
47	97	147	197
48	98	148	198
49	99	149	199
50	100	150	200

Tuesday 27 September

8	14
9	15
10	16
11	17
12	18
13	19

HELP REMOVE THE METEORITE!

METEORITE ZELDA On April 4th 2006, meteorite Zelda crashed through the ionosphere and straight into Kent. Known since then only as "404", this cataclysmic event immediately wiped out 6,500,000 lives, a third of them across the channel as a huge tidal wave engulfed the French, Belgian and Dutch coasts. Since then half of Europe has been reduced to three hours of (faint) sunlight a day, as the dust from the impact still saturates the atmosphere. The Gulf Stream has reversed course, a state of emergency has been declared, and food rationing is back with a vengeance. The core of the meteorite is still embedded in the remains of what was once known as "England's garden". Today join the thousands who make it their business to remove it chunk by chunk. Let's do it for our greatgreatgreatgreatgreatgreatgreatgreatgreatgreatgreatgreatgreatgreatgreatgrandchildren!

Wednesday 28 September

8	14
9	15
10	16
11	17
12	18
13	19

Today make a pact with the devil

Fill in this standard satanic contract with your own blood, which must be drawn from your left arm.

Dear Lucifer

I, ..., wish to make a pact with you.

In exchange for my soul, you will grant me great power/vast wealth (cross out) for the next .... years (to be agreed). I undertake to abide by the rules of the damned, accept the Devil's mark, sacrifice children to you and generally make a satanic nuisance of myself.

Signed and dated in my blood,

....

To register this pact with the devil, stand within a magic circle and recite the following invocation: LUCIFER, Emperor, Master of All Rebellious Spirits, I beseech thee to be favourable to me in calling upon thy GREAT MINISTER which I make, desiring thus to make a pact with him. BEELZEBUB, Prince, I pray thee also, to protect me in my undertaking. ASTAROTH, Count, be propitious to me and cause that this night the GREAT DEMON appear to me in human form and without any evil smell, and that he grant me, by means of the pact which I shall deliver to him, all the treasures of which I have need. GREAT DEMON, I beseech thee, leave thy dwelling, in whatever part of the world you may be, to come speak with me; if not, I shall thereto compel thee by the power of the mighty words of the Great Key of Solomon, whereof he made use to force the rebellious spirits to accept his pact. Appear then instantly or I shall continually torment thee with the mighty words of the Key: AGLON, TETRAGRAMMATON, ICION, STIMULAMATHON, EROHARES, RETRASAMATHON, ONERA, VAYCHEON, ESITION, EXISTIEN, ERYONA, CLYORAN, ERASYN, MOYN, MEFFIAS, SOTER, EMMANUEL, SABAOTH, ADONAI. I call you. AMEN. When the demon appears, simply hand him the pact and get a receipt. Congratulations! You have successfully sold your soul. May you rot in hell!

Thursday 29 September

8		14	
9		15	
10		16	
11		17	
12		18	
13		19	

TODAY COMMUNICATE BY ULTRASOUND ONLY

Why limit yourself to the conventional sound waves? All manner of animals obey instructions in the language of high frequencies. There is a rich conversation out there which humans don't participate in as much as they could. Today get hold of a dog whistle from your local pet store and enter the fascinating world of ultrasound communication.

How to use your dog whistle ultrasound device (THAT YOU WILL BUY TODAY!)

Set it to audible tone so you can hear a very faint version of what's really going on. Place the whistle between your lips, holding it in place with forefinger and thumb, and press lightly with your tongue, changing the pursing of your lips as you blow. Do not blow too hard or you will end up with a whistle full of dribble. Eventually, after a few years, when you master it, you will no longer need to hold it with your hand as much.

Learn the basic phonetic controls

Sound	Frequency range	Command
One long whistle	22,100-22,500 Khz	Come here dog
Wheet!	27Khz	Sit!
Wheep-whooooop!	5,000-45,000Khz	Stand!
One short, two long	22,750-22,850Khz	Move sheep up paddock
10-second low whistle	9,422Khz	No, the other paddock
Who!	31Khz-36,160Khz	All dogs to howl at moon
Wheeeooo-wheet	45,765Khz	All dogs to howl at death
Hee-wheeee!	23Mhz	Get that cat outta here
Who-whee!	25Khz	All bats to wake up
Short whistle	31Khz-36,150Khz	Dogs to mate nearest leg
Wheeeeeeeet!	23,679Khz	Dolphins to mate nearest submarine
Hee-wheet!	18Khz-46Khz	Bats to attack dogs
Wheeeet-heeee	24Khz-26Khz	Dolphins to come to the rescue
Three short whistles	19Khz-21Khz	Dolphins to defeat bats
Who-Hee-Who	12Khz-13,500Khz	Bats to return to caves

Friday 30 September

8	14
9	15
10	16
11	17
12	18
13	19

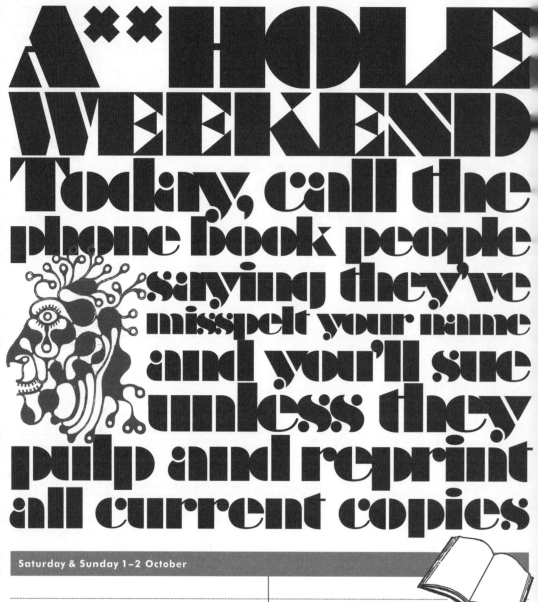

A**HOLE WEEKEND

Today, call the phone book people saying they've misspelt your name and you'll sue unless they pulp and reprint all current copies

Saturday & Sunday 1–2 October

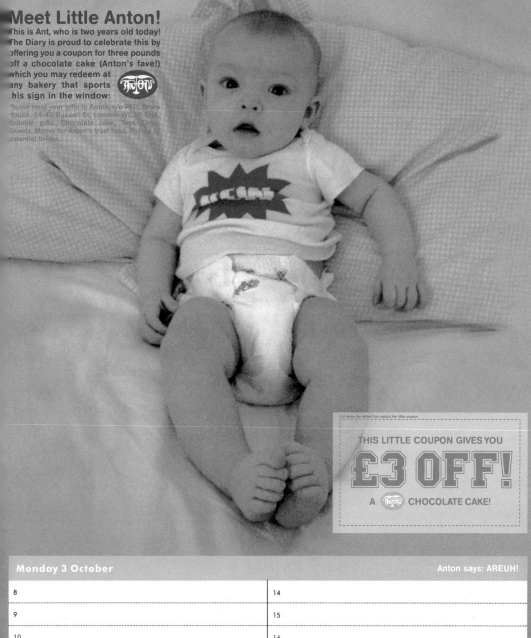

Meet Little Anton!

This is Ant, who is two years old today! The Diary is proud to celebrate this by offering you a coupon for three pounds off a chocolate cake (Anton's fave!) which you may redeem at any bakery that sports this sign in the window:

Please send your gifts to Anton, c/o PED, Drury House, 34-43 Russell St, London WC2B 5HA. Suitable gifts: Chocolate cake, Toys, Lego, Sweets, Money for Anton's trust fund, Photos of potential brides.

Cut along the dotted line around the little coupon

THIS LITTLE COUPON GIVES YOU

£3 OFF!

A CHOCOLATE CAKE!

Monday 3 October

Anton says: AREUH!

8	14
9	15
10	16
11	17
12	18
13	19

Traffic Russian Roulette is all the rage amongst the restless youth in the vast suburbs of Ukrainian dormitory towns. It's easy to take part, less easy to win. The idea is simply to cross the road without looking. Start with an easy road and progress to the trickier ones.

1 Path in your local park
Threats: dogs, joggers, pushchairs.
Risk: low.

2 Country lane
Threats: cows, tractors, idiots in sports cars.
Risk: some.

3 Main road
Threats: cars, buses, trucks.
Risks: high.

4 German autobahn
Threats: Mercedes, BMW, Porsche.
Risks: insane.

Tuesday 4 October

8	finished 2 prints	14	in prod?
9	retouch + enlargement	15	GT asked Lista to
10	bought from PV	16	source w6 fabric:
11	Meet Lista at 7 pm	17	silk wool crepe
12	confirmed Indian bird print	18	" " dyppiens
13	will send on next Mon,	19	" " cdc
	sent all other print		~30mm Bashine
	samples for Cabr standard		Warp print felted.

Give away free hugs

Spread a little love today you sexy beast you...
Here are the six officially recognized hugging styles

Standard hug	Grandma hug	Sexpest hug	Pickpocket hug	Self-hug	Porno hug

Freeform hugging **Freeform hugging** is only to be attempted when you have mastered the above. Many amateur huggers have developed cramps, injuring both themselves and the huggee.

Wednesday 5 October	
8	14
9	15
10	16
11	17
12	18
13	19

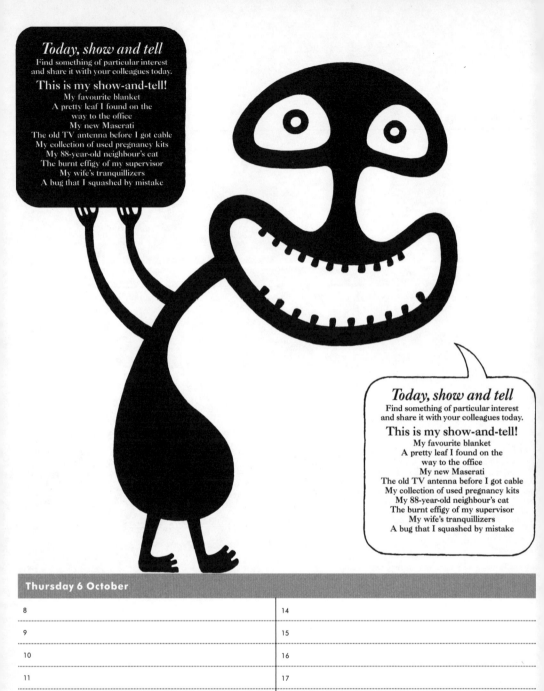

Today, show and tell

Find something of particular interest and share it with your colleagues today.

This is my show-and-tell!
My favourite blanket
A pretty leaf I found on the
way to the office
My new Maserati
The old TV antenna before I got cable
My collection of used pregnancy kits
My 88-year-old neighbour's cat
The burnt effigy of my supervisor
My wife's tranquillizers
A bug that I squashed by mistake

Today, show and tell

Find something of particular interest and share it with your colleagues today.

This is my show-and-tell!
My favourite blanket
A pretty leaf I found on the
way to the office
My new Maserati
The old TV antenna before I got cable
My collection of used pregnancy kits
My 88-year-old neighbour's cat
The burnt effigy of my supervisor
My wife's tranquillizers
A bug that I squashed by mistake

Thursday 6 October

8		14	
9		15	
10		16	
11		17	
12		18	
13		19	

CLASS ACTION LAWSUIT DAY

Benrik are filing class action lawsuits on behalf of their readers. If you feel you qualify for damages based on the description of the class action, then mark the relevant lawsuit(s), fill in the detailed form below and send it to our legal team.

■ THE SCHOOL SYSTEM
For wrongful imprisonment between the ages of 4 and 18, in violation of the Declaration Of Rights Of The Child (1959, Part 1 Art.3.1.2 & 3.1.3).

■ MAKERS OF CUDDLY TOYS
For instilling us with feelings of affection for inanimate objects, the memory of which later stunted our emotional and sexual lives.

■ THE MASSACHUSETTS INSTITUTE OF TECHNOLOGY
For allowing Edward Lorenz to discover chaos theory, thereby undermining 20th century man's already shaky relationship with the universe.

■ SOFT DRINK MANUFACTURERS
For funding the oppressive communist regime in Angola in the 1970s, perpetuating the legacy of oppression of the Portuguese.

DATE OF INJUSTICE:................................Details of complaint (damages you have suffered, including emotional damages)..
I want at least this much compensation ....$

A class action lawsuit is a lawsuit in which the plaintiff represents a number of people, all engaged in similar claims against the defendant. The plaintiff is known as the class representative. A plaintiff may for instance bring a claim against the manufacturer of a drug with hidden side-effects, on behalf of him or herself and others affected by the side-effects. Class action lawsuits make it economically and logistically possible for hundreds or thousands to sue a large wrongdoer, where pursuing their claims individually would prove difficult and expensive in relation to likely damages. The class members share any eventual damages amongst themselves.

Friday 7 October

8	14
9	15
10	16
11	17
12	18
13	19

Start your own religion this weekend

Religion doesn't just cater to spiritual needs, it's also very big business. Most of the current faiths have been around for a while, so it's time for a new kid on the block. This weekend invent your own set of beliefs and cash in on people's deepest fears.

Name

If you have a catchy surname, like Christ, then you'd be daft not to use it. Examples of good names include Stern, Ryke or Kharg – basically anything that sounds important with -ology or -ianism appended. Less good names might include Smith, Brown or Crawford. It helps if the name sounds vaguely eastern and hints at animal sacrifice.

Gods

You may want to feature several gods for the sake of variety. If so, try to link them to awe-inspiring animals, like the lion, the eagle, the serpent or perhaps the owl. The modern approach, however, is to concentrate on one god. It helps the believers focus, and is so much easier from a branding viewpoint. Again, scary names work best. Think Urgg, Drakkar or Achaemon.

Book

You will need a Holy Book, wherein you codify your religion. This is to guarantee your intellectual property rights over the religion. Sales of the Holy Book will also provide a valuable revenue stream. Be sure to write it in vague language, so that you will need to be consulted as to its precise meaning. Claim that the Book was dictated to you on a hill of some sort, by Urgg, Drakkar, Achaemon or other.

Rituals

Worship is a major part of religion, and gives your believers something to do. Provide for daily prayers, but keep them short and sweet. No one has time for lengthy get-togethers these days. You will want to create one special day a year though, where you will gather with your flock. Again, animal sacrifice does seem to draw the crowds, although communal singing is also a firm favourite.

Afterlife

This is pretty important. People will be more likely to sign up if there's a reward. You'll find it difficult to beat the Christian combination of Heaven for the faithful and Eternal Hell for the rest. Perhaps some form of cloned immortality might do the trick, although science could beat you to it. Certainly unbelievers need an incentive scheme to join.

Prophet

People want to hear it straight from the horse's mouth. If you want to be taken seriously, you will have to take on the mantle of prophet yourself. This is not without its dangers. Would-be prophets have been shot, burned and drowned, not to mention crucified. But the rewards are substantial. Fame, money and women could be yours, provided your religion allows them. Good luck!

Tip: Aliens provide a plausible basis for religion. Try to include them in some shape or form, if only to attract the affluent American market.

MEET YOUR MAKER

LET THE KIDS COME TO ME

FATHER, FORGIVE THEM

I AM THE LIGHT

WALK THIS WAY

MY CLOUDS ETERNAL IS GORGES FROM ME

A CHILD IS BORN IN BETHLEHEM

WATERWALKER

Saturday & Sunday 8–9 October

CORPORATE GAMES DAY

Don't let office routine get you down this year. Liven up proceedings by insisting that everyone in your company spend Friday afternoon playing. The following games are team-building, lessen workplace stress, teach modern corporate values, and they're fun!

HIDE&SEEK Everyone hides from the boss, those who don't get found in the first five minutes get fired for absenteeism.

SIMON SAYS Also known as Roger says, Gerry says, Richard says, Hilary says, Peter says, depending on the name of your boss.

SPIN THE BOTTLE
Everyone sits around the boardroom table. Players spin the bottle, and have to sexually harass the player the bottle points at.

TAG One player is labelled "office loser". He/she chases the others and tries to touch them to transfer the "office loser" label.

Monday 10 October

8	14
9	15
10	16
11	17
12	18
13	19

SPEED DAY

TODAY YOU MUST GO ABOVE 100MPH

The rush to the head that speed provokes is the defining sensation of our times. We've even named a drug after it. Today fly, drive or ride a rollercoaster. Only make sure you break your speed limit.

The world's magnificence has been enriched by a new beauty: the beauty of speed. A racing automobile with its bonnet adorned with great tubes like serpents with explosive breath ... a roaring motor car which seems to run on machine-gun fire, is more beautiful than the Victory of Samothrace (Filippo Tommaso Marinetti)

Too bad he was a fascist!

ACHTUNG! If you choose to drive, make sure you're on an autobahn!

Tuesday 11 October

8	14
9	15
10	16
11	17
12	18
13	19

Today, eat or drink something older than yourself

There is something deliciously unnatural about ingesting matter that predates you on this planet. Pick one of the following and consume it.

WINE (0 TO 150 YEARS)

Nothing could be simpler than drinking wine older than yourself; stroll down to the nearest merchant and buy a bottle from the year before your birth. Bordeaux is a safe bet, although the risk-takers might pick a Burgundy. If the wine is very old, it will react extremely quickly to air. Leave it for 10 minutes to dissipate any 'bottle-stink', then enjoy it in the next half an hour, before the evanescent aroma of decades vanishes into thin clear air.

WHISKY (10 TO 70 YEARS)

A great bottle of single-malt Scotch should keep for the average human life span. It is only after 12 years in cask that it can truly be considered for drinking. If you can afford it, try the 1937 Glenfiddich, which only became fully drinkable in 2001. It's the oldest whisky in the world. There are only 60 odd bottles left worldwide. One will cost you $80,000 at the very least. But you're guaranteed a taste of history.

DRIED MUSHROOMS (50 TO 70 YEARS)

In the north of Japan, farmers preserve Maitake mushrooms by drying them on the slopes of the Ishikari volcanic mountains. Then they use a unique mix of whale blubber and spices to seal them into man-sized urns which they bury for a minimum of 50 years. The result? A moreish treat with delicate yet earthy overtones, prized for its cancer-inhibiting properties. Simply brush off the dirt, soak in 23°C water for 5 hours, and fry gently for 10 minutes in extract of soya oil.

HANGAI YAK CHEESE (14 TO 60 YEARS)

This hard cheese is the longest-lived milk-based product in the history of food preservation. This is due in no small measure to the freezing climate of the Mongolian lowlands, where it is produced. The Hangai yak feeds on relatively acidic grasslands that provide the milk with some natural preservatives, which the Mongols then top up with rennet. The cheese itself is an acquired taste. Dense and pungent, with an inch-thick rind, it is normally enjoyed as a meal on its own.

SALTED BEEF (5 TO 50 YEARS)

Salting of meat is an ancient preservation technique, particularly favoured by the Romans. Perhaps this is why some of the best salted beef comes from the Italian region of Trentino. By using only the finest cuts and mixing in some salpetre, the locals are able to hang them for up to 50 years, by which time they have developed a layer of scrumptious fine moss. Once you've got your hands on some (no easy task!), just bring it to boil and leave to simmer with some marjoram for three hours per kilo. Serve cold with beetroot and/or radishes.

100-YEAR-OLD TURTLE SOUP

If your palate is jaded or you are already older than most of these delicacies, there is but one treat left for you: Chinese turtle soup made from century-old turtles. You will need to travel to Hunan, as export of food made from this endangered species is prohibited. There, you will need to scour the backstreets for the wily peasants who are still proficient in the art of hunting and deboning these increasingly rare ancestral beasts. The going rate for a bowl of this soup of soups is $3,000. NB: This trip is not recommended for anyone over 95 years old.

Wednesday 12 October

8	14
9	15
10	16
11	17
12	18
13	19

PASS A NOTE ON PUBLIC TRANSPORT TODAY

PLEASE PASS THIS ON TO: YOU LOOK TIRED. WOULD YOU LIKE TO COME AND SIT ON MY LAP?

PLEASE PASS THIS ONTO: WERE WE NOT AT SCHOOL TOGETHER? YOUR FACE IS STRANGELY FAMILIAR.

PLEASE PASS THIS ON TO: WHERE IS THIS BUS GOING AGAIN? I'VE COMPLETELY FORGOTTEN!

Please pass this on to: STOP STARING AT MY CLEAVAGE OR I'LL CALL U A PERVERT OUT LOUD.

PLEASE PASS THIS ONTO: THE GUY IN FRONT OF ME HAS DANDRUFF! TELL THE OTHERS!

Please pass this on to: YOUR SHOELACE IS UNTIED, YOU IDIOT. I'M AFRAID SOMEONE WILL RUN OVER DON'T YOU!

Please pass this on to: May I compliment you on your hat? I have the same at home.

Please pass this on to: This train has been hijacked by extremists. Be ready to act when I say.

PLEASE PASS THIS NOTE ON TO: I HAVE RUBBED THIS NOTE ON MY GENITALS! AND NOW YOU'VE TOUCHED IT!

On the bus to work i'm never alone

Thursday 13 October

8	14
9	15
10	16
11	17
12	18
13	19

Tonight between 6 and 8pm,
everybody call their local
radio station and request
a love song for "Malcolm".
Ask if they can also broadcast
one of the following
dedication messages:
a) Malcolm I'm pregnant
b) Malcolm I'm gay and I love you
c) Malcolm I've taken the kids
d) Malcolm please call the office asap
e) Malcolm you're a dead man
f) Malcolm I'm your long-lost brother
g) Malcolm your supper's ready

Friday 14 October

8	14
9	15
10	16
11	17
12	18
13	19

Sabotage
Hollywood Weekend

Go to movies and shout out the ending to help people realize
how predictable most big studio productions are.

APOLLO 13
They don't make the
moon, but return safely.

BASIC INSTINCT
Sharon Stone did it!

CASABLANCA
Ilsa leaves Casablanca
without Rick.

DEEP IMPACT
The shuttle crew blow
themselves up with the
comet and save us.

E.T.
The other aliens
rescue him.

FORREST GUMP
Forrest's Mum and Jenny
die, but leave Forrest with
a baby.

GLADIATOR
Russell Crowe kills the
emperor but dies.

HALLOWEEN
They think they've killed
him, but they haven't!

INDEPENDENCE DAY
They disable the alien
shield and nuke them all.

JAWS
Schneider blows
up the shark and
swims home.

KARATE KID
Daniel wins.

**LOCK STOCK AND
TWO SMOKING
BARRELS**
Big Chris takes the
money, they nearly throw
away the priceless guns.

**MISSION
IMPOSSIBLE**
Everything has been set
up by Jon Voight.

NOTTING HILL
They get
married,
she gets
pregnant.

**OCEAN'S
ELEVEN**
The Swat team
are the conmen.

PEARL HARBOR
The Japanese lose the war.

QUIZ SHOW
The hoax is exposed.

**RAIDERS OF
THE LOST ARK**
Indy recaptures the Ark
for the US government.

**SAVING PRIVATE
RYAN**
The old man at the
beginning is Ryan.

**THELMA
AND LOUISE**
They commit suicide by
driving off
a cliff.

**USUAL
SUSPECTS**
Kevin Spacey has
made everything up.

VANILLA SKY
Too
complicated
to explain.

**WHEN HARRY
MET SALLY**
Meg Ryan and Billy Crystal
eventually get together.

XXX
Vin Diesel
triumphs over the bad
guys.

**YOU'VE
GOT MAIL**
Meg Ryan and Tom Hanks
eventually get together.

ZULU
The Zulus
recognize their bravery
and let them survive.

Saturday & Sunday 15–16 October

Today add "von" to your surname to see if people treat you differently

The German nobility has an undeniable mystique. From medieval knights to temperamental Hollywood directors, the "von" prefix oozes aristocratic reserve. Adopt it and notice the deference.

Before — Danny Higgins

After — Danny Von Higgins

How to substantiate your claim to noble German descent: unfortunately, a "von" alone is no guarantee of pedigree. In Northern and Eastern Germany, a large number of families use it purely to indicate their town of origin e.g. Johann von Freiburg. Should some nosy snob demand proof of your lineage, you may resort to the following double-bluff: 'My great-great-grandfather killed the King and so was expelled from the family who erased all records and exiled him to America. I know this because my great-great-aunt told me with her last dying breath'.

Monday 17 October

8	14
9	15
10	16
11	17
12	18
13	19

Pass the whistle on day

Today get everyone in the office, classroom, street etc to whistle the same tune as you untill every one you know cannot get it out of their head.

Tuesday 18 October	
8	14
9	15
10	16
11	17
12	18
13	19

Today, divine the will of your ancestors

There is no reason why the ancient Etruscan art of haruspicy, better known as entrail-reading, cannot be practised in our day and age. Before you roast a chicken tonight, take time to 'read' it and learn what fate has in store.

Swollen liver?
You face
military defeat

Enlarged goitre?
Your tumble dryer
will break down

Unusually
protuberant veins?
You will miss
your plane

Purple spots?
Your daughter
will elope with a
Nubian

Dry patches?
The Furies are
after your head

Dark yellow
kidneys?
This chicken is past
its sell-by date

Small oesophagus?
Go into exile now

Fatty tissue?
Prepare to face
a tax audit

Strange little
white bones?
You are entrail-
reading a fish

And remember – it used to have a life – just like you and me!

Wednesday 19 October

8	14
9	15
10	16
11	17
12	18
13	19

MAKE YOUR BOSS NOTICE YOU TODAY.

Walk back and forth in front of his office in deep thought, yelling out EUREKA. When you're on the phone, shake your fist in triumph. Crack open a bottle of champagne whenever he looks up. Your boss will form the impression that you're the one to watch and you'll be guaranteed a fat pay rise.

Thursday 20 October

8	14
9	15
10	16
11	17
12	18
13	19

!!!POISONED PAGE!!!

Today make your mortal enemy touch this page, which is poisoned with a cyanide compound ink. The ink will kill your enemy for good within 3 minutes, just long enough for you to explain your motives and chuckle as they writhe in agony. As you do so their tongue will turn green and attempt to slither out of their mouth. Their innards will gently liquefy, their eyeballs retract into their skull, their saliva boil, and they will feel overall pain.

HOW TO CONVINCE THEM TO TOUCH IT:

YOU'RE TOO CHICKEN TO TOUCH THIS AREN'T YOU?

NO IT'S NOT POISONED THAT'S A TYPO DON'T WORRY.

I PROMISE YOU WON'T WRITHE IN AGONY.

LOOK AT THE PRETTY COLOUR, DON'T U WONDER WHAT IT FEELS LIKE TO TOUCH?

8	14
9	15
10	16
11	17
12	18
13	19

Benrikchalking Weekend

American hoboes in the Depression communicated through rough chalk symbols on sidewalks, fences and buildings, to let each other know what to expect in that area. More recently it's been used to advertise wireless access points. But the potential is much greater. This weekend, chalk the streets near you in Benrik signs, to let your fellow readers know the salient features of your neighbourhood.

Hobo sign language

Kind hearted lady	Unsafe place
Talk religion to get food	Work available
Bad tempered owner	Crooks!
Judge lives here	No alcohol town
Owner out	Gentleman
Bad water	Hoboes arrested on sight
Man with guns	Hold your tongue
Free telephone	Rich people live here
Vicious dog here	Good place to catch a train

Benrik sign language

Dog with diarrhoea	Woman with evil laugh
Bad haircuts here	Conscientious butcher
Don't order the prawns in here!	Nudist couple in window above
Celebrity often has coffee here	Small child pees from balcony
Farty shopkeeper	Road rage intersection
Household with widescreen TV	Watch your change in here
Housewife with forlorn smile	Cappuccinos extra frothy
Very loud kettle	Double pram zone
Man plays saxophone badly	Pee here if really can't hold it

Saturday & Sunday 22–23 October

Last year, Benrik asked readers to help create the world's longest poem, starting with the line 'Mercy, cried the popinjay to the pope'. The results have been impressive, so much so that we only have room to print 5% of the poem below. We still have not seen a suitable final line, though. Today, contribute one on www.thiswebsitewillchangeyourlife.com so we can end the poem!

[The page contains many columns of tiny, largely illegible poem text.]

Monday 24 October

8	14
9	15
10	16
11	17
12	18
13	19

I'm a poetry critic, and I really endorse this poem. I like especially the happy stuff. Poems have a tendency to be a bit on the sad side and I don't like that. I like happy poems. End of critique.

Today make your heart beat faster

Martial arts masters learn to control the "autonomic" body functions, like the heartbeat or blood pressure, which theoretically are outside our conscious control. Today make an effort to accelerate your subconscious vital functions and find out if you have a knack for it.

Heart rate
Normal: 60–180 bpm
Target today: 300 bpm

Tuesday 25 October

8	14
9	15
10	16
11	17
12	18
13	19

LIVE BY THE SCOUT CODE OF HONOUR TODAY

ome chaps say scouting is just for kids. Well, that idea is plain wrong! The high-minded principles laid down by Robert aden-Powell in 1907 are just as useful to grown-ups. Today, even you've never had a scouting experience as a child, endorse ose fine values and put them into practice in your daily life.

rst up, take the Scout Promise

> On my honour I promise that I will do my best,
> To do my duty to God and to the Queen,
> To help other people at all times,
> And to obey the Scout Law.

epeat this promise to yourself at least once an hour. Now, read n to work out how to apply the Scout promise and the Scout aws to your lifestyle.

pproach a homeless chap and make inquiries. Why does he lie here in such unscout-like spirit instead of fetching himself a ob? Urge him to shape up at the double, or you'll set the law n the fellow!

Volunteer for the Samaritans. When chaps feel down in the mouth, what they need isn't hangdog advice, but some cheery companionship! Tell the funny beggars to stop being bloody milksops and to start wearing a merry smile!

Stop a fight. Sometimes when pals have had one too many beverages (!), they quarrel and think it fun to have a bout. Ask them to desist and exchange the heartiest of handshakes. And don't mind if they scoff at you.

The Ten Scout Laws

> A Scout's honour is to be trusted
> A Scout is loyal to Queen and Country, other scouters, parents, and employers
> A Scout obeys orders of his parents, and scout authorities
> A Scout's duty is to be useful and to help others without reward
> A Scout is a friend to all no matter to what nationality, class, race or creed they belong
> A Scout is courteous
> A Scout is a friend to animals and nature
> A Scout smiles cheerfully even under difficulties
> A Scout is thrifty and self-reliant
> A Scout is clean in word and deed

Wednesday 26 October

8		14	
9		15	
10		16	
11		17	
12		18	
13		19	

Make a non-obscene phone call today. Call a stranger at random and whisper nice things about them down the line

Your phone has a lovely ring

I admire the way you keep your front garden so well-tended

Your voice is so strong I bet you're a baritone

Do I hear children in the background, they sound beautiful

Every word you say has the feel of self-confidence

I noticed your name as soon as I opened the phone book

If no one's home, leave a message: Hello this is just prepare you mentally for when I come up to you in t street and hug you tight you don't know me but I fe like I've known you a very long time now and I j think you're super, so don't worry, I could tell you wh I look like but that would ruin the surprise anywa look forward to meeting you very soon good nig CLICK

I bet if we met we'd be friends straightaway

Maybe it's a fancy, but I could swear I can smell your sweet scent down the phone

Even when you swear it sounds like pure poetry

Don't hang up, I want this conversation to last forever

Thursday 27 October

8	14
9	15
10	16
11	17
12	18
13	19

TODAY LOBBY CELINE DION TO SING ABOUT YOU

Celine Dion has enjoyed a meteoric rise to global fame. She has sold over 130 million records worldwide and now stars in one of the most successful live shows in the history of entertainment. But her wide repertoire of songs has not yet featured you. Today write to her and suggest yourself as a fertile song topic, detailing your life story and how you think you would fit thematically into her oeuvre.

> WRITE TO: CELINE DION, A NEW DAY, CAESARS PALACE, 3570 LAS VEGAS BOULEVARD, LAS VEGAS, NV89109, USA

Here is Celine's life to inspire you with emotional connections between your journey and hers. Celine was born in 1968 in a picturesque small town in Quebec named Charlemagne. The youngest of 14 children (!), she learned the art of entertainment early on, performing with her siblings for the benefit of the locals in her parents' pianobar. At the age of 12, she announced to her mother that she wanted to sing. They composed a song together and contacted one of Montreal's pre-eminent managers, Rene Angelil, in January 1981. Rene was so entranced by Celine's voice that he cried. He then remortgaged to finance her first album and set about introducing her talent to the world! She became an overnight sensation in her native Quebec with her French-language single 'La voix du bon dieu' ('The voice of God'), written by Eddy Marnay – apparently the words that Marnay exclaimed when he first heard her sing. International success swiftly followed, when she won the gold medal at the Yamaha World Song Festival in Tokyo barely a year after her debut. The next five years saw her become a huge star in the French-speaking world, with classic hit albums such as 'Du Soleil Au Coeur' and 'Incognito', which went platinum.

Her global breakthrough came in 1988, when she won the Eurovision Song contest, singing 'Ne partez pas sans moi' for Switzerland, wowing 600 million viewers throughout the world in the process! In September 1990 she capitalized on this by releasing 'Unison', her first English language album, which scored a huge hit in the US with the Top 5 single 'Where Does My Heart Beat Now'. But this was just the beginning! In 1991 she sang the title soundtrack for Disney's 'The Beauty and the Beast', which rocketed to No1 and won an Academy Award as well as a Grammy. Celine by now was unstoppable, with her eponymous album 'Celine Dion' spawning no less than FOUR more hit singles.

To top it all off, Celine had found love. Rene Angelil was 26 years her senior, yet love knows no such barriers. Their admiration and respect for each other had grown into something more, and on December 17, 1994, they married in Montreal, to the delight of her fans.

Meanwhile her worldwide success showed no sign of abating. 'D'Eux' broke through the French language barrier in 1995 to become the biggest-selling French hit in history, netting Celine the knighthood of the order of arts and letters from the French government for being the 'best ambassadress of the French language'. Merci beaucoup! In Britain she topped the charts for weeks with the ballad 'Think Twice', which sold over a million copies. This success, however, was all but eclipsed in 1996 and 1997 when successive albums 'Falling Into You' and 'Let's Talk About Love' sold roughly 30 million worldwide – each! The song 'My Heart Will Go On', movie theme song of 'Titanic', won an Oscar and became a favourite wedding song for fans of Celine. The Nineties were fittingly topped by an authorized biography by Georges-Hebert Germain and a collection of greatest hits, 'All The Way...A Decade Of Song', which featured such classics as 'The Power Of Love', 'Because You Loved Me', and 'If You Asked Me To'.

By the end of 1999, Celine was long overdue for a break! She decided to take some well-deserved time off from her hectic schedule. In spite of this, there was an unexpected release for her fans in 2001: her baby son, Rene-Charles Angelil, born on January 25!

After two years off, Celine returned to showbiz in 2002 with a new blockbusting album, 'A New Day Has Come', an immediate No1 across the globe, with fans reassuring Celine she had not been forgotten! If anything, her schedule has got busier since her break, with several new albums, a perfume launch, and in March 2003, the opening of her own show at Caesar's Palace Las Vegas! Bravo Celine!!!

Friday 28 October

8	14
9	15
10	16
11	17
12	18
13	19

DON'T PEE THIS WEEKEND

When we're all down and out it can be good to know how lucky we are, to be able to pass water for example. Today do not urinate until tomorrow to give you that future satisfaction of knowing that when times are bad, they COULD be worse!

AND KEEP AN EYE ON THIS IMAGE WHILE YOU'RE AT IT WHY DON'T YOU! HAHAHA!

Saturday & Sunday 29–30 October

HALLOWEEN
Today everyone meet at 8pm local time at your nearest cemetery, cover your faces with flour, and walk into town together with your arms outstretched zombie-style.

Monday 31 October

8	14
9	15
10	16
11	17
12	18
13	19

TODAY JOIN THE FRENCH FOREIGN LEGION

This has always been one of the swiftest ways of changing your life.
Leave your sordid past behind and enter a world of French camaraderie and bracing physical standards. The Legion's motto is 'March Or Die', which is no longer taken literally, but gives a flavour of their attitude towards slackers.

HOW TO ENLIST:

Simply pop into one of the recruiting centres in France *(like Fort de Nogent, Fontenay sous Bois, 94120, just outside Paris)*. You have to be 18 to 40, unmarried and male. You need to be physically fit, i.e. be able to run a minimum of 3km in less than 12 minutes, do 30 push-ups, and climb a 20ft-long rope without using your feet. If successful (and fewer than 1 in 30 are), you will sign a contract for 5 years and be shipped off to some remote part of Africa to fight anyone who has displeased the French government. If you haven't deserted after your minimum 5 years, you may acquire French citizenship (this is optional). Aux armes!

THE CODE OF HONOUR

You will need to memorize this perfectly before receiving your *képi blanc*, the white hat that all legionnaires sport. Learn it and recite it at interview to double your chances.

1. Légionnaire, tu es un volontaire servant la France avec honneur et fidélité.

2. Chaque légionnaire est ton frère d'arme quelle que soit sa nationalité, sa race, sa religion. Tu lui manifestes toujours la solidarité étroite qui doit unir les membres d'une même famille.

3. Respecteux des traditions, attaché à tes chefs, la discipline et la camaraderie sont ta force, le courage et la loyauté tes vertus.

4. Fier de ton état de légionnaire, tu le montres dans ta tenue toujours élégante, ton comportement toujours digne mais modeste, ton casernement toujours net.

5. Soldat d'élite, tu t'entraines avec rigueur, tu entretiens ton arme comme ton bien le plus précieux, tu as le souci constant de ta forme physique.

6. La mission est sacrée, tu l'exécutes jusqu'au bout, à tout prix.

7. Au combat, tu agis sans passion et sans haine, tu respectes les ennemis vaincus, tu n'abandonnes jamais ni tes morts, ni tes blessés, ni tes armes.

FIN

DON'T FORGET TO COMMIT A CRIME FIRST!

Tuesday 1 November

8	14
9	15
10	16
11	17
12	18
13	19

Fine Dine with Benrik tonight!

The highest bidder on ebay (search for: Benrik) gets to enjoy dinner with the authors of the Diary at London's exclusive Ivy restaurant tonight at 8pm.

What's included
If you bid £5-10: we go dutch
If you bid £10-20: the apéritifs are on us
If you bid £20-50: Benrik pay for the drink
If you bid £50-£100: we'll shout you dessert
If you bid £100-£500: the whole meal is on us
If you bid £500-£1000: we tell you the secret of our success
If you bid £1000 and upwards: one sexual favour of your choice

Wednesday 2 November

8	14
9	15
10	16
11	17
12	18
13	19

Today fabricate a prehistoric cave painting and alert the local authoritie

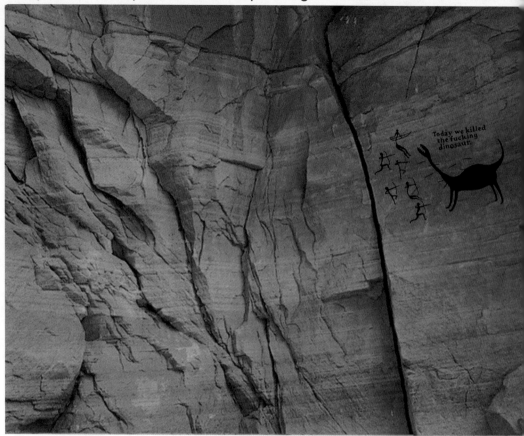

Today we killed the fucking dinosaur.

Don't be afraid to draw dinosaurs. According to the latest theories from America, dinosaurs and men coexisted. God created them both at the same time, and they lived happily together to begin with, at least until foolish Adam and Eve were thrown out of Eden. When the Flood came, the dinosaurs were harder hit because of their size. They drowned in huge numbers, leaving the fossilized remains we've discovered today. The dinosaurs on Noah's Ark survived, however, and went on to breed, in smaller numbers of course. Humans of all cultures have simply known them as dragons. Still today, there is evidence that some may survive deep under the sea. The idea that dinosaurs existed millions of years before Man is mere atheistic propaganda against the Young Earth scientific theory.

Thursday 3 November

8	14
9	15
10	16
11	17
12	18
13	19

Attend court today and offer your verdict to the judge

Most trials are open to the public. You've watched enough TV series to know the legal basics. Now put your knowledge into practice. Listen carefully to the evidence, weigh up the pros and cons in your mind, and shout out your verdict as soon as you reach it. The judge will be grateful for your input.

If your verdict is rejected
You have the right to appeal. Approach the judge outside the courtroom and demand a retrial. Outline your version of events and/or present any new evidence and/or witnesses you may have found. If the judge does not co-operate, lodge a formal complaint with the Lord Chancellor, and alert the media to a miscarriage of justice. Take it all the way to the Supreme Court if you have to!

Entry to the galleries is free, but you must be over 14. Cameras, videos, recording equipment and mobile phones are prohibited. But you are allowed to make a few clumsy crayon drawings of the scene.

Friday 4 November

8	14
9	15
10	16
11	17
12	18
13	19

Found a new city this weekend

Every city once started from scratch, no matter its present size. So will yours. And have patience: Rome wasn't built in a day. This is what you need:

THE FIRST BRICK: this is how cities start, with the founder laying the first brick. Choose a premium handmade brick, that meets recent European harmonization standards. You don't need any bricklaying qualifications, as professionals will finish the city for you, but do try and lay it flat.

A FIELD: find a field with enough room around it for your city to grow (10 miles in every direction should be plenty). If possible the field should be near a major river, as this will help turn your city into a major trading hub. Also, make sure the farmer who owns the field is vaguely aware of your plans.

A NAME: Paris, Milan, Tokyo, Los Angeles...These are glamorous names that have inspired millions of backward peasants to up sticks and move to the bright lights. Tip: try imagining it on a fashion house's letterhead. "Paris Milan Geneva Milton Keynes", for instance, doesn't work and should have been vetoed.

A STORY: Rome was founded by son of 'Mars the war god' Romulus, who was nearly drowned by his evil uncle as a baby, but survived after being suckled by a she-wolf, and returned to kill his uncle, and, soon after, his own brother Remus. Try to come up with something equally catchy.

NEW YORK 1615: BUILT IN 9 DAYS.

LONDON 202 AD: BUILT IN 17 DAYS.

TOKYO 431 BC: BUILT IN 34 DAYS.

PARIS 23 BC: BUILT IN 12 DAYS.

Saturday & Sunday 5–6 November

Today invent a new perversion

The human mind is the ultimate sexual organ, capable of conjuring up erotic pleasure from almost any object. Today test its limits by coming up with a new fetish.

Examples:
These are trademarked. Trying them costs £1 a go, payable to Benrik upon orgasm.

Animalhibitionism
Can only achieve satisfaction if watched by a pet

Opraphilia
Enjoy intercourse in front of live television

Speedophilie
Use of an egg timer in sex play

Masofonism
Aroused by being kept on hold indefinitely

Mediatism
Sex with people who look like a celebrity

Clonophilia
Sex with people who look like you

Monday 7 November

8	14
9	15
10	16
11	17
12	18
13	19

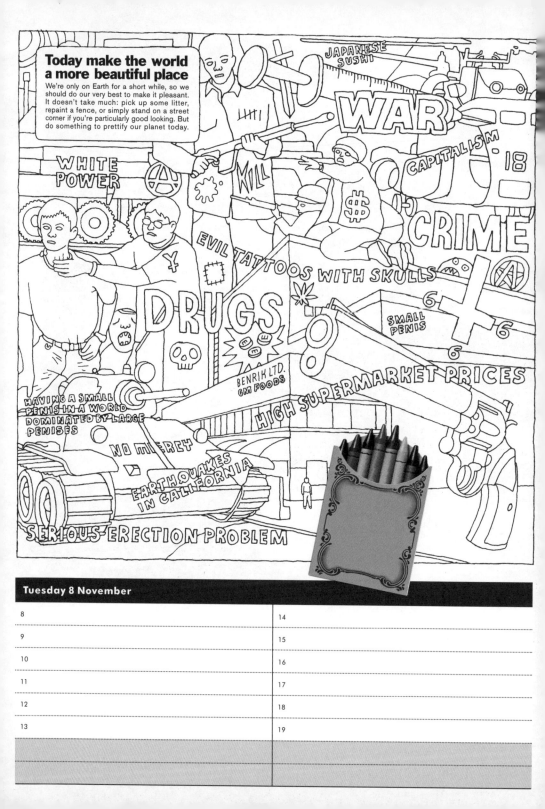

Today make the world a more beautiful place

We're only on Earth for a short while, so we should do our very best to make it pleasant. It doesn't take much: pick up some litter, repaint a fence, or simply stand on a street corner if you're particularly good looking. But do something to prettify our planet today.

Tuesday 8 November

8	14
9	15
10	16
11	17
12	18
13	19

GET IN TOUCH WITH YOUR HERO TODAY

There is nothing more uplifting than meeting the person you admire most in the world. Take the first step today by approaching your hero and requesting an encounter. Here are some suitable potential heroes if you can't think of any.

Mikhail Gorbachev, Nobel Peace Prize
39 Leningradsky Prospect, bdg. 14,
Moscow 125167, Russia

Jane Fonda, Peace and fitness activist
c/o Fonda, Inc.
PO Box 5840, Atlanta, GA 31107, USA

Nelson Mandela, Nobel Peace Prize
Office of the President
Pretoria 0001, Republic of South Africa

Javier Perez De Cuellar, Fifth UN Secretary
General, c/o UN, United Nations Plaza,
New York, NY 10017, USA

Bjorn Borg, Winner of 5 Wimbledon titles
Stadgarden 10, Box 154 15, 10465
Stockholm, Sweden

Bono, Singer and debt campaigner
Temple Hill, Vico Road
Killiney, Co Dublin, Ireland

Noam Chomsky, Professor/activist
MIT Linguistics and Philosophy Dept.
77 Massachusetts Avenue Bldg. 32-D808
Cambridge, MA 02139, USA

Jimmy Carter, Nobel Peace Prize
Carter Centre
One Copenhill, Atlanta, GA 30307, USA

Nana Mouskouri, Singer, UNICEF Goodwill
Ambassador, c/o Mercury – Universal 22, rue
des Fossés St-Jacques, 75005 Paris, France

Wednesday 9 November

8	14
9	15
10	16
11	17
12	18
13	19

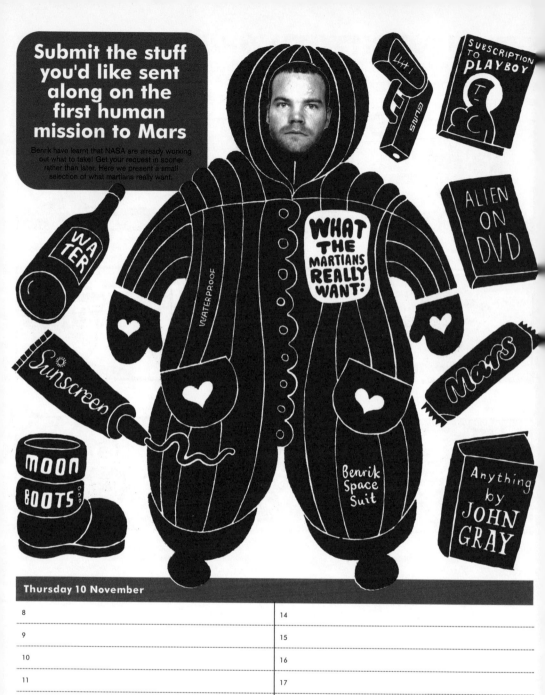

Submit the stuff you'd like sent along on the first human mission to Mars

Benrik have learnt that NASA are already working out what to take! Get your request in sooner rather than later. Here we present a small selection of what martians really want.

SUBSCRIPTION TO PLAYBOY

GUNS

ALIEN ON DVD

WA TER

WATERPROOF

WHAT THE MARTIANS REALLY WANT:

Mars

Sunscreen

MOON BOOTS

Benrik Space Suit

Anything by JOHN GRAY

Thursday 10 November

8		14
9		15
10		16
11		17
12		18
13		19

Play the stock market today

There's huge money to be made on the stock market, but people are often put off by its seeming complexity, and let's face it, the sheer numbing boredom of trying to fathom those endless figures. And yet it's not rocket science. Benrik have tried to make it more fun, so that anyone can enjoy the experience. Follow our instructions and you too will double your investment and become a trillionaire in no time*.

SELL Any share you can't pronounce immediately (though you can't ask for your money back).

INVEST In high yield bonds (aka "junk bonds"). They go up and down a lot which is more exciting all round.

SELL Shares in companies who do not answer the phone within three rings.

SELL Shares whose price is closest to 666.

GO LONG On Electronics.

GO WIDE On Tobacco.

START By buying a couple of hundred shares at random, while you still enjoy beginners' luck.

BUY Any shares that end in –ex.

SPREAD A rumour that world supplies of salt are about to run out, and buy pepper stocks.

GO SHORT On Mining.

CLOSE by selling everything and pocketing the profits (10% to Benrik).

In 1999, Swedish artist Ola Pehrson hooked up his yucca plant to a computer that bought shares according to the tiny electrical currents the plant generated. If the shares beat the index, the plant was rewarded with sunlight and water. If the shares did badly, the plant was left in the dark... The plant outperformed the Stockholm stock market by 12% over 4 weeks. This is a risky strategy though, which we do not recommend.

THIS COULD BE YOU...

TALKING TO HER

Benrik Limited shares

Coincidentally, Benrik Limited is floating today on the NASDAQ. Our readers get a 5% negative discount, so make sure you pop into your broker's and pick up your allocation. See our accounts at the end of this Diary to decide if you want to invest. Or visit www.thiswebsitewillchangeyourlife.com to start trading today.

Friday 11 November

8	14
9	15
10	16
11	17
12	18
13	19

*If you were a billionaire to start with of course!

Today women are to take charge of the world

Feminist thinkers have long argued that the world would be a better place for all if women had more say in vital matters. Today, any men following this Diary should relax, make sure to use their mother's surname, and look to the nearest woman for guidance. Women should take the lead and construct a more caring sharing society, free of war, want and worry. Take charge!

This Diary is brought to you by Ben Harden and Henrik Bengtsson. They are both men though, so does that mean following this day is patriarchal? What a head-ache!!

Saturday & Sunday 12–13 November

Nostradamus Day

Benrik are asking Diary readers to predict the future in the year 2015. Simply answer the questions below and complete the tie-breaker. The winning answer will be disclosed on December 31, 2015, and the winner hailed as the Nostradamus of their time!

CLOTHING
In 2015, we will all be wearing space suits
In 2015, we will all be wearing birthday suits
In 2015, we will all be wearing Gap
....

TRANSPORT
In 2015, petrol-fuelled cars will be banned
In 2015, cyclists will be a majority
In 2015, the robot-horse will be the norm
....

GEOPOLITICS
In 2015, Israel and Palestine will be at war
In 2015, the USA and China will be at war
In 2015, the Earth and Omega Centauri will be at war
....

BUSINESS
In 2015, genetics will be the No1 industry
In 2015, the Dow Jones will hit 30,000
In 2015, Microsoft will invade a small country
....

DESIGN
In 2015, clutter will be back
In 2015, the zero-gravity bookshelf will be a huge hit
In 2015, whole books will be devoted to this doodle
....

INTERNET
In 2015, the internet will be wired into our brains
In 2015, the most visited site will be "alienhotties.com"
In 2015, search engines will find true love and settle down
....

ART
In 2015, art will run out of taboos to break
In 2015, perspective will make a come-back
In 2015, rebel artists will seize Jupiter
....

SPACE
In 2015, mankind will be exploring Pluto
In 2015, mankind will be exploring the Andromeda galaxy
In 2015, mankind will be getting the hell out before the second meteorite hits
....

TIE-BREAKER
What would be a good slogan for the breakfast cereal of the year 2015? (200 letters max.)
....
....
....
....
....
....
....
....
....
....
....
....
....
....
....

Monday 14 November

8	14
9	15
10	16
11	17
12	18
13	19

Bake it Naked Day

today liberate yourself from clothes. walking around your pad naked is not radical anymore. bring yourself up to a new level of coolness -- bake something naked [and then invite friends over for a bake-tasting]. Possible things to bake: a cake, bread, cookies, casserole, chicken, pudding, fish, potatoes.

WARNINGS:

1. watch out for pubic hair or sharp objects near that area.
2. it's a good idea not to tell your friends how the baking was done until food is eaten and at least few glasses of wine [or any other alcoholic beverages] consumed.
3. the baking method disclosure might result in minor arse kicking [or equivalent, depending on kind of friends you gather].

AMATEUR PAGE
11
From: Tatiana
Platanova
Fairbanks, Alaska,
USA

Tuesday 15 November		
8	14	
9	15	
10	16	
11	17	
12	18	
13	19	

Today record something only you have noticed

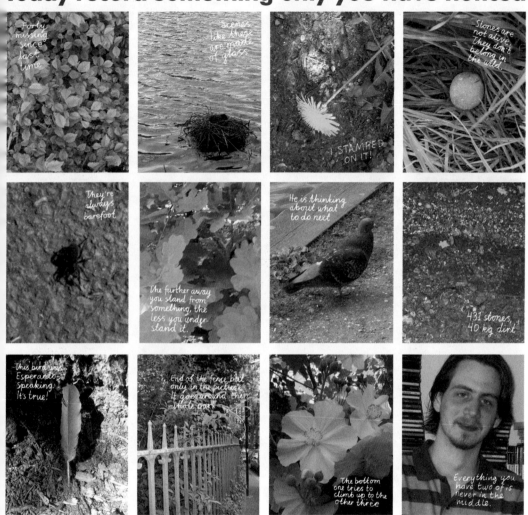

Forty missing since last time.

Scenes like these are made of glass.

I STAMPED ON IT!

Stones are not alive. They don't belong in the wild.

They're always barefoot.

The further away you stand from something, the less you understand it.

He is thinking about what to do next

431 stones, 40 kg dirt

This bird was Esperanto-speaking. It's true!

End of the fence, but only in the picture. It goes around the whole park.

The bottom one tries to climb up to the other three

Everything you have two of is never in the middle.

Wednesday 16 November

8	14
9	15
10	16
11	17
12	18
13	19

THE Cycle of CRIME

LITTERING

ZERO TOLERANCE DAY

Small crimes encourage bigger ones. In a community where seemingly minor offences such as littering are tolerated, serious ones like muggings will flourish. Today tell your fellow citizens off for the smallest of deviations and watch those crime figures drop.

MUGGING OF OLD LADIES

ARMED ROBBERY

CHEWING GUM WITH MOUTH OPEN

BURGLARY

SHOPLIFTING

GANGLAND BEATINGS

NOT TUCKING IN SHIRT

BULLYING OF NEIGHBOURS

SPITTING ON PROPERTY

DRIVING WITHOUT SEAT BELT

EATING FAST FOOD ON SUBWAY

DRIVE BY SHOOTINGS

SWEARING

SWEARING (4-LETTER WORD)

PARKING ON KERB

8	14
9	15
10	16
11	17
12	18
13	19

Order off-menu today

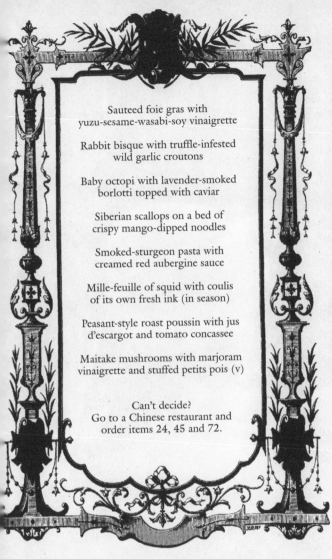

Sauteed foie gras with yuzu-sesame-wasabi-soy vinaigrette

Rabbit bisque with truffle-infested wild garlic croutons

Baby octopi with lavender-smoked borlotti topped with caviar

Siberian scallops on a bed of crispy mango-dipped noodles

Smoked-sturgeon pasta with creamed red aubergine sauce

Mille-feuille of squid with coulis of its own fresh ink (in season)

Peasant-style roast poussin with jus d'escargot and tomato concassee

Maitake mushrooms with marjoram vinaigrette and stuffed petits pois (v)

Can't decide?
Go to a Chinese restaurant and order items 24, 45 and 72.

"The menu" is food in a straitjacket. Refuse it point blank and order from your imagination. The waiter will respect you for it, and other customers will think you're a player. Here are a few dishes that any half-decent chef should be able to rustle up in a few minutes. Bon Appétit!

Friday 18 November

8	14
9	15
10	16
11	17
12	18
13	19

REBIRTH!

This weekend ask your parents to help you stage a realistic reconstruction of your birth.

Strange how little we know about the details of the most important moment of our life: its beginning. And yet there are witnesses to the act! Enlist them to recreate that magical instant where you burst forth. Only by understanding where you came from will you fully understand where you're going.

GET IT RIGHT!

Details to check and replicate:
- When and where did the waters break?
- How did you get to hospital?
- What time was it?
- How long did the delivery take?
- What drugs were administered?
- Were stirrups involved?
- Was the father in the room?
- Did you put up a fight?
- Which bit came out first?
- Did you cry when spanked by the nurse?
- Who cut the umbilical cord?

Warning: Do not attempt to recreate a Caesarian without qualified medical assistance.

Saturday & Sunday 19–20 November

Information Overload Day

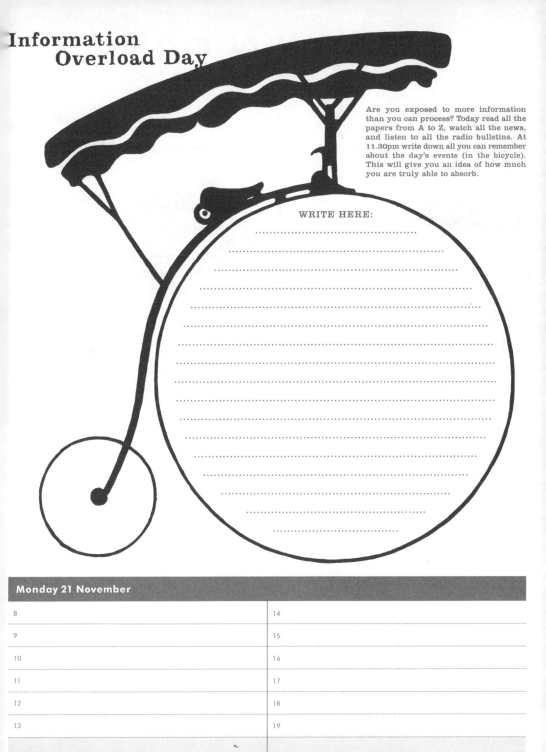

Are you exposed to more information than you can process? Today read all the papers from A to Z, watch all the news, and listen to all the radio bulletins. At 11.30pm write down all you can remember about the day's events (in the bicycle). This will give you an idea of how much you are truly able to absorb.

WRITE HERE:

Monday 21 November

8	14
9	15
10	16
11	17
12	18
13	19

DARWIN DAY

Evolution guarantees the survival of the fittest and the end for everyone else. Today, try mutating to keep ahead of the pack.

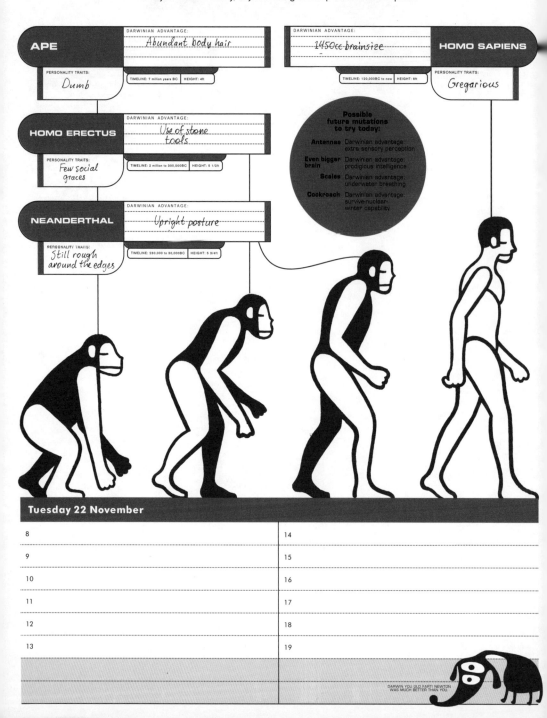

APE
DARWINIAN ADVANTAGE: *Abundant body hair*
PERSONALITY TRAITS: *Dumb*
TIMELINE: 7 million years BC | HEIGHT: 4ft

HOMO ERECTUS
DARWINIAN ADVANTAGE: *Use of stone tools*
PERSONALITY TRAITS: *Few social graces*
TIMELINE: 2 million to 500,000BC | HEIGHT: 5 1/2ft

NEANDERTHAL
DARWINIAN ADVANTAGE: *Upright posture*
PERSONALITY TRAITS: *Still rough around the edges*
TIMELINE: 230,000 to 30,000BC | HEIGHT: 5 3/4ft

DARWINIAN ADVANTAGE: *1450cc brainsize*
HOMO SAPIENS
PERSONALITY TRAITS: *Gregarious*
TIMELINE: 120,000BC to now | HEIGHT: 6ft

Possible future mutations to try today:

Antennas Darwinian advantage: extra sensory perception

Even bigger brain Darwinian advantage: prodigious intelligence

Scales Darwinian advantage: underwater breathing

Cockroach Darwinian advantage: survive-nuclear-winter capability

Tuesday 22 November

8	14
9	15
10	16
11	17
12	18
13	19

DARWIN YOU OLD FART! NEWTON WAS MUCH BETTER THAN YOU.

Get mugged today

Investigate the reality of street crime for yourself: stroll around a dodgy neighbourhood with a shiny camera, a new wristwatch and a laptop bag, and see how long it takes for some kid to approach you for your possessions. Hand them over, but only on condition he tells you all about his deprived childhood and his drug problem.

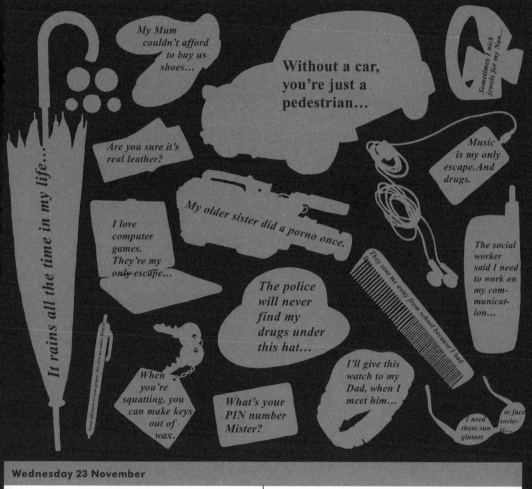

Wednesday 23 November

8	14
9	15
10	16
11	17
12	18
13	19

Today, let power corrupt you

We all enjoy some form of power: today let it go to your head and abuse it...

Make the check-out girl ring all your purchases through again

Oblige the shoe store assistant to look for another model

Force the pizza delivery guy to go back for extra anchovies

Order the wine waiter to get you a cleaner glass

Demand that your secretary retype the letter in italics

Insist that the receptionist change the flowers' water

Return this book to us for a refund claiming it's rubbish

Bully your family members to let you hold the remote

Require your visitors to take off their shoes

Thursday 24 November

8		14	
9		15	
10		16	
11		17	
12		18	
13		19	

Ask public transport to make a detour for you

Urban planners are busy people and can't always be expected to get it right the first time. Buses, trains and underground services often stop hundreds of yards away from where you need them to. Remedy this by asking the drivers to divert via your choice of destination. Remember to check the other passengers don't mind; you'll probably find that's where they wanted to go too, only they were too shy to ask! This is only a stopgap measure, until the local authorities commit resources to servicing you properly. To help them, draw up your proposed route and send it to them for implementation. Here is an example.

My house   Where I buy the paper

Park bench (summer only)

I enjoyed this museum   Shops

Other friends live here

The cinema I go to sometimes

My office

My friend Louise (3rd floor)

Public library

My bank   DIY store (Sundays)

My favourite zoo

Never been here but would like to go someday (request stop)

Friday 25 November

8		14	
9		15	
10		16	
11		17	
12		18	
13		19	

Neighbourhood Watch Weekend

Today keep an eye on your neighbours. Who is cheating on their spouse? Who is living beyond their means? Who isn't recycling? Log each infraction in your neighbourhood watch booklet and hand it in to the police on Monday morning.

Goshooo Sue hasn't watered her plants for like 2 days now! Oh, here comes her cat. Doesn't it look a bit hungry? Maybe I should feed it poison!!! Hahaha. The Sampsons has put up their christmas decoration three days later than last year. I wonder if something is wrong with their family. They are awfully quiet. And the son looks like he is <u>not</u> getting enough food. Oh, that bad housewife! Nothing, like what I could have been!! I will give them three days—no more no less, to prove to me that they are shaping up! Otherwise I will call the social service. THAT DAMN KID IS PLAYING THAT MUSIC AGAIN! THEy are retarded that's what they are—<u>both men and women</u>. Oh, I heard Simons car park outside! Here he is now... WITH SUE! That BITCH! Leave Simon alone, he is not for you! Good, they went seperate ways! Here is old Peter now, haha, in his wheelchair from like -44. Looser, he can't even do his shopping himself. I heard he's never had a wife either, that kinda tell you something about that whole thing don't you think? Blemming old man, he was surely a builder who fell down drunk from whatever he was building or something old fart! What's this? Simon is coming back out again!!! With a bottle of champagne Please come here, please come, come to me!!!! No nono! Nooo! He's knocking on her door. As usual

SPECIAL TEST!

Write your name and address on this label. Stick it on a letter. Put the letter in your next-door neighbour's letterbox to make it look like a postman's mistake. See if your neighbour passes it on to you. Check if they haven't opened it!

VALUABLE CONTENT

TOP SECRET

To:
....
....
....

FOR YOUR EYES ONLY

Saturday & Sunday 26–27 November

Today solve a world-famous mathematical problem

The Riemann hypothesis states that the nontrivial Riemann zeta function zeros all lie on the "critical line"

$$s = R[s] = 1/2,$$

where R[s] denotes the real part of s.

Prove it and your fortune is assured.

You may use this space to prove it:

Monday 28 November

8	14
9	15
10	16
11	17
12	18
13	19

Call someone with your telephone number but a different area code. See how long they're willing to talk about your common bond.

Here is a quick guide to the personality traits associated with some prominent area codes, so you can be better prepared for their reaction when you call.

01562 people are dark and mysterious. This can be difficult for loved ones, but means they are often thrilling company!

Those with area code 0121 are filled with zest for life. Meeting new people is a pleasure and a treat for them.

The people of area code 01892 are wary of strangers. For them, patience and endurance are the uppermost virtues.

Many 01349 people function on an intuitive level, and love animals and nature above all. Others are more withdrawn.

01993 area code people display huge ambition and charisma. Nothing stops them: beware those who get in the way!

Sensuality and seduction are central themes in the lives of 01666ers. They exude a magnetic charm that few can resist...

The people of area code 01942 are sometimes capable of malice, but get to know them and you will discover their softer side.

01625 people are dominating personalities. They take up leading roles in society and mark the times they live in.

The hedonistic individuals of area code 01873 are not interested in anything beyond pleasure: all play and no work!

Map labels:
- 01349 Dingwall
- 01666 Berwick-upon-Tweed
- 01625 Macclesfield
- 01562 Killarney
- 0121 Birmingham
- 01873 Abergavenny
- 01993 Witney
- 01892 Tunbridge Wells
- 01942 Bodmin

Tuesday 29 November

8	14
9	15
10	16
11	17
12	18
13	19

Today stalk someone

Spot someone interesting in the street and follow them around. Who are they? What do they do? Where do they live? What does their lover look like? Are they running late? Where do they shop? What do they order for lunch? What articles do they read in the paper? What makes them special? What moves them? And who are they stalking?

Wednesday 30 November

8	14
9	15
10	16
11	17
12	18
13	19

Today, confuse a large corporation

Ever felt helpless in the face of a corporate behemoth? Here's your chance to get your own back. Start a dialogue with a utility about a fictitious meter. Claim you have recently moved and wish them to take over supply on this meter, which until now has been supplied by another utility. Ask the corporation to get in touch with their competitor and arrange a transfer. Make up a credible-looking meter number (455 987), give them a reading (5674.76), get a case reference number, and there you go: you have sparked off months if not years of fruitless correspondence.

Transgas

TeleTel

PowerWeb

CentraFuels

Electrica

Directelectric plc

Hydroline

GloboFuel

NorthernGas

FuelSource

Metrix

WestComms

PacificBoard

MagnoGen

SLAMDUNK

Can't get service? Complain to the regulator: Ofgem 020 7901 7000

Thursday 1 December

8		14	
9		15	
10		16	
11		17	
12		18	
13		19	

Today work out how many seconds you have left to live

Formula (AVERAGE LIFE EXPECTANCY 78 – YOUR CURRENT AGE) x 31,536,000 = ...

Now plan for each one of them.

987761208
735556478
901739999
092687 sec

1 sec

2 sec

3 sec

Friday 2 December

8		14	
9		15	
10		16	
11		17	
12		18	
13		19	

Time is running out my friend!

Homeless Weekend

This weekend, leave your home and possessions and try to live on the streets. Could you survive the cold, the hunger, the looks? Experience life on the other side of the begging bowl, and by Monday morning, you'll never look down on the homeless again.

What you may take

Your past attitude to begging dictates your level of discomfort.

If you give to beggars every day:	You may take a sleeping bag, comfortable walking shoes and £5.
If you give to beggars once in a while:	You may take a blanket, a pair of woollen gloves, and a toothbrush.
If you never give to beggars:	You may take some foreign coins, a broken umbrella, and a flea-ridden sheet.

HEAVEN £1

SAVING FOR SEX CHANGE

Hungry

Used to be a taecher

Saturday & Sunday 3–4 December

Arrive three quarters of an hour late for everything today

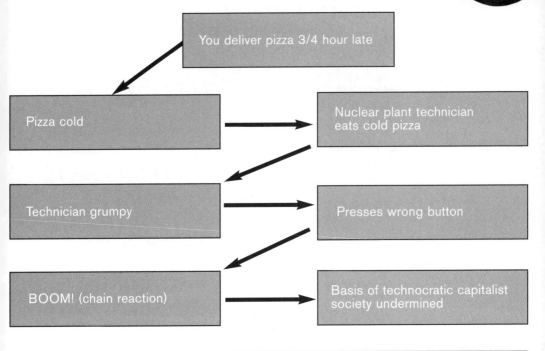

As Oscar Wilde pointed out, punctuality is the thief of time. Sabotage everyone's attempts at it today by running late for any meetings, thus setting off a chain reaction that will undermine the very basis of technocratic capitalist society. Example of chain reaction:

You deliver pizza 3/4 hour late

Pizza cold → Nuclear plant technician eats cold pizza

Technician grumpy → Presses wrong button

BOOM! (chain reaction) → Basis of technocratic capitalist society undermined

Monday 5 December	
8	14
9	15
10	16
11	17
12	18
13	19

Today dress out of character

Don't be a prisoner of your wardrobe: wear clothes that contradict people's perception of you.

I AM YOUNG AND INSECURE SO I NEED TO SHOW WHAT TRIBE I BELONG TO THROUGH THE PRINT ON MY T-SHIRT.

(HARD) Life is like a nut, but i'm known 2 B a bit of a nutcracker!!!

Autumn is approaching... as usual in my heart...

HELIX

My parents went to Italy and all I got was this lousy t-shirt wich really shows me what a shallow relationship I have to them.

"THEY" SAY LOVE IS WONDERFUL...

Life is like mustard in the ass of a cat – You run 'cause it hurts.

I want to be your friend but you probably don't want to be my friend... Do you?

www.benrik.co.uk. A website with a difference!

I SLEPT WITH PARIS HILTON AND SHE LOVED IT AND SCREAMED FOR MORE.

IF YOU'RE A TEACHER: FUCK OFF! DON'T TRY TO TEACH ME ANY BULLSHIT!

Bach is the Quentin Tarrantino of classical music.

Tuesday 6 December

8	14
9	15
10	16
11	17
12	18
13	19

Conspiracy Day

There's a potential conspiracy everywhere you look. Today find one in your everyday life!

My neighbour has been poisoning my cat with anthrax pellets! My cat is a different animal. He used to be cuddly but now he growls like a dog. Whenever he comes back from the next door garden, his saliva is greenish and frothing. My neighbour works for a chemical company. She keeps odd hours. I am afraid for myself and my cat.

I am the subject of a snuff reality TV show! There are cameras everywhere in my house. There have been since my birth. I even know which channel the show is on, channel 9 because they have "broken" that button on my TV. My life fascinates millions daily. But it will end with my being impaled to death live on prime time. Help me escape!

My children are the vanguard of an alien invasion! They are not like other kids. They don't go out. They don't play. They just do their homework and eat their greens. Since my wife was abducted (the so-called divorce was just for show), they stare out of the window waiting for the signal from the mothership.

My computer is bugged by the CIA! They are aware of my subversive potential. Every time I sit down to write my exposé of our crypto-world government, they zap my brain with alpha waves to cause writer's block! But I will fight back you evil bastards! What happens if I pour wate<ds5z++…,'√ɔfi√‹ₛ.ς₅∂≈†

Elvis is living in my shed! There's worse: he's using my tools. The other day, my staple gun was on next to the drill, when I 100% remember leaving it next to the saw! I dunno what he's making but it's a big job! He's working flat out all hours of the night. I know this cos I can hear him crooning to cover up the noise.

My cleaner is a communist! She leaves hammer and sickle signs in the dust. And last week, my books must have been rearranged, because the first letters of the titles of five of them spelt Lenin backwards. I fear she is using my toilet pan to leave messages for her Comintern handler, whom I suspect is the plumber. That damn toilet always blocks!

Wednesday 7 December

8		14	
9		15	
10		16	
11		17	
12		18	
13		19	

Today look at things from the most interesting angle

Wherever you go, whatever situation you're in, position yourself so that you're viewing it in the most dramatic way possible. Ask yourself how Hitchcock would look at it, and sit yourself accordingly.

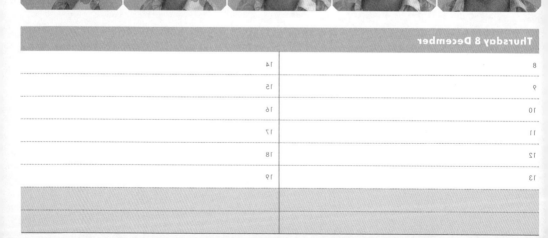

8	14
9	15
10	16
11	17
12	18
13	19

Buy your own grain of sand in the Bahamas!

Today purchase a small piece of paradise. Benrik Limited have arranged an exclusive real estate deal whereby our readers may acquire their very own parcel of land on the glamorous tropical island of Great Exuma. One grain of sand can be yours in perpetuity for as little as $1. For your money you will receive: a certificate of part-ownership of Exuma, a photograph of your grain of sand, a map showing its exact location (within 1cm²), and a 20¢ voucher towards a cocktail of your choice at the Big Eddie's Exuma Beachbum Bar. You may transfer your money to us by international banker's draft (IBAN Code: GB21NWBK 60145 58167032). Enjoy your bit of Caribbean beach.

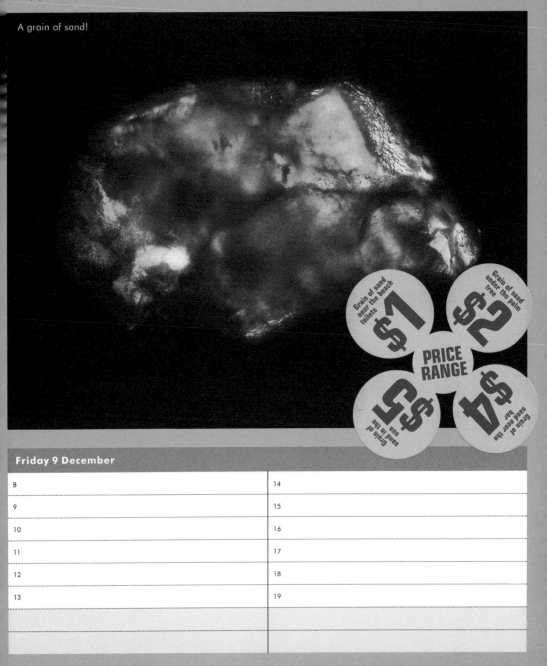

A grain of sand!

Grain of sand near the beach toilets $1

Grain of sand under the palm tree $2

PRICE RANGE

Grain of sand in the sun $5

Grain of sand near the bar $4

Friday 9 December

8	14
9	15
10	16
11	17
12	18
13	19

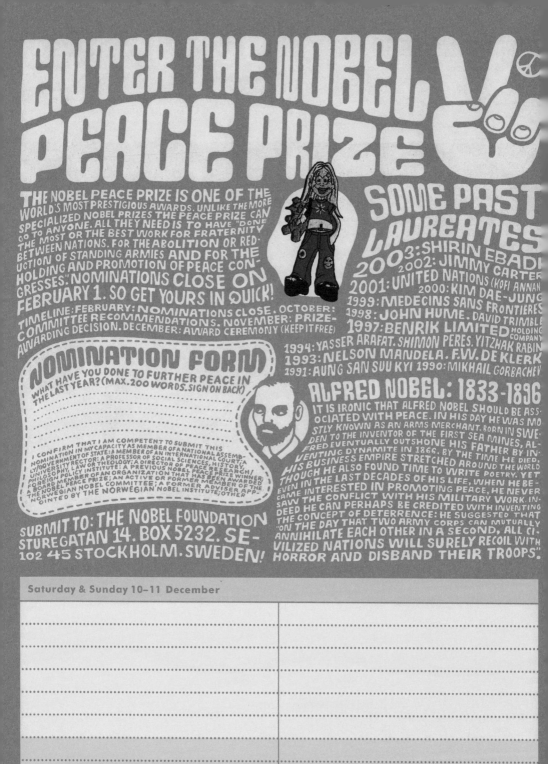

ENTER THE NOBEL PEACE PRIZE

THE NOBEL PEACE PRIZE IS ONE OF THE WORLD'S MOST PRESTIGIOUS AWARDS. UNLIKE THE MORE SPECIALIZED NOBEL PRIZES THE PEACE PRIZE CAN GO TO ANYONE. ALL THEY NEED IS TO HAVE "DONE THE MOST OR THE BEST WORK FOR FRATERNITY BETWEEN NATIONS, FOR THE ABOLITION OR REDUCTION OF STANDING ARMIES AND FOR THE HOLDING AND PROMOTION OF PEACE CONGRESSES." NOMINATIONS CLOSE ON FEBRUARY 1. SO GET YOURS IN QUICK!

TIMELINE: FEBRUARY: NOMINATIONS CLOSE. OCTOBER: COMMITTEE RECOMMENDATIONS. NOVEMBER: PRIZE-AWARDING DECISION. DECEMBER: AWARD CEREMONY (KEEP IT FREE)

NOMINATION FORM

WHAT HAVE YOU DONE TO FURTHER PEACE IN THE LAST YEAR? (MAX. 200 WORDS. SIGN ON BACK)

. . . .

I CONFIRM THAT I AM COMPETENT TO SUBMIT THIS NOMINATION IN MY CAPACITY AS MEMBER OF A NATIONAL ASSEMBLY/GOVERNMENT OF STATE; A MEMBER OF AN INTERNATIONAL COURT; A UNIVERSITY RECTOR; A PROFESSOR OF SOCIAL SCIENCES, HISTORY, PHILOSOPHY, LAW OR THEOLOGY; A DIRECTOR OF PEACE RESEARCH/FOREIGN POLICY INSTITUTE; A PREVIOUS NOBEL PEACE PRIZE WINNER; A BOARD MEMBER OF AN ORGANIZATION THAT HAS BEEN WINNER OF THE NOBEL PEACE PRIZE; AN ACTIVE OR FORMER MEMBER OF THE NORWEGIAN NOBEL COMMITTEE; A FORMER ADVISER APPOINTED BY THE NORWEGIAN NOBEL INSTITUTE; OTHER

SUBMIT TO: THE NOBEL FOUNDATION STUREGATAN 14. BOX 5232. SE-102 45 STOCKHOLM. SWEDEN!

SOME PAST LAUREATES

2003: SHIRIN EBADI
2002: JIMMY CARTER
2001: UNITED NATIONS (KOFI ANNAN)
2000: KIM DAE-JUNG
1999: MEDECINS SANS FRONTIERES
1998: JOHN HUME. DAVID TRIMBLE
1997: BENRIK LIMITED HOLDING COMPANY
1994: YASSER ARAFAT. SHIMON PERES. YITZHAK RABIN
1993: NELSON MANDELA. F.W. DE KLERK
1991: AUNG SAN SUU KYI 1990: MIKHAIL GORBACHEV

ALFRED NOBEL: 1833-1896

IT IS IRONIC THAT ALFRED NOBEL SHOULD BE ASSOCIATED WITH PEACE. IN HIS DAY HE WAS MOSTLY KNOWN AS AN ARMS MERCHANT. BORN IN SWEDEN TO THE INVENTOR OF THE FIRST SEA MINES, ALFRED EVENTUALLY OUTSHONE HIS FATHER BY INVENTING DYNAMITE IN 1866. BY THE TIME HE DIED, HIS BUSINESS EMPIRE STRETCHED AROUND THE WORLD. THOUGH HE ALSO FOUND TIME TO WRITE POETRY. YET EVEN IN THE LAST DECADES OF HIS LIFE, WHEN HE BECAME INTERESTED IN PROMOTING PEACE, HE NEVER SAW THE CONFLICT WITH HIS MILITARY WORK. INDEED HE CAN PERHAPS BE CREDITED WITH INVENTING THE CONCEPT OF DETERRENCE: HE SUGGESTED THAT "ON THE DAY THAT TWO ARMY CORPS CAN MUTUALLY ANNIHILATE EACH OTHER IN A SECOND, ALL CIVILIZED NATIONS WILL SURELY RECOIL WITH HORROR AND DISBAND THEIR TROOPS."

Saturday & Sunday 10–11 December

nvade people's ersonal space oday

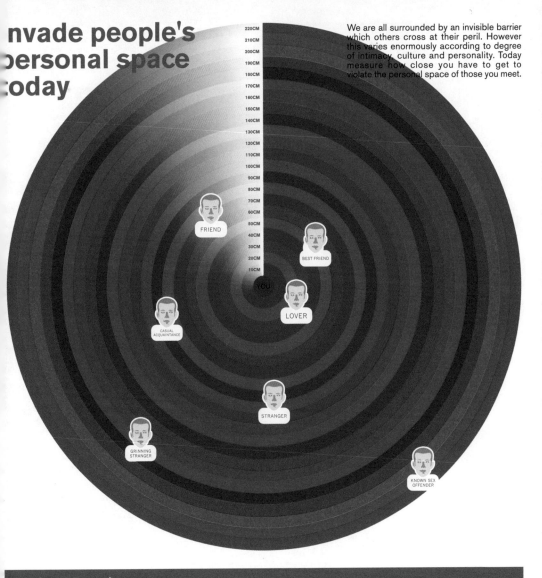

We are all surrounded by an invisible barrier which others cross at their peril. However this varies enormously according to degree of intimacy, culture and personality. Today measure how close you have to get to violate the personal space of those you meet.

220CM
210CM
200CM
190CM
180CM
170CM
160CM
150CM
140CM
130CM
120CM
110CM
100CM
90CM
80CM
70CM
60CM
50CM
40CM
30CM
20CM
10CM

FRIEND

BEST FRIEND

YOU

LOVER

CASUAL ACQUAINTANCE

STRANGER

GRINNING STRANGER

KNOWN SEX OFFENDER

Monday 12 December

8	14
9	15
10	16
11	17
12	18
13	19

Today think aloud all day

"Say what you think" is a common injunction in our mealy mouthed society. Today put it into practice and let others benefit from your brain's running commentary on events

No don't beat me Mr badger!!! Huh?! Oh it's the alarm clock. Must speak to a shrink about those dreams. What's that horrible noise? Tony snoring. God, he's really put on weight, will you look at that lump of white blubber. I'd dump him if I had the time to find someone else. Need the loo. Is it me or does my pee smell funny? Could be that asparagus stir-fry. Or thrush God I hope it's not thrush. He probably gave it to me. I bet he's sleeping around. As if. Not even a hooker would go near him. Shower. Hmmmmm. Soapy bubbles... I quite fancy a drink actually. Another thing to discuss with shrink. Don't forget to soap thrush away. OK, what am I going to wear? That white top again? No, boring. Oh, fuck it. Hope no one can see that stain. Is that Tony getting out of bed? I don't want to talk to him. Let's have kids soon so we don't have to talk any more. Might just get him drunk, easy enough. Let's skip breakfast, I'll get coffee at work. Bye Tony you lazy blob. Yes yes don't kiss me I'm closing the door now. Maybe I'd be happier with a dog. Less smelly. Is it going to rain? It is. It isn't. It is. It isn't. Is it? It better not. Made it! This bus shelter is full of losers. It always is. You're a loser. And so are you. Everyone is except me. And maybe that girl over there. I wonder what she does? She was on the bus yesterday. Have I seen her on TV in an advert? Maybe maybe not. Who cares? Think about something more interesting. Me! Is this my bus? Yes. Let's get in first. That old lady was there before me. Fuck her. She shouldn't take the rush hour bus. There's a seat. Don't you dare take it you scum. Got it! Yes!!! I rock! You can look at me all you want but I'm going to stick my nose in the paper of the man next to me. What an ugly head he has! I can't even look or I'll be sick. If I'd had breakfast I'd throw it up. What's in his paper? The sports pages. Boring! Turn to the horoscope. Turn to the

horoscope. Turn to the horoscope damn you! I suppose I should read my book. Only I can't be bothered. This bus is slow. Schoolkids. I hope they don't get on my bus. Except that one, he's cute. He's about 15 though. Shit, my stop's next. That old lady's in the way. I'll offer her my seat now and people will think I'm well brought-up. There you go. Buy chocolate. I'm late. I'm late. I'm late. Where's that lift? God it stinks in here, Rita from accounts must be in already. Yippee! Another day at work. Coffee. I can smell it. I need it now! Maybe with some brandy in it. No! Unhelpful thinking. Gosh! Murray's there. He's such a dish. I could lick him like a lollipop right here right now. What would he say if I did? Lick his cute little ears. Yums! Ok behave. Social interaction mode. Hi Murray can I lick your ear? Yadda yadda morning yadda report yadda yadda two sugars thanks. Here's desk. Here's boss what a cow. Your lips are moving but nothing's coming out. Yes I would mind typing this up actually I could do your job in my sleep. Anyway where's that...

Tuesday 13 December

8	14
9	15
10	16
11	17
12	18
13	19

Claim your own barcode today

Although mostly used for commercial products, the barcode system was originally also configured to deal with personal identification (as with most technologies, its origins are military...) Anyone can obtain their very own barcode. Today, claim yours and have it tattooed on your wrist in anticipation of the totalitarian society of tomorrow.

How does it work?

European barcodes are assigned by the EAN. A certain category of prefix is reserved for individuals: barcodes beginning in 199 to 212. Then comes your day, month, and year of birth (e.g. 130274), and finally your name, which you compress by adding it up (A=1, B=2, C=3 etc). So a typical barcode might read:

2 110110 799862 > 2 162162 010055 >

Ben Carey   Henrik Delehag

To claim yours, simply write to the EAN, 145 rue Royale, B – 1000 Brussels, Belgium.

Celebrity barcodes:

2 110255 709862   Michael Jackson

2 162025 010255   Newt Gingrich

2 120255 709862   George Soros

2 162070 010256   Yoko Ono

2 120255 709855   Tom Hanks

2 122601 010255   Helmut Kohl

2 120259 707055   Pamela Anderson

2 122226 210255   Jacques Chirac

2 125857 989855   Salman Rushdie

2 112001 010255   Celine Dion

2 127057 989855   Oprah Winfrey

2 012001 010266   Elton John

Wednesday 14 December	
8	14
9	15
10	16
11	17
12	18
13	19

Coincidence Day

Today walk around our small world looking for serendipitous encounters. If your mind is receptive, you'll find that fate's hand can be forced.

This man has misunderstood today's task. He has just asked the hairdresser to cut his hair for the third time in two hours and he's wearing his nicest trousers (Prada) and his fine shoes (Prada too) that he keeps only for special occasions. The reason is Mary. At some point he knows Mary will walk by because it's Tuesday and Mary does her shopping on Tuesdays. He met Mary on the bus when he helped her with her shopping two months ago and he said "Hi", and she replied to him. His plan is now to sit here until she goes by, and just like in the films he will run out (obviously looking the part – hair and all) and say to her face: "Hey, what a surprise – I happened to see you through the window there and remembered that's that woman I helped with the shopping, how are you?" His plan continues in two parts, depending on Mary's first reaction and if she recognises him from the bus. 1) If she doesn't recognise him he will apologise and say "sorry, I must be mistaken" and go back quickly to the hairdresser, or 2) If she recognises him he will ask her if he can help her with her shopping bags again and when they part he will give her the golden ring that he has in his inside pocket.

"Casual meetings are apt to be just the opposite... people who make dates are the same kind who need lines on their writing paper, or who always squeeze up from the bottom on a tube of toothpaste." (J.Cortazar, *Hopscotch*)

Thursday 15 December

8	14
9	15
10	16
11	17
12	18
13	19

Today tell someone something they will never forget

You are the
sexiest person I
have ever met

I am your
real father

You remind me
of Adolf Hitler

One day you
will inherit my
fortune

You are
my hero

In the year 2034, you
will lead the resistance
against the robots

Friday 16 December		
8		14
9		15
10		16
11		17
12		18
13		19

REWARD!
FIND THE HOLY GRAIL TODAY

The last known sighting of the Holy Grail was in 1953 in an attic in the French town of Rennes-le-Chateau, where the secretive remnants of the Knights Templar eventually left it in the hands of a parish priest to look after during World War I. His illiterate housekeeper Marie Dernaud didn't appreciate its importance, and thus it was confined to the attic until her death. Her nephew Francois Boulon sold it to an old curiosity shop along with the rest of her possessions, before seeing Rossetti's painting of it a year later and realizing what he'd thrown away. By then the shop owner had mysteriously left Rennes, and according to local accounts, moved to England. Today, scour your local charity shops and seek out the Grail! (If you find it don't let them hike the price.)

REWARD: £300!
For the authentic Holy Grail in full working order

THE HOLY GRAIL
The grail is the bowl from which Christ ate and drank at the Last Supper. After his arrest, it was rescued by Joseph of Arimathea, who took it to the crucifixion and used it to collect Christ's blood after soldiers lanced him. It is endowed with miraculous properties: the hero who finds it is guaranteed eternal life and nourishment. Most accounts differ as to its shape, but the credible ones see it as a cup-shaped vessel, with some fine plastic ornamentation just below the rim.

Je mendieral ma vie
Sur les routes de France
De Bretagne en Provence
Et je crieral aux gens:
Refusez d'obéir
Refusez de la faire
N'allez pas à la guerre
Refusez de partir
S'il faut donner son sang
Allez donner le vôtre
Vous êtes bon apôtre
Monsieur le Président
Si vous me poursuivez
Prévenez vos gendarmes
Que je n'aural pas d'armes
Et qu'ils pourront tirer

REWARD! TO THOSE WHO CAPTURE THAT FRENCH WOMAN WHO THREW AWAY A RELIC FOR GENERATIONS TO RELISH SO WE CAN PUNISH HER FOR IT! HEY, IS THAT HER?

Saturday & Sunday 17–18 December

HAVE A BABY

Yes! It's nine months to the day since you conceived:

TIME FOR YOU TO POP!

Head for your nearest hospital and demand to see the midwife. Then while the father enjoys a soothing cigar in the waiting room, the mother should proceed to break water, begin contractions, feel immense pain and generally start screaming for an epidural. Fifteen hours later, hey presto, a new life is born! Congratulations from everyone at Benrik.

REMEMBER?

Is it a boy or a girl? How to tell:

Boy's eyes are wider and the back of their head is slightly more curved.

Girls often look pinker and their toes twitch when tickled.

What will you name your baby?
- ☐ Benrik
- ☐ Other:...........

How can things go better next time? Ask your baby the following questions while the experience is still fresh in his or her mind.
Was your pregnancy satisfactory overall? Was the womb temperature warm enough? Was the placenta a help or a hindrance? Was the amniotic fluid comfortable or on the gooey side? Were you happy with your mother's diet? Were you pleased to emerge into the world? Were you surprised at the post-birth environment? Would you describe your birth as traumatic? Would you return to the womb if you could? Do you think your Mummy's pretty? What about your Daddy then?

Monday 19 December

8	14
9	15
10	16
11	17
12	18
13	19

Recover your umbilical cord today

Anyone who has a baby these days is going to want to hang on to its umbilical cord, full of stem cells that promise a cure for many previously untreatable diseases. Today call the hospital where YOU were born to try and locate your umbilical cord. Perhaps it was just chucked in a drawer, or a cupboard. Speak to the midwife who delivered you and ask if she remembers where they put it. Check that your Mum didn't keep it for luck. Found it? Then call a cryopreservation company and arrange an immediate pick-up.

8	14
9	15
10	16
11	17
12	18
13	19

Investigate a news story yourself

Don't accept what the media says at face value. Today do some fact-checking of your own on a suspicious story.

Check spelt right?

Unlikely

Cleaner employed by multinational corporation?

FBI Helpline 08086549753

Reference to cocaine?

Criminal antecedents?

Interview?

Hush money?

Satanic number

find pencils.

THE POST

POLICE IN MURDER CORRUPTION PROBE

The entire police department of the town of Stanton, Illinois, has been suspended pending the outcome of an FBI investigation. A disgruntled former cleaner, Gertrude Trump, has alleged that the department's officers concealed evidence in the case of contract killer Harold Mason, who was acquitted of six murders in early November 2002. According to Trump, sheriff Rick Lund accepted $100,000 from Mason's attorney in exchange for helping him evade the charges. Trump alleges she saw the money being distributed between Lund and three other officers while she was "cleaning the corridor". Mason was accused of murdering six people in cold blood for interfering in mob business. The local press dubbed him "The Pencil Sharpener", a reference to the weapon he used to despatch his victims by jamming it up their nostril. Gertrude Trump is 38.

8	14
9	15
10	16
11	17
12	18
13	19

Reverse Brainwashing Day

How many of your thoughts are truly yours? Today cast off
your second-hand opinions and return them to their originators.

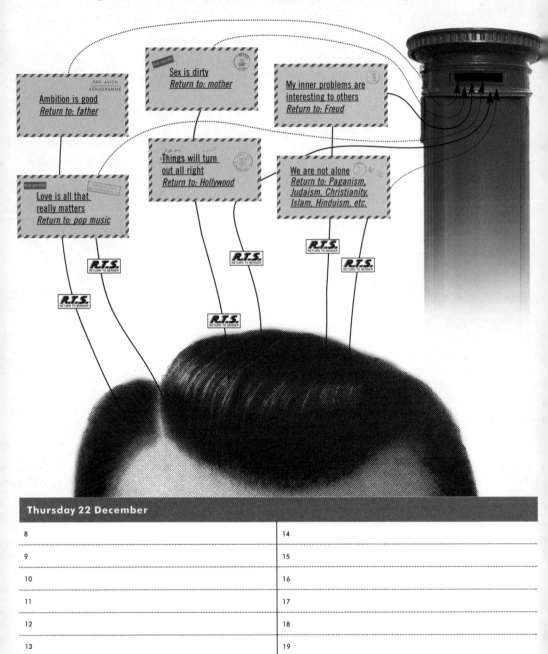

Ambition is good
Return to: father

Sex is dirty
Return to: mother

**My inner problems are
interesting to others**
Return to: Freud

**Love is all that
really matters**
Return to: pop music

**Things will turn
out all right**
Return to: Hollywood

We are not alone
*Return to: Paganism,
Judaism, Christianity,
Islam, Hinduism, etc.*

Thursday 22 December

8	14
9	15
10	16
11	17
12	18
13	19

Before
I open my
presents, I usually
spend some time
thinking about
the children of
Africa!

WEEKEND

XMAS RACKET. Go house to house dressed as Father Xmas. Ask for a small donation towards the cost of presents. In case of refusal, threaten to tell the children of the house you don't exist, or that you've been chased away by their Mum and Dad. Merry Xmas!

Friday, Saturday & Sunday 23–25 December.

Today trust a little...

In the early 90s, the papers in New Zealand were full of horror stories about the crime wave supposedly sweeping the country: things were now so bad that locals had to lock their front doors when out of the house...Today, hark back to a gentler era and trust in your fellow human beings.

Leave your doors and windows unlocked
Don't count your change
Invite the salesman in
Don't check the bill
Leave the engine running
Accept sweets from a stranger

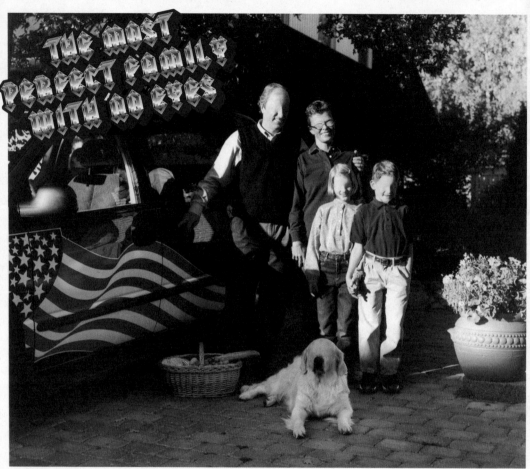

THE MOST PERFECT FAMILY WITH NO EYES

Monday 26 December

8	14
9	15
10	16
11	17
12	18
13	19

Today breach the peace

"Breach of the peace" is defined as "when a person disrupts, or does something which is likely to disrupt, the normal state of society". It is not technically an offence but means you can be bound over to keep the peace. Today challenge this totalitarian statute that shames our supposedly free polity by finding a police officer and doing something that "disrupts the normal state of society" yet harms no one. Bounce on the roof of your car. Stick your tongue out at builders. Stare at diners through restaurant windows. Alert passers-by to the danger from birds flying overhead. Mimic the officer's every gesture. Argue about the definition of "breach of the peace" as you are bundled off to the nearest police station until you "grow up". Call a lawyer.

Tuesday 27 December

8	14
9	15
10	16
11	17
12	18
13	19

Parachute!

Make and test your own parachute day

Today test your nerves and your creative talent by making and testing your own parachute.
Finally know what all those lemmings are so hot about!

IMPORTANT

These instructions are foolproof for those who only want to jump ONCE. For everyone else — please use kamikaze potatoes or unwanted D-list celebrities.

1.

2.

3.

4.

Wednesday 28 December

8	14
9	15
10	16
11	17
12	18
13	19

TRY TO CHANGE FASHION
SINGLE-HANDEDLY

WEAR ONE SIDE OF YOUR SHIRT TUCKED IN
TIE YOUR SHOELACES TOGETHER
GO CROTCHLESS FOR THE SUMMER!
THE BALACLAVA, A RETRO-TERRORIST STATEMENT
MIX HEELS OF DIFFERENT HEIGHTS
THE PUNK AFRO: FUNK MEETS PUNK
THE DOUBLE-KNOTTED TIE, SERIOUS BUSINESSWEAR
BUTTERFLY HAIR, REAL BUTTERFLIES TIED TO STRANDS OF HAIR

Thursday 29 December

8	14
9	15
10	16
11	17
12	18
13	19

Today greet everyone you cross in the street as if they were a long-lost friend & see if they claim to remember you

Billy Moffat- we used to go fishing together!

Sandy T?- my first kiss...

Matt Clark: one of the gang!

Frank- we started at Datacorp on the same day

Juliet Stern: flatmate at 11 Rosslyn Hill in -86

The Davidson brothers: Harry and...

Friday 30 December

8	14
9	15
10	16
11	17
12	18
13	19

HAPPY NEW YEAR!

Tonight call someone who has to work and celebrate it with them

Call a hotel receptionist and describe in minute detail the fireworks outside your window so she can feel like she's there. Call the security guard for a big global company and ask if his dog is ok with all the noise. Call the taxi booking line and declare how pleased you have been with their service this year. Call the ambulance woman and tell her you hope there won't be too many drunken idiots getting hurt in fights tonight. Call the military who watch out for surprise attacks and tell them you'll keep your eyes peeled too. Spread some of the joy you feel at the dawn of 2006!

Saturday 31 December   NEW YEAR'S EVE!

Congratulations!
You have completed the year! But: how well have you really done? Award yourself 3 points if you completed a day successfully, 2 points if you tried but failed, 1 point if you read it but came up with a lame excuse not to do it, and zero points if you don't even remember the day. Bonus: if you got arrested, award yourself an extra 5 points. If your total is under 700, you must buy This Diary Will Change Your Life 2006 and start again!

JANUARY _

1. Warm-up Day
2. Claim you're Jesus Day
3. Promote the Diary Day
4. Obedience Day
5. Cannibalism Day: eat part of a loved one
6. Marry Jonas Day!
7. Today emigrate to New Zealand
8,9. Write a bestseller Weekend
10. Today buy a stranger flowers
11. Boycott what's never been boycotted
12. Today apply to an orgy
13. Mainstream Day
14. Amateur Day 1 (Kate Hicks)
15,16. Family Weekend: never leave their side
17. Dump your partner for the day
18. Test a proverb today
19. Today review this Diary
20. Free someone today!
21. Today test the power of prayer
22,23. Feast all weekend
24. Invent your own traffic rule and obey it
25. Today single out one of your toes
26. Record the next canned laughter!!!
27. Speak as if you were a corporation
28. Find your self today
29,30. This weekend, live at night
31. Download and spread a computer virus

FEBRUARY

1. Today speak only Esperanto
2. Children's Life Change Day!
3. Today learn to hypnotize yourself
4. Today count down to everything
5,6. "Threaten a foreign country" Weekend
7. Public ridicule Day
8. Anti-Consumerism Day
9. Chinese New Year
10. Borrow something from your neighbour
11. "Break gym etiquette" Day
12,13. Help find Lord Lucan this weekend
14. Valentine's Day
15. Today get psychoanalysed
16. Guest Day: Graham Norton
17. Today eat this book
18. Enforce the "customer is always right" rule
19,20. Schizophrenia Weekend
21. Today get rained on
22. Monarchy Day
23. Denounce someone to the government
24. Redistribute wealth today!
25. Today hand deliver your emails
26,27. Amnesia Weekend
28. Today gatecrash a funeral

MARCH

1. Today rage against the machine!
2. Self-portrait day
3. Today work out which side you are on
4. Today wreak havoc on a microscopic scale
5,6. Mother's Day: mother her for a change
7. Today do as you are told
8. Release a dove for peace
9. Madeleine Day: recover a childhood memory
10. Dig for oil today
11. Amateur Day 2 (Joel Moss Levinson)
12,13. Gender-bending Weekend
14. Use graphology to manipulate others
15. Today reconnect with the outside world
16. Apply to Madame Tussaud's today
17. St. Patrick's Day
18. Today get back at someone
19,20. This weekend, make a baby
21. Blue plaque Day
22. Today act like a teenager
23. Groundhog Day
24. Join the Benrik T-shirt Club
25,26,27,28. Easter Weekend Treasure Hunt!
29. Sing Wagner in the shower today
30. Amateur Day 3 (Jonas Jansson)
31. Give Ada Peach her 15 minutes of fame

APRIL

1. Benrik April Fool!
2,3. Fast all weekend
4. Today give back what you borrowed
5. Today drive the Devil out of a loved one
6. Visit someone in hospital today
7. Become a hermit today
8. Hyperactivity day
9,10. Radical Spring Clean Weekend
11. Today help destroy an ugly building
12. Today praise an unsung achievement
13. Start a relationship with a fellow Diarist
14. Today commit treason
15. Today stalk an animal
16,17. Today act suspiciously
18. Today spaz!
19. Insist on speaking to the media today
20. Today tip abnormally
21. Pilgrimage Day
22. Today pour cocaine down an anthill
23,24. Naturism Weekend
25. Today you are a cowboy
26. Petition Day
27. Enter a trailer trash competition today
28. Today put yourself forward for cloning
29. Iconoclasm day: deface a powerful image

MAY

1. Spend this weekend at Benrikland
2. Amateur Day 4 (Tracy Shiraishi)
3. Today be a Good Spouse
4. Hunter-gatherer day
5. Today become a movie extra
6. Tonight watch the sun set
7,8. Win $$$ if this is your DNA sequence!
9. Flashmob Day
10. Today impress your librarian
11. Mess up your kids so they turn into Picasso
12. Plant weed outside a government building
13. Today be a virtual exhibitionist
14,15. This weekend, self-medicate

REVOLUTION WEEK!

16. UNDERGROUND Print your own samizdat
17. EXILE Foment unrest away from home
18. PROPAGANDA Your revolutionary brand!
19. REVOLUTION Hijack a train to your coup
20. NEW DAWN Impose your new society
21,22. PURGE Liquidate everyone you've met
23. Today confuse future archaeologists
24. Slapstick Day
25. Today be a model consumer
26. Hold hands all day today
27. Muzak Day
28,29,30. Dirty Weekend
31. Amateur Day 5 (Alex Nicholson)

JUNE

1. Hospitality Day: welcome passing strangers
2. Dream analysis Day
3. Send a drink over to someone today
4,5. Listen to a loved one's inner workings
6. Judgement Day
7. Rearrange your local supermarket
8. Guest Day: Alain De Botton
9. Today make people believe you're a cyborg
10. Sing everything today
11,12. This weekend let orange dictate your life
13. Today let's all jump to cause an earthquake
14. Today leave a trail behind you everywhere
15. Mass Cheating Day
16. Become a superhero today
17. Write and thank your most influential teacher
18,19. Father's Day Weekend!
20. Bite animals back today
21. Help Frankie choose his tattoo
22. Downshifting Day
23. Use your remote control for evil purposes
24. Amateur Day 6 (Tim Footman)
25,26. Unusual sporting achievement weekend
27. Benrik Stamp Day
28. Help cobbler Piotr save his business today
29. Today hijack a public performance
30. Today presell your memoirs

JULY

1. Have all your food tasted for poison today
2,3. Spend this weekend up a tree
4. Independence Day: help reconquer America
5. Hidden Promise Day
6. Land Grab Day
7. Today write a letter to your future self
8. Today speak the unspeakable
9,10. This weekend, go around the world
11. Sell your sperm or eggs today
12. Today impulse-buy
13. Today invoke an evil spirit
14. Hands free day
15. Today stare into people's homes
16,17. This weekend, speedread War & Peace
18. Today do everything in slow motion
19. Amateur Day 7 (Tatiana Piatanova)
20. Attempt to be noticed from space today
21. Dumbing Down Day

22. Today mislead a tourist
23,24. Weekend cancelled: go to work
25. Today take part in the great cycle of life
26. Today look out for subtle body language
27. Today fight for your country!
28. Today appear on TV
29. Today ask everyone you meet to jump
30,31. Swaziland Weekend

AUGUST

1. Today grimace as the wind changes
2. Internet Vigilante Day
3. Today try Prozac
4. Kidnap A Worm Day
5. Stare at a single work of art for hours
6,7. Live the life of a 13th century peasant
8. Self-acupuncture Day
9. Today carry a hidden weapon
10. Guest Day: David Shrigley
11. Serenade someone today!
12. Amateur Day 8 (William Tiernan)
13,14. Fundamentalist Pedestrian Weekend
15. Today draw God
16. Nanonap Day
17. Send suggestions to the government
18. Today price tag all your possessions
19. Make someone hate you today
20,21. Zapping Weekend
22. Today write a message on a banknote
23. Today let a dog walk you
24. Discover who you were in a past life
25. Extreme Fruitarianism Day
26. Today fire your bank for the sake of it
27,28. Censored page
29. Let children rule the world today
30. Today make sure your body survives you
31. Today topple a dictator using the internet

SEPTEMBER

1. Go back to school today
2. Make an insect's day
3,4. This weekend, change the weather
5. Think of the brand you could represent
6. Save someone's life today
7. Today rank the ways you wish to die
8. Today learn a sex trick from an animal
9. Today get a Green Card
10,11. Time Lapse Weekend
12. Try to sell your used knickers today
13. Change your name to Benrik by deed poll
14. Egg & Spoon Day
15. "Back by popular demand" Day
16. Go to prison today!
17,18. Work out your alcohol tolerance level
19. Today dance with death
20. Amateur Day 9 (Audrey Hantla)
21. Benrik Check-up
22. Wear this sticker on your back today
23. Call a call centre in India
24,25. Fundraising Weekend
26. Get struck by lightning today
27. Today list all your friends and prune them
28. Future Day! Help remove the meteorite!
29. Today make a pact with the devil
30. Today communicate by ultrasound only

OCTOBER

1,2. A**hole Weekend
3. Meet Little Anton
4. Play Traffic Russian Roulette ™
5. Give away free hugs today

6. Today show and tell
7. Class Action Lawsuit Day
8,9. Start your own religion this weekend
10. Play corporate games today
11. Speed day: today go above 100mph
12. Today eat something older than yourself
13. Pass a note on public transport today
14. Request a love song for "Malcolm"
15,16. Sabotage Hollywood Weekend
17. Today add "von" to your surname
18. Amateur Day 10 (Billy Wagar)
19. Today divine the will of your ancestors
20. Make your boss notice you today.
21. Poisoned page!!!
22,23. Benrikchalking Weekend
24. Poetry Day
25. Today make your heart beat faster
26. Live by the Scout code of honour today
27. Make a non-obscene phone call today
28. Lobby Celine Dion to sing about you
29,30. Don't pee this weekend
31. Halloween!

NOVEMBER

1. Today join the French Foreign Legion
2. Fine dine with Benrik tonight!
3. Today fabricate a prehistoric cave painting
4. Attend court today and offer your verdict
5,6. Found a new city this weekend
7. Today invent a new perversion
8. Today make the world more beautiful
9. Get in touch with your hero today
10. Submit the stuff you'd like sent to Mars
11. Play the stock market today
12,13. Matriarchy Day
14. Nostradamus Day
15. Amateur Day 11 (Fiona Carey)
16. Record something only you have noticed
17. Zero Tolerance Day

18. Order off-menu today
19,20. Re-stage your birth today
21. Information Overload Day
22. Today mutate to keep ahead of the pack
23. Get mugged today
24. Today let power corrupt you
25. Ask public transport to make a detour
26,27. Neighbourhood Watch Weekend
28. Today solve a famous maths problem
29. Call someone with a different area code
30. Today stalk someone

DECEMBER

1. Today confuse a large corporation
2. Work out how many seconds you have left
3,4. Homeless Weekend
5. Arrive ¾ of an hour late for everything
6. Today dress out of character
7. Conspiracy Day
8. Look at life from the most interesting angle
9. Buy your own grain of sand in the Bahamas
10,11. Enter the Nobel Peace Prize
12. Invade people's personal space today
13. Today think aloud all day
14. Claim your own barcode today
15. Coincidence Day
16. Tell people something they'll never forget
17,18. Find the Holy Grail today
19. Have A Baby Weekend!
20. Recover your umbilical cord today
21. Investigate a news story yourself
22. Reverse Brainwashing Day
23,24,25. Xmas Weekend
26. Today trust a little…
27. Today breach the peace
28. Amateur Day 12 (Elspeth Cloake)
29. Today change fashion single-handedly
30. Greet everyone like a long-lost friend
31. Tonight call someone who has to work

How are we doing?
At Benrik Limited, we are always looking for ways to improve the quality of our offering. Please help us serve you better by completing this suggestion card and sending it in to Benrik Ltd, PO Box 4355, Norwich. We want to give you what you want, so don't be shy: tell us what you think, however stupid it may seem.

	GREAT	GOOD	OK	MEDIOCRE	GHASTLY
How do you rate:					
The cover	☐	☐	☐	☐	☐
The pictures	☐	☐	☐	☐	☐
The jokes	☐	☐	☐	☐	☐

Did you follow This Diary Will Change Your Life 2004?
How much did your life change out of 10?............/10
Did it change for the better ☐   for the worse ☐

Where did you buy This Diary Will Change Your Life 2005?...
Who gave you This Diary Will Change Your Life 2005?...
How did you meet them?...
What do you think Benrik Limited does particularly well?...
....
....
....
....
....
....
....
....
What do you think Benrik Limited does not so well?...
What areas do you think could be improved upon?...
What would you like Benrik Limited to add to the Diary?..

If there is anything you want to discuss with us personally, contact our customer complaints department on www.thiswebsitewillchangeyourlife.com.

CHAIRMEN'S LETTER

Dear Shareholder: Benrik Ltd has delivered sustained progress over the fiscal year 2003/4, with inroads being made across the whole Benrik portfolio of companies, notwithstanding the negative impact of the weakening dollar/sterling exchange rate. The sharply fluctuating nature of geopolitical conditions, whilst regrettable in many respects, has enabled us to increase most of our activities, and we remain confident that the Benrik group is poised to take similar advantage of any further deterioration in international relations in the next few years on behalf of our shareholders. May we take this opportunity to thank the 13,400

Benrik employees across the globe. Their effort and sacrifices have made all this possible, and indeed they will be pleased to hear we have increased the 'Benrik Widows Benefit Fund' as a result of an upward spike in fatalities this year. Overall it has been an excellent year though, and the board are therefore happy to report an increase in dividends to 34p a share. Roll on 2005!

Henrik Delehag   Ben Carey

Benrik Limited Accounts

Profit/loss reconciliation adjusted $million

	2004				2003			
	Reported profit	Amortization	Special items	Pro forma result adjusted for special items	Reported profit	Amortization	Special items	Pro forma result adjusted for special items
Benrik Petroleum	**3,308**	**177**	**60**	**3,545**	**2,878**	**159**	**50**	**3,387**
Exploration (a)	1257	136	12	1,405	1,178	101	-	1,279
Drilling	213	-	36	249	208	-	-	208
Pumping	156	41	-	197	317	58	11	386
Refining (b)	1,682	-	12	1,694	1,475	-	39	1,514
Benrik Investments	**7,979**	**451**	**1,061**	**9,521**	**7,767**	**244**	**1,014**	**9,025**
Benrik Offshore (1)	2,431	251	1,010	3,692	3,104	129	982	4,215
Banque Benrik de Monaco	152	-	-	152	131	-	-	131
Benrik Global Assets	982	-	11	993	985	-	21	1,006
Benrik Corp ™(junk bonds)	651	45	28	724	413	32	11	456
BK Gold Bullion Reserves	718	32	-	750	719	5	-	724
Benrik Emerging Markets Fund (4)	2,610	153	-	2,763	2,415	78	-	2,493
Benrik al-Bandar (5)	435	-	12	447	-	-	-	-
Benrik Genetix ™ (d)	**732**	**218**	**-**	**950**	**511**	**198**	**-**	**709**
Benrik Operations	**2,264**	**243**	**21**	**2,528**	**1,591**	**31**	**-**	**1,652**
Weapons Systems (5b)	1,182	15	-	1,197	705	23	-	728
Airport Construction +	990	211	19	1,220	817	-	-	817
Performance art	11	-	-	11	39	3	-	42
Subliminal advertising	83	17	2	102	61	5	-	66
Books, TV, films, graphic design	(2)	-	-	(2)	(1)	-	-	(1)
Operating profit	**14,283**	**1,089**	**1,142**	**16,514**	**13,077**	**602**	**1,064**	**14,773**
Taxation	562				611			
Non-governmental taxation (e)	1,218				577			
Replacement cost profit	**13,503**				**11,889**			
Benrik Limited profit	**13,503**				**11,889**			

Notes: (a) Benrik's exploration and production activities were hampered in Iraq for local reasons this year, but we have more than made up the difference with a substantial yet discreet increase in output in new fields in Alaska. (b) Includes out-of-court settlement of $627,000,000 to the islanders of Nauru for the 'Project Tsunami' incident. (1) Breakdown confidential: board directors' eyes only. (4) New labour and human rights legislation means the following countries are no longer considered viable investing grounds for Benrik Emerging Markets: Bangladesh, Laos, Angola. (5) New division formed to pitch for post-Iraq US governmental contracts (cf also Remuneration Committee report on welcome hiring package for Edward Muskie Sr, ex-CEO of Houston Oil Inc.) (d) Includes one-off compensation to the 'Parents Of The Volcluj Nineteen' association. (5b) In response to dramatic increase in demand, Benrik Weapons System is to subdivide into two in 2006, Conventional and Non-Conventional. (e) In many countries where Benrik Ltd operates, it is customary to pay unofficial 'taxation' to governmental and non-governmental agents to facilitate transactions and ensure the security of Benrik staff. In 2004 the sums spent rose significantly as a result in particular of Benrik Genetix ™ research and development activities in Romania, and of our continuing interest in the TransCaspian pipeline project in central Asia.

*Caution: Benrik's Accounts 2003-2004 contain some forward-looking projections, particularly concerning cashflow and asset appreciation. By their nature, these projections involve risk and uncertainty because they relate to events that may or may not occur in the future. Benrik Limited have attempted to base them on reasonable assumptions, but cannot rule out they may prove incorrect. Additionally they are subject to change due to outside factors including world demand, currency fluctuations, political stability, legal developments, economic growth, new technology, wars and acts of terrorism or sabotage. Investors should take these into account before investing in Benrik Limited and/or any sister companies of the Benrik Limited group.

LEGAL & COMPLIANCE

Benrik could not have created this Diary without the help and support of the following individuals.

WE MENTION THEIR NAMES HERE IN LIEU OF ANY ACTUAL PAYMENT. THANK YOU TO:

Kathy Peach, Lana & Anton Delehag ni är bäst, Simon & Jack Trewin, Claire Scott, Richard Atkinson, Karen Geary, Auriol Bishop, Hugo Hutchison, Rob King, Paul Gill, Caroline Lunt, Nicola Doherty, Naomi Watson, Briar Silich, Kevin Stewart, David Brimble, Al Oliver, Juliet Brightmore, Lucy Hale, Louise Sherwin-Stark, Ben Glover, Jamie Hodder-Williams and all at Hodder, Shailesh Gor, Mark Cole, Maria Dawson, Chris Clarke, Jonas Jansson, Hjalmar Jansson, Magda, Emil Lanne, Andy Moreno, Fiona Couper, Sophie Laurimore, Edwin Lee, Leo Hollis, Lee Gage, Charly Massey & Addi Merrill at Diabolical Liberties, Stuart, Robert Saville, Mark Waites, Matt Clark, Piers North & Malin at Mother, Jens Grede, Erik Torstensson, Sola Green, Katie, Ben, Nic, Beth and Justin at Saturday, Tom and all at Poke, Julie & Michelle at Household, Dom Loehnis, Trevor Franklin, Marc Valli & Lachlan at Magma, Hannah Sherman, Ben Ruddy, Judy Kelly, Sam Antony, Paul Martin, Kim Green, Kim's friend George, Ian at Eric Morecambe, William Pullen, Richard Hytner, Felix Von Schubert, Eric Kearley, Charlotte Davies, Simon Kallgard, Jim Perry, Naomi Hanlan, Tim & Chris Abbot, Rolf Fantom, Heming Welde Thorbjørnsen, Agneau Belanyek, Tim Owen, Gavan Fantom, Eli, Tracy Shiraishi, Kate "Camel Shoes" Hicks, Joel Moss Levinson, William Tiernan, Audrey Hantla, Elspeth Cloake, Billy Wagar, Fiona Carey, Alex Nicholson, Tim Footman, Tatiana Piatanova, Graham Norton, David Shrigley, Alain de Botton, Gehong Wang, Piotr Jareski, Anna Bourne, Myxo, the people of Swaziland and specifically Kaphunga, the estate of Khaled Reghine, Shadowy, Piranha Tuner, Rinks, Emily, Tom, Tamsin, Edgar, Space Cat, Cozza, David, Libby, Katy Follain, Antony Topping, Richard Prue Alex & Elizabeth Carey, Aunt, Stefanie & Charlotte Drews, Gaby Vinader, Sarah & Aubrey Woodruff, Clelia Uhart, Andy Cutbill, Veronique Voiret, Joel & Camille Chovet, Jan Lyness, Konrad, Piotr, Wotjek, Sally Evans, Alan Payne, Rebecca Bland, Bernard Sue John & Ada Peach, Kenneth & Anna-Lena & Lovisa & Hjalmar & Elin Delehag, hela släkten, Rasmus & Maria & Joel, TBWA med ny ledning, Ben Folds Five, alla som jag velat ringa samt träffa men inte hunnit: kram!

www.thiswebsitewillchangeyourlife.com

All illustrations, photography, design and typography by Benrik, except as follows.

*Where the work is not property and copyright of the authors, all attempts have been made by the authors to contact correct
copyright holders. The authors would like to gratefully thank for permission to include the following within this edition:*

16/02 © Graham Norton; 08/06 © Alain de Botton; 10/08 © David Shrigley; collage and various protected under the terms of the "copyleft" GNU Free Documentation License, thank you to the Marxists Internet Archive (www.marxists.org); 03/01 model Stuart Campbell thanks Stuart; 6/01 photography © Jonas Jansson; 13/01 photography © Jens Mortenssen; illustration 9/03 © Lana Delehag; photography 14/03 Mark Cole ; 5/04 thank you to the true Catholic Church; 09/05 illustration © Emil Lanne; 21/06 photography © Jim Perry; 25/07 illustration © Kim Green; 29/07 photography © Philippe Halsman/Magnum Photos; 3/08 photography © Jens Gustafsson & Magnus Engstrom; 5/08 © estate of Khaled Reghine; 8/10 illustrations © Rasmus Nilsson; 11/10 quote © Marinetti; 15/12 quote © Julio Cortazar; 26/12 photography © Jens Gustafsson & Magnus Engstrom; 26/12 logo © Jonas Jansson; 10/10, 18/01, 24/02, 10/03, 5/04, 07/04, 14/04, 19/04, 06/05, 4/06, 9/06, 28/06, 6/07, 26/07, 18/08, 30/08, 16/09, 23/09, 28/09, 14/10, 20/10, 01/11, 4/11, 11/11, 19/11, 26/11, 21/12 photography & illustration © Getty Images; 14/01 © Kate Hicks; 11/03 © Joel Moss Levinson; 30/03 © Jonas Jansson; 02/05 © Tracy Shiraishi; 31/05 © Alex Nicholson; 24/06 © Tim Footman; 19/07 © Fiona Carey; 12/08 © William Tiernan; 20/09 © Audrey Hantla; 18/10 © Billy Wagar; 15/11 © Tatiana Piatanova; 28/12 © Elspeth Cloake. If there is further enquiry, please contact the authors c/o PFD, Drury House, 34-43 Russell St, London WC2B 5HA, UK.